empathic intelligence

ROSLYN ARNOLD is Professor and Dean of Education, and Head of School, at the University of Tasmania. Prior to this, she was Pro-Dean and Head of School in the Faculty of Education, Fellow of Senate, and Deputy Chair of the Academic Board at the University of Sydney. She is currently Chair of Loreto Education Board, the governing council of Loreto Schools in Australia.

She has been actively involved throughout her career in English and Drama education, teacher education and issues relating to students' learning and literacy, and is frequently invited to address national and international audiences live and through radio and television.

Professor Arnold is regularly consulted on policy matters by education agencies and has written several reports for Ministers of Education.

Her publications include *Timely Voices*, *Writing Development: Magic in the Brain* and *Mirror the Wind* (a collection of her poems). She is currently working towards her second collection of poems and completion of her novel *Laugh at Gilded Butterflies*.

*e*mpathic *i*ntelligence
teaching, learning, relating

ROSLYN ARNOLD

UNSW PRESS

A UNSW PRESS BOOK

Published by
University of New South Wales Press Ltd
University of New South Wales
Sydney NSW 2052
AUSTRALIA
www.unswpress.com.au

© Roslyn Arnold 2005
First published 2005

This book is copyright. Apart from any fair dealing for the purpose of private study, research, criticism or review, as permitted under the Copyright Act, no part may be reproduced by any process without written permission. Inquiries should be addressed to the publisher.

National Library of Australia
Cataloguing-in-Publication entry

Arnold, Roslyn M., 1945- .
　Empathic intelligence : teaching, learning, relating.

　Bibliography.
　Includes index.
　ISBN 0 86840 591 4.
　1. Teacher-student relationships. 2. Empathy. 3. Effective teaching.
　I. Title.
　371.1023

Design Di Quick
Cover Arthur Boyd *Bathers and Pulpit Rock,* 1984/85, Oil on canvas, 244 x 457 cm. Collection: Queensland Art Gallery

Extracts from Inga Clendinnen's *Reading the Holocaust* and Robert Manne's 'The Holocaust as a Fairy Tale' reprinted with permission.

The author and UNSW Press undertook to obtain permission to use copyright material reproduced in this book, but in some cases could not trace copyright holders. Information from copyright holders that will enable the author and publisher to rectify an error or omission would be welcome.

CONTENTS

Foreword *by Maxine Greene* — 7

Acknowledgments — 9

Preface — 11

Chapter One — 15
The Concept of Empathic Intelligence

Chapter Two — 31
Empathy as a Function of Mind, Brain and Feeling

Chapter Three — 63
Empathy, Narrative and the Imagination

Chapter Four — 92
Theoretical Antecedents of Empathic Pedagogy

Chapter Five — 119
Empathic Literacy for Effective Leadership

Chapter Six — 162
Developing Empathic Cultures of Learning

Chapter Seven 191
  Creating Empathically Intelligent Organisations

Conclusion 223

Bibliography 225

Index 233

FOREWORD

This eminently readable book appears at an opportune moment in the development of psychological, philosophical, and pedagogical thinking with regard to human lives and growth. Until recently, it will be recalled, inquiry in the several fields was dominated by technicism, or what might be called positivism. No sentence or claim, it was believed, would be considered meaningful if it could not be empirically verified. This carried with it a bifurcation of human reality, a dualism or a separation of mind and body, a split between reason and emotion. Lately, in the sciences and various social sciences, there has been a recognition of the emptiness of dualisms and the need to bring, as Virginia Woolf would say, 'the severed parts together'.

Virginia Woolf had metaphors in mind; and Roslyn Arnold's book, like her focus on 'empathic intelligence', is deeply metaphorical. She moves from classroom stories to questions of relationship and caring. She touches on problems of leadership, motivation, self-awareness – all of great relevance to an understanding of pedagogy and the complexities of teaching and learning. Referring to pioneers in the several fields of her concern, Professor Arnold delves into the works of Antonio Damasio, Stephen Rose, Howard Gardner and a number of others (occasionally with quotations from case histories or anecdotes) and discovers themes common to such thinkers and to emerging pedagogical theorists as well.

By the end of the book, we cannot but find a kind of polymath in Roslyn Arnold, reaching towards the humanities as well as the human sciences, reappearing as a dynamic educator in the very real contexts of public school classrooms and college seminars. As someone long committed to an existential pursuit of freedom and authenticity, to the arts and their arousing us to wide-awakeness, to a consciousness of empathic membership in a democracy, I am grateful to Roslyn Arnold and her effort to make us whole.

Maxine Greene
Professor Emeritus
Teachers College
Columbia University

ACKNOWLEDGMENTS

This book has had a genesis as long as my life. It is common to talk of an academic's scholarly output as a 'body of work'. In a sense, the attribution solely to scholarly work is too narrow. An academic's body of work, in an empathically intelligent model, is really every significant conversation and experience embodied through life.

Much of this book draws on my relationships, teaching, researching, reading and reflecting. Many significant others have mirrored something through a word, a look or a tone of voice. So I am deeply grateful to my family, friends, colleagues and students for providing the texture and shape of my life and work. In particular I thank:

The English class 1968–71 at North Sydney Girls' High School (Wendy, Alex, Jane, Robin, Karen, Linda). The boys at North Sydney Boys' School 1973 – memorably Andrew Spearritt, John Darling and the ever-practising Allan Border.

Postgraduate students at the University of Sydney and University of Tasmania, Les Cartwright, Janine Kitson, Gloria Latham, Sue Marks, Susan Nicolson, Steve Reissig, Clare Wearring.

Su Baker, Rob Burnett, Anne Inall and Neil Inall, Craig Judd, Ray Misson, Brian Muir, Brian Scott, Don Spearritt and Jean Spearritt, Ross Steele, Nancy Swortzell and Lowell Swortzell, Ken Watson, Julie Weedon and Mark Weedon, Marilyn Wilson and Diana Mitchell; the

Loreto nuns at Mandeville Hall, Toorak, Veronica Brady, Deirdre Browne, Meg Hannan, Brigid Jones, Ruth Winship.

Kerry James who urged me to publish, John Hughes who has always been an empathic friend and inspiration, Jo Le Grew and Daryl Le Grew, Louise Mayne, Carole Miller, Juliana Saxton, Christopher Strong, Jill Hickson Wran and Neville Wran, AC, and Janice Folletta. Her Excellency, Quentin Bryce, AC, cares and inspires in equal measure.

Karen Jennings and Joan Cunningham (She'll Be Write) are brilliant, expert and empathic editors to whom I am indebted. They engaged sensitively with the spirit of the text. However, the shortcomings remain my own.

Linda Callahan, Amanda Sundstrup and Kerri Wells in my University office have given valued practical and moral support. Special thanks to Pamela Page for her help with managing and editing the manuscript. I thank Marianne Vick and Penny Stewart for research assistance.

Special thanks to Debbie Lee of University of New South Wales Press for her creativity, warmth, insight and daring.

Affectionate thanks to caring Christian Avramides.

Cynthia Gregory-Roberts, my sister, and Simon, Emily, Nicholas and Lucy, along with Kristin Boag, my cousins and the extended McDonald family are always a source of warmth and insight.

Professor Maxine Greene's 'Foreword' is a generous response to friendship and a shared love of imagination. Her conversations are always heart-warming, thought-provoking and energising.

Finally, this book is dedicated to the loving memory of my empathic mother, Meg, and my poetic father John, who taught me to read and write stories. It is, of course, dedicated also to Louisa Meg, my beloved daughter, and the best poem I will ever write. I live better for the delight of your presence.

PREFACE

PURPOSE AND SCOPE OF THIS BOOK

Once upon a time ... the classic opening phrase beloved by storytellers. You may be wondering what it has to do with a serious, scholarly book on empathic intelligence. I hope as this book unfolds you will see its relevance and appreciate how the phrase evokes many aspects of the topic I am exploring. In the pages that follow I will explain how empathic intelligence thrives on curiosity, reflection and memory of emotional and learning experiences, relationships and narratives. I will suggest that it is stimulated by your engagement in imagined worlds and real encounters and that it is dependent on a capacity to engage and identify with the thoughts and feelings of others. A timelessly evocative and paradoxical phrase, *Once upon a time* connects the past, the present and the future. It hints at endless permutations of plot lines, infinite variations on universal themes, and multiple and complex truths.

Empathic intelligence attests to the complexity of human dynamics and provides a framework to describe that complexity. In this book I ask what it is that makes exceptional educators and other professional leaders so effective? I suggest that the concept of *empathic intelligence* helps us to answer this question. Empathic intelligence is a theory of

12   *Empathic Intelligence*

TSRQ

relatedness. It is relevant to person-centred situations and professional contexts such as teaching and learning. It explains some of the salient skills, abilities and attitudes that underpin effectiveness in these contexts – things such as enthusiasm, expertise, capacity to engage, and empathy itself.

My aim is to provide new and experienced teachers, leaders and those involved in influencing others with a conceptual framework to enable their further professional development. I hope that my discussion of empathic intelligence will resonate with those who are attracted to it, affirm your practice, challenge you, and encourage you to develop a personally meaningful, ever-growing theoretical position.

Central to the concept of empathic intelligence is the argument that learning is effective when educators are attuned to their own thinking and feeling processes, are able to imagine how others might be thinking and feeling, and use their sensitivity and imagination to create purposeful and energising learning experiences. Enacted in a climate of care, these skills are all part of professional expertise and have the potential to transform both relating and learning.

I see empathic intelligence as underpinning the ethical and curriculum frameworks of transformative pedagogies in the United States, Canada, the United Kingdom and Australia. In this book, I demonstrate that it informs these pedagogies because it articulates how to create learning experiences of deep impact and personal significance. I argue that teaching and learning which goes beyond transmitting knowledge into the realms of creative experiences, and which mobilises deeply-felt shifts in consciousness, can transform our understanding of self, of others and the complexities of the life of the mind.

Naturally, not all learning experiences will be cognitively complex or emotionally powerful. Yet they might well lay the foundations for later experiences. It is an important part of an educator's expertise to have a vision of a vast range of learning experiences from the simple to the profound, the mundane to the transformative, depending on students' needs, hopes and interests. In an empathically intelligent model of learning, every experience can add to the sum of the whole, and provide important data about learning patterns and preferences for both the educator and student.

One of my central arguments is that learning can be enhanced by educative processes that recognise how thoughts (cognition) and feelings (affect) can work together to enhance both intellectual and

Cognitive + affective engagement

emotional maturity. When thoughts and feelings can be encouraged to interact in dynamic ways, better learning, communication and leadership can occur.

An early version of empathic intelligence was called *psychodynamic pedagogy*, but as the concept has grown, a new more comprehensive term – empathic intelligence – has evolved to describe it. I have developed my concept of empathic intelligence as a theory of high level pedagogy from a number of sources: empirical and qualitative research; reflections on professional and personal practices; engagements with colleagues and students; and extensive reading across a number of disciplines, including philosophy, linguistics, psychology, psychotherapy, sociology, arts education, English literature, drama and poetry. The motivations for that reading have been a curiosity about the phenomena of relatedness between people as individuals and in engagements with their culture and environment.

While I ground the theory in well-established concepts of effective teaching and learning, I elaborate it in language that I hope leaders, educators and parents will recognise as familiar, yet also new, challenging and evocative. In that sense it might be called a *poetry* of leadership and pedagogy, creating new metaphors and energies to enhance relating and learning.

I aim to provide readers with sufficient reference points for you to see, hear or feel yourselves reflected within its pages in different places. I then encourage you to observe yourselves more closely in interaction with your own students, clients or significant others. You will then appreciate the complex dynamics within your own practices and engagements. At the same time, you should develop a greater capacity to recognise and understand the phenomena of relatedness. With renewed confidence in such capacity, you might then seek to enhance your own professional practices in beneficial ways. Committed educators tend to engage life-long in an existential quest of becoming. With such a mind-set, significant experiences in both professional and private life can seamlessly influence that becoming.

It is my belief that once teachers better understand what constitutes empathic intelligence, they will cultivate these qualities in their students through modelling. Ideally, the kind of commitment involved will not mean more work or stress, but rather, less fruitless labour and deeper satisfaction. It will improve student learning because their abilities and interests will be mobilised. As with most developmental experiences, progress will not follow a straight upward trend. There will be encouraging progressive periods, and periods of regression, testing the resilience of both the educator and the student. But these are realities in any human growth experience. Hopefully, and that word is used very deliberately, this book and its perspectives will support the quest for more person-centred, more enriching, more informed and more effective professional practice. This can occur wherever interpersonal, public and private interactions occur – for example, in the arts, health disciplines, parenting and leadership situations.

While I attempt to articulate how the skills, attitudes and abilities of empathic intelligence can contribute to deeply effective teaching and learning, I can only make a start towards accounting for the deeply complex cognitive and emotional dynamics involved in engagements between individuals. My aim here is to pursue the quest for understanding while being ever aware of the improbability of comprehensively coding complex human behaviour. In this pursuit I consider a range of phenomena which have a role in developing and reflecting empathic intelligence and which facilitate effective teaching and learning. These include narratives, the arts, prior experiences, personal dispositions and the nature of care.

In the early stages of the book, I have kept referencing to a minimum to help readability. At the end of each chapter I outline hypotheticals that can be done individually or as part of a group experience. These can be helpful to those reading the book as individuals or those engaged in teaching, training, or leading professional development courses and postgraduate seminars. They require memory work, observation, reflection, contemplation and reading. They require commitment to self-reflection and observation.

Ideally, those students or educators seeking to experience or create empathically intelligent and transforming experiences, will find sufficient stimulation here to embark on learning with a sense of anticipation and leave with a sense of tantalising satisfaction and longing. The human mind seems capable of seeking its own growth, continually prompting the brain to cooperate in the enterprise.

CHAPTER ONE

THE CONCEPT OF EMPATHIC INTELLIGENCE

Quality relationships are the foundations of excellent pedagogy. As we move beyond an age that idealises technology, with good reason, we'll move into a period in which quality relationships are recognised, affirmed and researched in ways appropriate to their nature. This book aims to enhance that change process.

Much has been written about effective teaching and learning, so what more, in this postmodern age, needs to be said? What is new about a concept of empathy? Isn't it merely a kind of sympathy? Isn't empathic intelligence just emotional intelligence with compassion thrown in? And, anyway, how can a busy educator handle more theory when education is already overloaded with theories and content? If the Internet provides all the information we need, who needs teachers? Why worry about students' feelings when there isn't time to cover mandated content?

This chapter answers many of these questions. In it, I explore various definitions of empathic intelligence and argue that a false dichotomy between feeling and thinking has clouded and limited definitions of intelligence. I examine the role of empathic intelligence in transformative learning and teaching and identify its attributes, differentiating it from other intelligences. I advocate a theory that democratises intelligence, and suggest that a compelling reason for formulating the concept of empathic intelligence is to provide a useful framework for educators and students facing the challenges of rapid change. Such a framework anchors the processes of learning, maturing, developing, and integrating and transforming life's intra- and interpersonal experiences. It privileges the tacit abilities of humans to direct their own learning, supported by empathic others.

FEELING AND THINKING

One of the promising developments in science at the beginning of this new century is the increasing interest in the nature and function of human emotions. For many reasons, including the difficulty of studying them in traditionally scientific ways, the emotions have tended to be the domain of poets, artists, philosophers and females. There has been a mistaken belief that rationality, an important indicator of intellectual maturity, necessitates the subjugation of feelings. Feelings have been regarded as unreliable indicators of mature human responsiveness, particularly in intellectual pursuits. Similarly, art and science have been regarded as dichotomies rather than potentially complementary ways of perceiving the world. However, once we become interested in the interplay between feelings and thought, we move into a potentially creative and dynamic space in which deep reflective thought is possible.

Now that brain neural imaging and research on the development of consciousness have illustrated the interconnectedness of thought and emotion in the brain, the concept of rational thought is being re-conceptualised. The brain and mind research of neuroscientist Antonio Damasio (1994, 2000), J. Le Doux (1992), L. Williams (2001) and others is helping us to understand better that the relationships between the cognitive and emotional parts of our brains are infinitely more complex than is generally realised.

A profound belief in the existential need for humans to access both their rational and their felt or emotional responses to the world of experience underpins the framework of empathic intelligence. The depth of psychic 'colour' created by this interplay of thought and feeling derives from the dynamism between them. Each needs the other.

The concept of empathic intelligence

TRANSFORMATIVE LEARNING

Attitudes to human thinking and the nature of intellectual maturity are changing as they become increasingly influenced by scientific research into human consciousness (Damasio, 2003, Le Doux 1992, Schwartz 2002, Siegal 1999, Rose 1998). Furthermore, postmodern thinking about the nature of intelligence and the phenomena of human experience has stimulated debate about the best educational methods for a humane, global and electronically wired world. Since information itself is readily accessible to those in the wired world, the management of information and the judgment to select from overwhelming choices, become the major challenges, not only for educational leaders, but also for other client-based professionals and for parents. It is now acknowledged that the best educative processes will match information-seeking with imaginative and open-ended outcomes. Such processes model and encourage mindful, *care*-ful participation in this challenging, ever-changing world. Education for the best and fullest human consciousness requires that we understand and respect the inner world of individuals, in which thought and feeling are complementary psychic processes. It is equally important to understand how individuals interact with others, and how they derive significance from such interactions.

While individuals bring their own biographical history to their social encounters, they can together inhabit a shared, meaningful, psychic landscape. Watch an infant and mother engage in intense contact through eye-gazing, smiling and verbalising. Often the infant initiates the moves and the mother follows; at other times the mother initiates an affective response and the infant follows. They waltz together with their eyes and choreograph their special relationship. So it can be in potentially transformative learning experiences when students and teachers, leaders and followers focus beyond their roles and status to create new meanings and shared insights.

As educators in classrooms and lecture halls around the world face their students day after day, the students study the teachers' faces, listen to their voices, read their dress and body language for clues to the teachers' biographies and predispositions. In doing so, they are fine-tuning an expertise started in infancy of interpreting what the other really means, and determining whether it matters. If it does matter, then there is the potential for a transformative experience to occur. Such an experience will be long remembered and cherished because it affected an important development in the psychic life of the student, and possibly, the teacher.

The rich world of interpersonal life between humans and the equally rich intra-personal life enjoyed by those of a reflective or contemplative disposition, are the foundations for deep and meaningful learning. Such learning can modulate and reflect complex understandings of the world, its shapes, patterns, order, irregularities, ambiguities and mysteries. Such deep learning, and the contexts which give rise to it, are the subject of this book. The qualities of empathy, enthusiasm, the capacity to engage, and expertise constitute empathic intelligence and enable transformative learning and its associated relational caring.

EFFECTIVE TEACHING

At last, the positive influence of teacher quality upon pedagogy is well established through research. To determine the attributes of excellence, educator John Hattie (2003) studied 'America's very best teachers' (p. 1). He argues that while resources are often deployed to reducing class sizes, introducing new testing methods, encouraging parental assistance in the school and focusing on problem students, the ingredient that makes the most difference is the classroom teacher. He elaborates that our attention therefore must be primarily directed at higher quality teaching. To that end, we need to 'identify, esteem, and grow those who have powerful influences on student learning' (p. 4).

Learning is an interactive experience best achieved in a climate of relatedness, care and mutual respect. Such care is offered, not imposed, and respects humans' need for autonomy, self-determination, and challenge as well as security. In this empathic model, learning is a dynamic, democratic process. An understanding of this process and the ability to put it into effect generally mark an empathically intelligent and effective educator. Such a person harnesses complex intellectual, affective and interpersonal skills for the benefit of students and others for whom they are responsible. In a typical classroom, high-level skills are required to manage constructively all the variables and dynamics. Sensitivity, attunement to others, acute observation skills and robust self-scrutiny and self-understanding are precursors to empathic intelligence and effective teaching.

Educators, in particular, need to be encouraged to respect what many of them already know intuitively – that students' motivations and feelings about learning are just as important as the content of their learning. It is not just *what* we learn, but how we *feel* about what we learn, which counts in the long term. When we care about a learning experience, it tends to influence us more strongly, for positive or negative effect. When we don't care, the learning tends to be perfunctory. This goes some way to explaining why some people remember very little from their school days, or recall with delight or regret, those emotionally charged moments of personal significance, such as failing or succeeding against expectations, or winning or losing the esteem of peers, parents or teachers.

DEFINING EMPATHIC INTELLIGENCE

Empathic intelligence is a way of using various intelligences and sensitivities to engage effectively with others. Typically there will be an awareness of purpose and effect in these engagements, and a capacity to shift dynamics if necessary. For example, an educator may engage in a pleasant conversation with a student about something unrelated to work at hand, and in so doing, exercise a measure of empathic intelligence to build rapport and relatedness.

Empathic intelligence is a sustained system of psychic, cognitive, affective, social and ethical functioning, derived from an ability to:

- differentiate self-states (both thoughts and feelings) from others' states through-self awareness, reflection and applied imagination;
- engage in reflective and analogic processing to understand dynamics;
- mobilise a dynamic between thinking and feeling in self and others to enhance learning;
- demonstrate enthusiasm, expertise and an ability to engage others;
- work creatively, guided by observation, attunement and adaptive capacity;
- demonstrate intelligent caring;
- use mirroring and affirmation effectively; and
- commit to the well-being and development of self and others.

This definition describes a sophisticated system of psychic functioning developed through affective sensitivity, a habit of self-reflection, knowledge about the ways humans learn and process experiences, and certain philosophical assumptions about human values and human potential. In this definition, precursors to the development of full empathic intelligence are both affective, and cognitive. It reflects an educator's view of the world.

Empathic intelligence is not the same as emotional intelligence or cognitive intelligence, because it is essentially concerned with the dynamic between thinking and feeling and the ways in which each contributes to the making of meaning. The word *dynamic* is important because it highlights the psychic energy generated when one mobilises both thought and feeling in understanding experience. When there is an intensity of feeling matched with intensity of thought, transforming learning experiences may occur.

Clearly those with abilities in other intelligences – be they analytical, interpersonal, artistic, metaphoric or spatial – will have special capacities to bring to, and derive from, empathic intelligence. As the argument in this book develops, you will be able to see how various emotional, kinaesthetic, intellectual, physical and aesthetic abilities can contribute to the development of empathic intelligence.

With its underpinnings of affectivity, imagination and logic, empathic intelligence, is fundamentally generative, dynamic and analytical. It is both hopeful and realistic. Imagination is fundamental to contemplating the thoughts and feelings of others, as is an analytical capacity to underpin judgment. It is inspired by intuition – that ability to notice what logic might tell you to ignore – and supported by reflective practice. It can function in situations where intelligent, reflective people are engaged in relationships, creative and performative enterprises, client-centred work, leadership or other spheres of influence, or education. Empathic intelligence functions well where excellence or high performance is inspired to, and it grows through recognition.

Empathic intelligence is theorised and elaborated here to explain some of the phenomena involved in teaching and influencing others. While specific attributes of empathic intelligence can be identified, in practice empathic intelligence functions in an integrated way. For example, a teacher challenged by a student's behaviour might well engage in an internal dialogue such as: 'I need to understand better how to tap into his/her interests here … I'm feeling anxious myself that he/she won't succeed and I'll feel incompetent, but then again I remember when this strategy did work ... ' In recalling that success, the teacher's return to confidence might well mobilise the student's interest or it might provoke resistance. All this happens quickly, and often imperceptibly, as inter/intra-subjective processes interact in the engagement between the teacher and student. Whatever happens, the teacher's expertise is needed to interpret the best approach and to provide a range of strategies. These might include acknowledging, with the student, a need to work together to find the best way forward.

Ideally, readers will discover here echoes of their own stories of life and work which will both hearten and encourage them to take risks and be rigorously sceptical – to question what matters most in solving a problem or engaging in influencing others; to determine what values inhere in experiences and what matters most as we struggle to lead meaningful personal and professional lives. While scepticism and rigour may sound hard and cold, they can enhance the logic and intuition which inform empathic intelligence and lend it robustness.

Empathic intelligence is a complex system of functioning supported by culture and human responsiveness. For example, it can be supported by the associative link that narratives can provide. Imagination and emotional sensitivities can expand through reflections upon personal or cultural narratives, through films, music, drama or art. Cultures can provide a kind of cognitive and emotional scaffolding for the development of their members. Hence the importance in education of promoting various symbolic systems (music, dance, drama, sculpture, art, design) as sources for aesthetic, affective and cognitive development. One-dimensional approaches to teaching and learning will not promote the rich intellectual development that comes from responsiveness and its sensitive communication. Those skilled in composing and articulating within various symbolic systems are often required to communicate verbally about their practices. It follows that their understanding of the needs of their audiences requires a certain amount of sensitivity and communicative skill, alongside their specialist expertise. Empathic educators, therefore, take seriously the need to develop in their students, those skills, attitudes and communicative abilities necessary for complex, global worlds.

The concept of empathic intelligence is an outcome of liberal, democratic, student-centred educational philosophy. Influenced by the pioneering work of philosopher John Dewey (1916, 1963, 1964, 1971), the decades of the 1960s and 1970s saw the development of a pedagogy which encouraged teachers to engage students in learning through experience (Polanyi, 1959, 1969, 1974, 1983; Bruner, 1972; Vygotsky, 1988). Once it was accepted that students could learn through exploration and direct experience, teachers were no longer expected to simply transmit information and check the accuracy of students' memories. It was recognised that teachers' true worth lies in their ability to be well-informed, engaging, flexible facilitators of meaningful learning experiences, sensitive, attuned and reflexive in managing interpersonal relationships and complex dynamics in the classroom.

In this theory of empathic intelligence, the medium for experiencing is the self, a complex, dynamic, unique constellation of familiar and felt experiences that constitute our individuality. The sources of a development of self are biological, psychological, cultural, social and linguistic, at the very least. The sources of stimulation for self-development are self-awareness, other-awareness and repeated, meaningful experiences of engagement with the world of objects and persons, affirmation from that world, and reflection upon those interactive processes.

ENTHUSIASM, EXPERTISE, ENGAGEMENT AND EMPATHY

Four qualities of relatedness – enthusiasm, expertise, capacity to engage and, of course, empathy – are identified here as attributes of empathic intelligence. While it might seem redundant to include empathy within the definition, we need to remember that people can be empathic without necessarily functioning as empathically intelligent practitioners. For example, they may lack expertise in theory, content, skills or other qualities. Or they may not apply their empathic abilities for the well-being of others. To simplify the concept of empathic intelligence, it can be helpful to consider how teachers might exemplify each of its attributes in their practice.

Enthusiasm
(En – theos = God/Spirit within)
A personal energy conveyed to others
Motivated by belief and hope
Cousin to passion and desire

Expertise
Mobilises imagination/perspective-taking/hypothesising
Theoretically informed about teaching, effective in practice and competent in discipline area
Able to attune to others' learning needs
Can recognise both regressive and developmental states – spiralling development
Can see the universal, particular and affective characteristics of different symbolic systems (such as art, design, language, mathematics, dance)
Has expansive repertoire of approaches
Can model best practices and can tolerate own and others' mistakes

Engagement
Ability to attract and hold students' attention through centered, purposeful interactions
Ability to mirror others to enhance communication
Ability to channel/teacher-power/authority/charisma for the benefit of students' learning
Communicates a vision beyond the here and now

Empathy
Empathy is an ability to understand your own thoughts and feelings and, by analogy, apply your self-understanding to the service of others, mindful that their thinking and feeling may not match your own
It is a sophisticated ability involving attunement, decentring, conjecture and introspection: an act of thoughtful, heartfelt imagination

Enthusiasm is an attractive concept because by its very nature it draws attention to itself. Enthusiasm refers to the sense of spiritedness, joy, resilience, confidence and warmth which people demonstrate as they work and engage with others. It is not essential for enthusiasm to be highly energetic, though it can be. At times it can manifest as a deep-seated, emotionally charged, but managed, commitment to whatever is happening. It is relatively easy to recognise overt enthusiasm. But where students have learnt to mask enthusiasm, for whatever personal or cultural reasons, it can take some sensitivity to read enthusiasm or to stimulate it.

The sustained enthusiasm of professionals for their work can mobilise positive outcomes for those they relate to. In teaching, parenting and coaching contexts, provided it is modulated appropriately, enthusiasm can sustain students through periods of self-doubt and disbelief. Caring enough to listen to doubting or disaffected students, even when their messages are unpalatable, can be a form of enthusiasm.

Enthusiasm can spark and sustain engagement, but in contexts where learning is the desired outcome, expertise also has to function to make the engagement purposeful and focused, as distinct from merely entertaining or diverting. This is not to suggest that pedagogy has to be earnest. Rather, it is to suggest that in a functional engagement, at least one participant has to have the expertise to monitor the dynamic. This attribute may not be exclusive to the teacher or professional. Ideally, the student will respond to the teacher's cues and be stimulated through modelling, to be enthusiastic and engaged too. Sometimes, the student's enthusiasm and engagement will be directed differently to the teacher's, or be masked or dormant. Then the skilled teacher works to create a synergy between them through a process of adaptation and informed improvisation.

Transformation involving major shifts in understanding and changes to the affective templates guiding behaviour, can be gruelling at times as the mind shifts gears to accommodate new experiences. Such transformation may have to be carefully anticipated, mindful that intellectual and emotional growth do not necessarily occur apace. Despite the quick fixes offered in self-help literature, this book argues that sustained achievement in intellectual development is more likely to be achieved in the long term, and often through the informed encouragement, persistence and mentoring of professional educators. Those committed to achieving professional excellence through quality engagements with their students are likely to be empathic at least, and at best empathically intelligent.

FINE-TUNING PSYCHIC DEVELOPMENT

At the heart of the empathic, transformative model advocated here, is a principle that educators who can engage students in a dynamic exploration of thought and feeling, can promote increased differentiation in both modes of being. In this model, thought becomes increasingly more complex and feelings become more accessible and finely tuned. Their expression in language, movement and aesthetic artefacts records experiences, reflects both moments of insight and points in development, and in turn stimulates further thought and feeling.

An image that might help explain the concept of differentiation is that of a very thick cable rope such as might tie an ocean liner to a wharf. The cable is composed of multiple strands of fibre, twisted into cords. In turn those cords are then wound together to create one very thick cord. By cutting through the cord and looking at the cross-sectioned end of the cable, you could observe hundreds of fibre ends bunched tightly together. Were you to unwind the cable strand by strand, you might be said to 'differentiate' it. You would be able to understand the whole – its overall function and component parts – as well as recognise how the parts contribute to that whole.

This analogy proposes that thinking and feeling can continue to develop as holistic structures, capable of increased complexity and increased differentiation throughout a developing psychic life. While regular learning experiences can add to the sum of memories and strands of experience that constitute a sense of self as a learner, transformative experiences have strong emotional impact. They reformulate the strands in significant ways, influencing, in their own reformulation, related memories or associated strands of experience. That is, they have a deep and lasting impact. At the heart of this model is a philosophy which affirms the inherently person-centred nature of effective pedagogy and a psychology which understands human development as dynamic, experiential, self-enhancing and both inter-dependent and self-driven. A high-order human desire to create personalised meaning from experience, through both individual reflection and relatedness with others, links the philosophy with the psychology.

RETHINKING INTELLIGENCE

A question that is often asked is: *Is empathic intelligence the same as emotional intelligence?* I hope it is clear from the discussion so far that while emotional intelligence is a necessary part of empathic intelligence, there are two key differences. One is that empathic intelligence relies for its functioning on the creation of a dynamic between both cognitive and emotional intelligence. The second distinction is that empathic intelligence has an ethical intention – it is the application of cognitive and emotional intelligences to a creative or beneficial outcome, even if the motive is not entirely altruistic. So, empathic intelligence could be functioning when one undertakes some intellectual or creative pursuit for the primary purpose of self-development; but importantly, the boundaries of empathic intelligence are transgressed if its insights are deliberately applied to a purpose that diminishes another person.

It is helpful here to provide some history of *emotional intelligence* – a concept that has been given public currency by educator Daniel Golman's popular books (1995, 1998). John Mayer and Peter Salovey (1997) argue that emotional intelligence should refer 'in some way to heightened emotional or mental abilities' (p. 5). They define emotional intelligence as 'the ability to perceive emotions, to access and generate emotions so as to assist thought, to understand emotions and emotional knowledge, and to reflectively regulate emotions so as to promote emotional and intellectual growth'(p. 5). They point out that this definition 'combines the ideas that emotion makes thinking more intelligent and that one thinks intelligently about emotions' (p. 5).

This definition of emotional intelligence supports my argument in this book that thinking and feeling need to cooperate in the development of intellectual life. However, it is important to emphasise that, within a framework of empathic intelligence, emotional intelligence refers to the ability to perceive, access and generate emotions to assist *more than thought*. Emotional knowledge, in an empathic framework, is applied to thought in order to plan and work towards *outcomes*. For example, in a classroom a teacher might use emotional knowledge of herself and her students to determine the best classroom dynamics and tasks likely to achieve an outcome such as student mastery of a concept or skill. The process of managing the reflective and anticipatory thinking involved here would engage the teacher in a dynamic cognitive and emotional process. It is the complexity of this kind of process, involving thought, emotion, commitment, reflection, care, enthusiasm, expertise, the capacity to engage students, and empathy, which indicates the necessity for a concept like empathic intelligence.

Mayer and Salovey (1997) argue that emotional intelligence should refer to heightened emotional and mental abilities, as opposed to simple emotional awareness or responsiveness. However, the nature of educative leadership suggests that it is appropriate and timely to differentiate those heightened abilities. Hence my focus in this book on the relatedness of cognitive, emotional and empathic intelligences. Since the word 'intelligence' has strong emotional and cultural impact, it is worth considering how and where it might reasonably be used.

Within psychology one of the rationales for identifying a 'new' intelligence is to document its partial or complete independence from known intelligences. Mayer and Salovey (1997) point out, that in a given individual, most intelligences are moderately correlated with one another, at levels that are closer than one would expect by chance. The correlations among intelligences are only moderate, however, not high, and this allows for a moderate amount of difference among intelligences in the same person. This may mean that identifying the 'new' intelligence 'will tell you something new about a person' (p. 6). They also point out that psychologist Howard Gardner avoids the correlational approach in his work on the theory of multiple intelligences.

I accept that the correlational approach may well be useful to test the existence, or otherwise, of a new intelligence, but I would argue that it is not useful to over-rely on it in pedagogical contexts. In dealing with people engaged in learning through social interactions, there is some educative value in identifying intelligences that may or may not meet accepted psychological criteria for a new or distinct intelligence. I contend that the real value in the identification of complex, multi-layered intelligences, such as empathic intelligence, is that through identification and definition, people who possess something like these intelligences can be encouraged to understand and differentiate their functioning. For example, when it was thought that intelligence was similar to a good memory, rote learning was over-emphasised in classrooms. Now that it is recognised that intelligence can be a manifestation of complex functioning, educators can look for and encourage learning experiences which value and develop such intelligences. In so doing, they reach beyond the known and may bring into awareness, concepts known only tacitly or subliminally.

There is also a danger that the cultural values attributed to certain intelligences can influence the resources directed towards their development. For example, it is only a fairly recent phenomenon that interpersonal abilities such as empathy have begun to appear in job advertisements. This is perhaps recognition in the work community that problem-solving ability alone is rarely a sufficient criterion for a position involving work with others.

Another definitional complexity concerns the distinction posited between emotional *intelligence* and certain *traits* (characteristic or preferred ways of behaving) and *talents* (non-intellectual abilities such as skill at sports). On this point, Mayer and Salovey quote psychologist Sandra Scarr (1989):

> There are many human virtues that are not sufficiently rewarded in our society, such as goodness in human relationships ... to call them intelligence does not do justice either to theories of intelligence or to the personality traits and special talents that lie beyond the consensual definition of intelligence (p. 78).

Mayer and Salovey argue that emotional intelligence could be considered an actual intelligence as opposed to, say, a highly-valued social trait. Scarr's *goodness in human relationships* might indeed be a preferred way of behaving, composed of the traits of sociability, trustworthiness, and warmth. But in addition, there might exist actual abilities or mental skills, such as knowing what another person is feeling, that may involve considerable thinking, and consequently could be considered an intelligence.

However, I suggest that these distinctions are not so simple. For example, I would challenge the idea that talents such as sporting skills are non-intellectual. In most sports, especially at very high levels, intelligence comes into play in decision-making processes, game plans, coping with public pressure and all the complex management of feelings and thought involved in competitions such as the Olympic Games. Another complexity is that in certain contexts, the very knowledge that a trait such as *goodness in human relationships* is highly valued and socially functional, might motivate a strategic alignment with that trait. To take the point further: the *goodness in human relationships* which Scarr has called a trait, might actually be the result of considerable observation, reflection, mental effort, empathy and communicative ability. It seems limiting to argue that the term *intelligence* cannot be applied to the combinations of functioning that make up such highly complex behaviours, largely on the grounds that current measurement methods preclude their identification.

Educator Joe Kincheloe (1999) argues that one of the ways to rethink intelligence is to expand the boundaries of what is called sophisticated thinking:

> When such boundaries are expanded, those who had been excluded from the community of the intelligent seem to cluster around categories based on race (the nonwhite), class (the poor), and gender (the feminine).

> Mainstream educational psychology tends to construct intelligence as fixed and innate – a mysterious quality found only in the privileged few … When we begin to challenge these perspectives in the process of democratising intelligence, dramatic changes occur in our perceptions of who is capable of learning (pp. 7–8).

At its best, empathic intelligence functions to mobilise new meanings and potential from the experience of engagement between individuals, either singly or in groups. It can function between individuals and within the spaces in which they engage. For example, empathic intelligence can inform curators in museums who need to anticipate how patrons might think and feel in visiting an exhibition, and it can function when attuned patrons, alive to sensory stimulation, engage with an exhibit. Their silent conversation with an art work or an exhibit might well be shaped by the imaginative capacity of the artist and curator to shape the dynamics of space in intelligently caring ways.

This complex phenomenon of creating distinctive meanings from interpersonal and intrapersonal engagements is cued by mind-sets open to phenomenological experience and the emotional risk-taking involved. To that end, participants involved in empathically intelligent learning need to feel confident that they can manage their feelings and interpersonal relationships, and be supported in a quest to satisfy intellectual curiosity about the world of people and experience.

Empathic intelligence creates the possibility that the ineffable might well become the visible and tangible, given the potential of imaginative minds to create and explore new psychic worlds. The position I take in this book is that it is helpful to elaborate a complex theory for those who function in complex ways. Although the elaboration will be incomplete, possibly flawed, hard to test and sometimes elusive, at least some aspects of the elaboration may resonate sufficiently with known or felt experience to encourage you to engage with it.

HYPOTHETICALS

Some of the points made in this chapter may have stimulated some memories of significant past experiences. No matter how fleeting those memories are, jot down when and where they occurred and who else was involved in the scenario. If possible, replay the scenario in your imagination, and replace the remembered self with your self now. How would the scene change?

- Imagine you belong to a professional reading group, or a university seminar group designed to develop your identity as an educator, teacher or member of a profession involved in engaging with clients. Write down three or four dot points that sum up for you the important points in this chapter. If you are working in a group, share your points with a colleague and note the similarities/differences in your work.

- Observe a variety of people who demonstrate enthusiasm. How do you detect their enthusiasm? Does it engage you, threaten you or even mystify you?

- Now observe those who demonstrate expertise and a capacity to engage. How do you detect these qualities? How do you feel and think in response to your observations? To what extent, in what circumstances and with whom do you demonstrate enthusiasm, expertise and a capacity to engage others? Do you know how to modulate these qualities according to feedback?

- The concept of intelligence is loaded with emotional, social and cultural significance. How would you define an intelligent person? What are your own intelligences? What kinds of intelligence does a well functioning society need?

- Advertisers are skilled at applying empathic insights for commercial benefit. They understand human needs, and the desire for power, status and prestige. They know how to manipulate feelings to create a sense of need. They even manipulate the ethic of care to create a sense of doing consumers a favour by persuading them to purchase goods and services. How can educators develop students' sensitivity and discernment so that they can engage in their culture without becoming victims of consumerism?

- Analyse the interpersonal qualities of key radio or television interviewers or presenters. Consider how they engage their audiences and note the qualities that might contribute to aspects of empathic intelligence.

FURTHER READING
Rowe, CE & Mac Isaac DS (1991) *Empathic Attunement: The Technique of Psychoanalytic Self Psychology*, Jason Aronson Inc, London.
Tansey, MJ (1989) *Understanding Counter-Transference: From Projective Identification to Empathy*, The Analytic Press, London.

CHAPTER TWO

EMPATHY AS A FUNCTION OF MIND, BRAIN AND FEELING

In this chapter I elaborate some of the characteristics of empathy, in particular the way in which it integrates thought and feeling. I differentiate empathy from other related abilities, and discuss some of the ways in which it translates into action, especially in educational and other professional contexts.

A DYNAMIC BETWEEN THINKING AND FEELING

If the concept of empathy resonates with significant aspects of an individual's professional and personal life, it might well, over time, become internalised. When this occurs, empathy becomes an inner reference system in which actions, thoughts and feelings are integrated and generated. In this way, internalised empathy acts as both a support and information source that impacts dynamically on a person's life. It guides reflection, it supports action and it informs thought. Operating from an internalised system of empathy involves high levels of attunement and response.

Empathy has its genesis in child-centred pedagogy and was promoted through the self-psychology movement emanating from the work of Heinz Kohut, an American self-psychologist and analyst. One of the pivotal ideas in his work was that, in order to understand experience from another's point of view, we need to empathise with that person's reality and their interpretations of their experiences. This stance was a radical departure from earlier psychoanalytic work, which tended to view people and their behaviour from a scientific point of view. One of the outcomes of this new focus was the beginning of the child-centred approach to learning.

Student-centred pedagogy has encouraged educators to respect and promote imaginative responses to learning. However, the concept of empathy in education incorporates imaginative approaches but exceeds them. You could be an imaginative teacher without necessarily being empathic, but it would be difficult to be empathic without having imaginative capacities. Imagination is a necessary but not sufficient characteristic of empathy.

In current student-centred pedagogy, educators encourage students to engage in cognitive experiences such as: visualising, hypothesising, re-conceptualising, speculating, lateral thinking, creating and problem-solving. Such strategies are now orthodoxy in pedagogy, designed to develop students' thinking abilities. Empathic approaches to education differ in that they are designed to encourage a dynamic between thinking and feeling in order to promote learning more effectively.

Beyond identification

In common parlance, 'empathy' means being able to imagine, often intuitively and instinctively, how the other feels. Psychoanalyst Heinz Kohut (1959) described empathy as 'vicarious introspection'. As a more complex process than 'identification', this definition includes both affective attunement and the cognitive capacity to judge how best to respond empathically to another's emotional and cognitive state. It is important to note as we explore this concept of empathy that it is not sufficient to imagine that we can know how another is thinking or feeling based solely on awareness of how we think or feel ourselves.

If we reflect on the notion of 'vicarious' in Kohut's definition, we can appreciate the feeling of embodiment the word suggests. A vicarious experience feels as if we are sharing something with another, even when rationality would tell us that we are not. For example, people watching quiz shows or reality television may feel as though they are sharing the fate and fortunes of the contestants they watch. The experience can become extremely absorbing – but that process is much closer to a form of identification than it is to empathy.

However, without the capacity to identify, it might be difficult to move into an empathic relationship. When I watched the movie *Titanic*, I left the theatre exhausted! All that vicarious swimming in freezing water wore me out. I over-identified with the characters and events in the movie. But if I exercise empathic intelligence, a reality check quickly tells me my experience wasn't anything like that of the victims of the *Titanic*. I experienced my own physiological and emotional responses to events viewed as a spectator.

The capacity to identify enhances my ability to develop empathy, but such empathy is more complex than that of simple, vicarious viewing and identification. Nonetheless, we can embody or internalise effects (cognitive templates) and affects (emotional templates) from both real and imagined or vicarious experiences.

For all the limits of vicarious experience, it is still an important capacity in developing imagination and, ultimately, empathy. When we move to the 'introspection' part of Kohut's definition, the concept of empathy gains more balance. Introspection here refers to the capacity to reflect deeply on one's experiences in the service of gaining guidance to action.

Introspection

To introspect is to work through the mass of stored, embodied, often unconscious memories, to seek significance from them. It calls on analytic skills as well as emotional awareness. It allows us to determine the differences between our role as a spectator, albeit one who is vicariously attuned to witnessed events, and the nature of the role being played by active participants.

Another way of thinking about introspection is to regard it as the process which functions to give perspective to experiences – to distinguish between their personal and public importance, their temporal and their lasting significance. Introspection can secure the links between affect and cognition by promoting awareness of their symbiotic or interdependent nature.

Kohut's definition of empathy is especially relevant to pedagogy where internalisation of learning is required, as distinct from rote learning or mechanistic drilling of information. For example, if a student downloads factual information about the World War I from the Internet, it is a relatively straightforward task to read through the material to determine a sequence of events. If, however, the aim is to draw out the significance of that war to international events of the twentieth century, a deeper kind of thinking, analysing and feeling about the war and its consequences, is required. Introspection and evaluative capacities come into prominence when seeking to determine the significance of events, be they private or public. The psychic energy needed to sustain that kind of introspection is the dynamism fundamental to transformative pedagogy and leadership.

Dynamism

Dynamism, as it is theorised in empathic pedagogy, refers to the sense of energy, tension or movement that is present when we internalise or relate with deep thought and feeling to a situation. Empathic attunement underpins this process. The kind of dynamism I am talking about is recursive – it is energy that moves both outwards and inwards. Think of a dynamic person you know – someone who enthuses you with their aliveness. You may pick up their energy and feel energised yourself (provided they are not so 'over the top' as to be exhausting!) By the same process, lack-lustre individuals can sap our energy and can seem to call on our own reserves to replenish theirs. Similarly, as we engage in certain activities we can feel revitalised or depleted, according to the balance or imbalance between the reciprocal energy flows.

Interpersonal relationships, work and play involve dynamic experiences, alongside the personal dynamics of our own mental and physical states. It is inherent in life that things change constantly. Reflective people monitor their own internal dynamics closely. For them, it is second nature to notice, reflect and analyse their own thoughts and feelings, as well as their interactions with others and the environment. Such people tend to develop a rich inner life – the product of that recursive, dynamic process of inner and outer engagements.

As we perceive events around us, we access both physiological responses, such as impulses from the vagus nerves or an adrenalin rush, as well as rational thoughts that help us monitor what is going on. In a steady state of equilibrium, for example when we are routinely monitoring emails, we may not be paying particular attention to the task at hand until a familiar name appears on the screen.

Depending on our past experiences or current expectations, our state of apparent equilibrium might suddenly change. Feelings and thoughts might compete for attention in our mind as we decide whether to open the email or ignore it, or whether to read the letter from a friend before opening the bill from the credit card company. Choices might have to be made about whether the day will be spoiled or enhanced by the decisions we make in the next few seconds.

An important factor comes into play here and that is our own understanding of our responses to life's daily challenges. We might soothe our anxieties about opening the credit card account with a helpful self-reminder that we had actually been very careful that month. In pressing this reminder into the service of our own emotional states, we are using empathy for our own benefit.

We might know how to soothe our anxiety with a realistic reminder of our pre-emptive strategy of thrift. It may be that in experiencing anxiety at the sight of a bill or invoice, we fleetingly recall witnessing a parent's anxiety at such times. We may recognise that we are actually mimicking our own parents who first modelled this response, rather than reflecting our own reality. If we introspect further, it might become apparent that a parent's response is derived from circumstances very different from our own. It could be that we gain insight, through introspection, about an internalised influence upon our habitual behaviour. We are then in a position to make choices about that behaviour.

This elaboration serves to suggest that our daily responses to experience are infinitely dynamic and complex. We don't need to analyse every moment of the day with the kind of attention and detail I have suggested above. Most of the time we move through the day in a habitual pattern of observation, movement and response, until something demands attention and change. Nonetheless, if we want to manage our own inevitable development, it helps to acknowledge our potential to tap into the underlying dynamism of cognitive and affective states. To suggest that dynamism is an important part of the empathic process is not to suggest that we exist, or should exist, in a state of manic psychic activity. Rather, it is to argue that dynamism functions to fuel deep learning, insight and psychic development.

Companionable stillness and silence can also be empathic. There are times, such as in a meditative or deeply contemplative state, when we might be exquisitely poised between thinking and feeling, and barely conscious of inner movement at all. Even within the concept of dynamism as outlined here, there is a role for stillness, and for attuned listening, to self and to others. Dynamism in the case of poise or stillness might be thought of metaphorically, as potential, rather than actual energy.

EMPATHY, ATTUNEMENT AND RECIPROCITY

It stands to reason that it is easier to attune to those whom we can see, hear and even touch. Mothers gazing at their infant are affirmed if the child returns or initiates the gaze. That communicative dance is mutually regarding. However, there are times when the attunement is disrupted. Not all students in a classroom care about the teacher's agenda, no matter how attuned the teacher wants to be. University lecturers in large lecture halls have to search for affirmation when proximity is difficult and attunement is a matter of imagining the audience's needs. Writers have to imagine the responses of their silent, distant, diverse readers and cater for their responses through imagined projection and the empathy of experience.

This raises the issue of reciprocity within the dynamics of relationships. It is likely to be easier for a teacher to be engaged in a caring and attuned relationship with a student if the teacher's responses are reciprocated. Indeed, such a relationship can often operate in a mutually intuitive way.

If the student is not responsive however, or actively resists such engagement, there are important issues for the teacher to consider. One issue is, arguably, that students who are not responsive to care may be the very ones who are most in need of it. And another is that the strategy of withdrawing care from those who do not reciprocate is questionable on both ethical and pedagogical grounds. It is important that a teacher who is committed to empathic engagement reflects deeply in ways previously described, in order to go beyond immediate reactions to the situation. It is quite possible, for instance, that a student yearns for some sort of caring contact, but is entirely unused to experiencing it and therefore not comfortable with it.

Depending upon their level of maturity and readiness, students might well be able to discuss notions of caring for, caring about and dependency/independence as part of understanding the dynamics of relationships. Role-plays can effectively demonstrate how dynamics can be manipulated through the giving or withholding of response, approval or affirmation. Even subtle modulations in voice can signal reciprocity or a blocking of response.

Most people are susceptible to the responses of others, all the more so during periods of psychic vulnerability such as: adolescence; transition to a new career role; retirement from the workforce; or entering into a new relationship. At such times of identity shift, there is increased sensitivity to inter-personal engagements and closer than normal monitoring of others' affirmation or rejection. It helps if the more robust partner in a caring relationship is aware of the contextual influences on reciprocity or its absence.

The development of ability to experience and differentiate affects can continue throughout life. This ability is commonly expressed through language but it informs all kinds of expressive and creative work, including musical composition and performance, drama, literature and even higher-order calculus and science. The expression of emotions though language and other symbolic systems is not only cathartic; it allows us to recognise feelings, share them, modulate them and resolve them. When accompanied by reflection, such processes can be very meaningful. The search for understanding and meaning is rarely a cognitively-driven process. It is impelled by curiosity, imagination and hope – qualities that are inherent to empathy.

Drama of the new
SOURCE **David Moore Photography Pty Ltd**

Being there

There is a function of empathy that tends to defy analysis, even though it is intuitively recognised as important. It is the form of empathy that is simply 'being there' for another in a time of need. Children know they need such empathy when they insist that someone significant watches them perform some trick. Just witnessing the attempt can enhance its success or soothe the effects of its failure. Sports fans recognise the power of group and individual moral support and the symbolic support of mascots that embody desirable attributes.

This function of empathy can occur between friends and intimates even when it is not acknowledged or understood. In that sense it is a sub-set of empathic intelligence: a necessary precursor to its development, but not necessarily a guarantor of its development. This form of empathy, which might be thought of as silent witnessing, is fundamentally important to emotional well-being, and in turn, to learning about oneself as a learner.

I would like to consider first the role of empathy in emotional well-being. It is claimed that one of the most painful psychological torments is the fear or actuality of abandonment. The force of this claim is exquisitely captured in the story of the agony of Christ in the garden the night before his crucifixion. In that powerfully insightful story of psychological suffering, Christ, abandoned by his human companions, experienced the torture of feeling that he had been abandoned by his father, God. In the way that narrative, drama and religion can symbolically represent fears and hopes, this story attests to the interdependency of humans, particularly when our very sense of self is threatened.

Why this is so defies explanation, but life, culture and wisdom attest to the need. We maintain our sense of self, agency, coherence and hope through interactions with others and our environment. When emotional upheavals upset the equilibrium of self, empathic others can help restore that balance. The rituals of graduations, funerals and public processions enshrine the tacit knowledge that the ceremonial mirroring of significant events creates meanings of public and private significance. Such meanings create a sense of belonging and of timelessness, comforting feelings that help to assuage the terror of aloneness and the vacuum of death.

On a simpler scale, the child's experience of an attentive other as a listener, or reader of their writing, can give them a sense of audience and purpose. These concepts are fundamental to literacy development

(Moffett, 1968; Britton et al. 1975; Arnold, 1991). The audience does not have to be sophisticated or informed; it just has to be attentive and attuned.

Just being there can be constructive for the performer, whether at times of success or difficulty. Even silent witnesses have their place in the human drama of development. They attest to the importance of an event by their readiness to give it attention. Like the chorus in a Greek drama, they act as echoes to the theme, reinforcing symbolically, if not actually, the importance of these moments. The parent or teacher who watches and listens attentively honours the student in ways that seemingly stimulate tacit abilities. Patience is more than just a passive virtue; it has a dynamic, educative function in pedagogy.

THE ROLE OF MIRRORING

We have discussed the infant's need to connect with others in order to thrive, develop and experience a sense of self. That need for connectedness with self and others is a life-long need, for many important reasons. Self-psychologists talk about 'mirroring' as the process which infants experience as they feel the mother's touch, hear her voice and see her facial expressions.

Sensory mirroring is an important way in which we connect with others, soothe our feelings and reassure ourselves that we exist. The fact that solitary confinement is designed as a painful punishment is recognition of that need. Our sense of self can be relatively stable. Most of the time we may feel that we are an okay human being/adult/parent/friend/worker/spouse or student, but it is a sense that can also fluctuate in manageable, or sometimes, unmanageable ways.

When the fluctuations are unmanageable we experience a crisis in confidence. When the fluctuations are manageable but demand attention because we feel disconcerted, we might employ a range of strategies to re-establish a sense of equilibrium. One common strategy is to talk to someone else, seeking self-reassurance. A sensitive listener recognises the underlying need and mirrors back positively. The insensitive listener might settle an old score by reminding us that we are every bit as bad as we are feeling!

Mirroring is a powerful form of self/other modulating. It is the means by which we manage our relations with others, and with our inter-subjective world. Well-balanced individuals seek constructive ways to modulate their relationships with others and to experience a sense of agency and purpose in life. Unbalanced individuals may seek ways that are ultimately destructive to achieve a sense of agency or purpose. In the extreme case of the psychopathic personality, the desire for self-gratification through the annihilation of others can be catastrophic.

The concept of mirroring is powerful, because it is ever present in our lives. Elio Gatti, an excellent educator, actor and director, working with inmates in a prison system, was captivated by the concept. He drew my attention to the opening of the Bible, as a powerful example:

> And God said, Let us make man in our image, after our likeness: and let them have dominion over the fish of the sea, and over the fowl of the air, and over the cattle, and over all the earth, and over every creeping thing that creepeth upon the earth.
>
> So God created man in his own image, in the image of God created he him; male and female created he them (*The Bible*, King James Version. Genesis, 26–27)

The inspiration in the myth of creation is profound. The spiritual and creative nature of both empathy and mirroring is poetically articulated here. The story of creation is more than an imagined narration of events, it encapsulates our hope that we can aspire to divinity by reflecting and enacting the purposes of a transcendental being. This theme is a universal one and is reflected, for example, in Jung's work on myths and archetypes and their influence on the human psyche.

It is not possible to imagine such transcendence without an image or concept to aspire to. God is a creation of the imagination, though embodied in the figure of Jesus Christ. Mirroring as recorded in *Genesis* is a mutual engagement between God and humans, promising transcendence. Whatever the origins of the Bible, the imagination and hope which 'once upon a time' inspired writers to tells its stories, can both comfort and challenge the creatures of the earth destined to enact its myths. Even if God were nothing more than the creation of prodigious imagination, the power of that imagination is deeply inspiring.

Mirroring and engagement in the service of self/other development can take many productive and expressive forms. Reading a novel or watching a play can provide imaginative engagement with people beyond our immediate time and place. Through multiple identifications with characters or roles we can extend and project our sense of possible selves. Could I be like him/her? Would I act in that way? Am I as courageous/ruthless/loving/sad as that character?

While those experiences provide us with mirroring through cultural artefacts and texts, listening to music can provide us with mirroring for affective modulating. We might experience the music as matching our current mood, or as elevating it or soothing it. Cultural experiences that are also aesthetically pleasing might also stimulate reflections about the nature of existence or the effects of particular patterns in the experience. At a deeper level, such experiences affirm our sense of self and attest to the presence of the ineffable.

The physiological responses to such experiences serve to affirm our sense of self as an engaged individual. This sense of engagement satisfies a basic human need to connect with others and the world around us. At the same time, it can promote further cognitive, affective and skill development.

Mirroring in educational settings

Mirroring can function as an expression of bonding between individuals, and it can act as a form of unconscious or conscious reinforcement. If you observe people who are together in a street or in a social setting, often styles of dress, posture and speech symbolise connectedness between them. In a formal sense, the ways educators respond to students can function to reinforce, positively or otherwise, the value of their work.

Since we engage in mirroring from birth, it stands to reason that we become accomplished at it. Students who are accustomed to sitting quietly observing teachers have plenty of opportunity to become connoisseurs of mirroring. They read the sub-texts of teachers' comments with unerring accuracy. The instances where they are likely to make mistakes in interpretation are when they unexpectedly receive feedback that is at odds with their own self-concept as learners. Such instances merit considerable attention because they offer the teacher and student opportunities to explore the nature of such concepts.

It may be that such a reassessment can occur by engaging the student in tasks that are likely to be successful and self-enhancing. Engagement and mirroring can occur in all kinds of ways, symbolically and structurally. Educators' modelling and subtle use of engaging tasks can allow covert re-assessments of a student's sense of agency, competency and mastery. In this area of pedagogy, drama enactments can be a powerful tool.

The work done by my colleague John Hughes (2000) on the positive influence on students' language development of assumed mastery through role enactments, speaks about the role of self-concept in language competence. Leaders, even those whom we do not particularly like, can attest to a vision or image of a future beyond our own boundaries. Their sense of beyond can entice us, in spite of our scepticism. We can suspend disbelief and harness our energies to their cause, as if it were our own. We might even prefer to be mistaken rather than directionless.

Clearly, engagement has a vital role in pedagogy, but how do educators learn to engage students in experiences which the educator values but which the students do not? This issue lies at the heart of pedagogy as an art. It is never more in evidence than when an educator stands before a group seeking to engage their attention. Reputation might well have preceded the educator. But as the educator stands poised to gain attention, his/her deepest feelings about students and the educative process send subliminal messages to the audience.

Those who work with student teachers in classrooms recognise the truth of this observation. Fundamental attitude issues that work against the development of professionalism of an educator require remedies beyond simple changes in technique. It is not inexperience that students disparage; it is that they can sense a lack of deep concern for their learning and the processes of effective pedagogy. At the risk of seeming facetious, children and dogs know their friends and enemies because they pick up signals that more rational adults tend to edit out.

Experienced educators know that attracting and holding students' attention long enough to establish the purpose of a lecture or activity can be one of the hardest moments. Establishing credibility with students is a major challenge. Enthusiasm, expertise, sensitivity to the students' emotional states and their psychological readiness all help, as does having something worthwhile to present. Kristen Lippincott (1998), now director of the Royal Observatory in Greenwich, and a former student of the controversial feminist, Camille Paglia, was asked to comment on Paglia's teaching. She replied:

> She was a fabulous teacher. Her classes were always over-subscribed … she would weave it all together so that it made sense. She is very passion-

ate about ideas and irritated with people who are intellectually lazy. If you were slouching at the back she would shake you out of your adolescent complacency. She had the ability to teach by grabbing students and making them take notice (p. 58).

Of course, not all educators have highly developed attention-grabbing strategies. Determining the best methods of attracting attention has occupied the advertising industry for decades, mindful as it is of the fickleness of novelty. Not surprisingly, performers and arts educators have much to offer educators on the matter of gaining attention from an audience.

Janet Karin, of the Australian Ballet School, addresses this issue in her education of ballet dancers. Dancers are encouraged to observe how a skilled, highly focused, utterly poised, perfectly still dancer can attract attention through postural attitude. How this feat is achieved depends upon the dancer's ability to visualise that anticipated outcome. Paradoxically, rather like a self-fulfilling prophecy, that expectation becomes communicated subliminally to the audience.

In education, there has to be a measure of cooperation and reciprocity between participants in the process. Much as we would wish it were otherwise, education is rarely as aesthetically satisfying or as entertaining as cultural experiences, so the challenges for educators are differently demanding. In innovative and highly effective pedagogical contexts, students have been well educated to understand their responsibilities as learners. In such contexts, the reciprocal nature of teaching and learning is well understood and educators are seen to have responsibilities more complex than that of transmitting information. They are able to monitor students' learning, scaffold increasingly challenging experiences and provide mirroring or feedback which is constructive and informed.

An aura of professionalism can imply that educators have little difficulty engaging students' attention. In spite of movie images of educators as charismatic personalities with enthusiasm and patience, such as Robin Williams in *Dead Poets' Society* or Michelle Pfeiffer in *Dangerous Minds*, charisma can wear thin after a few performances. To be sustained, it needs to be supported by an understanding of how to maintain engagement and how to structure pedagogy along developmental lines. Importantly, teachers also need to be authentic in the teaching interaction. Some critics of the films previously mentioned, for example, readily identified problems of authenticity in their representation of reality.

Consistent with the dynamism that underpins the concepts discussed here, engagement is also dynamic. It not only operates between people but also on the concept of self. Increasingly we recognise that the boundaries between participants in pedagogical exchange often share more similarities than differences. Educators are subject to fluctuations in their sense of competence in role, as are students. Students who succeed usually provide positive mirroring for their teachers. Those who thwart their teachers' best efforts can accelerate the downward spiral of defeat.

Sometimes students respond positively to appropriate explanations about the reciprocal nature of pedagogy and can enjoy analysing the dynamics involved. Classrooms, laboratories, workshops and sites where formal learning occurs are microcosms of broader social and work place settings. Relationships, power plays, feelings, self-concepts, personal narratives, hopes, fears and ambitions all meet at that site.

The Commonwealth Government of Australia has recognised the importance of schools as sites in which the emotional and mental health of students is particularly important and potentially vulnerable. One initiative that illustrates this awareness is the *Mind Matters* resource that has been distributed to all secondary schools in the country. It is a resource that contains 'whole of school' planning resources, curriculum materials and a professional development program for teachers. The curriculum materials are extensively researched and address key mental health and well-being issues. Importantly, the aim of the program is to:

> Enhance the development of school environments where young people feel safe, valued, engaged and purposeful. Social and emotional well-being has been linked to young people's schooling outcomes, their social development, their capacity to contribute to the workforce and the community and to reducing the rate of youth suicide. (*Mind Matters publicity brochure 2000*)

Clearly, there is some support for the development of affective learning within educational environments. Indeed, it is suggested within the *Mind Matters* resources, that mental health and well-being is greatly enhanced when schools develop a whole culture of sensitive engagement and connection between staff, students, parents, caregivers and community members. Such a notion implies that empathic intelligence should be at work in interpersonal communication and pedagogical processes. It also reassures us that when we work with students to explore the nature and implications of their affective world, we are indeed engaged in very important educative work. The lived experiences and meanings that students bring to the learning site offer a rich source of learning for teachers and students alike.

Even if an educator had nothing tangible to work with except the students and their interactions within a group, there would be sufficient material for analysis, observation and reflection. The theatre of pedagogy is rich in significance.

EMOTIONAL TEMPLATES AND EMPATHIC ATTUNEMENT

The work of physician Daniel Stern (1985) on the role of empathy in infancy illuminates the importance of empathic attunement in early learning, emotional development and socialisation. Stern writes about the development of 'inter-subjective relatedness', that ability to experience one's self as a separate being from others, but also as a dependent being. The process by which a mother's empathic responsiveness evokes, stimulates, validates and maybe names the infant's emotional and physical state, ensures that her underlying affective response is encoded in the baby's brain.

According to Stern, and others, the degree to which the major affect states (interest, joy, surprise, anger, distress, fear, contempt, disgust and shame) are encoded in the baby's brain influences the development of their core relatedness. That sense of core relatedness is the basis for the development of inter-subjective relatedness. Stern argues that in the pre-verbal stage infants seek to share joint attention, intentions and affect states with significant others. Stern refers to the process of organising the affect responses of the mother to the infant, and indeed, possibly, the infant's own physiological responses, as the laying down of templates into Representations of Interactions that have been Generalised (RIGS) (1985, p. 97). It is the mother's (and others') empathic responsiveness to the infant that influences the integrations of 'agency, coherence, and affectivity' to provide the infant with a unified sense of a core self and a core other: 'the existential bedrock of interpersonal relations' (p. 125).

It might help to think of the significance of this concept of RIGS in the following way. Reflect upon a very affecting experience in your own personal history. It might be a serious bereavement, or a divorce, or a major career disappointment. It could even be something less extreme such as 'loss of face' in a humiliating situation. As you reflect upon that experience, more than likely you suffer not only the pain of the present circumstances, but a resurgence of other, similar experiences which your mind has codified under a certain pattern, or RIGS, in Stern's terms.

It is sometimes difficult to disentangle the present experience from the past experiences, so persistent is the brain's ability to codify experience in apparently manageable ways. The trick is to apply an empathic method to your own case. This can be achieved by noticing, analysing and reflecting upon the thoughts and feelings aroused by the present situation and disentangling them from those factors that belong to the past. Through a process of introspection it is possible to determine what belongs to the experiences of the past, and what appropriately belongs to the present experience. It requires some skill and perseverance to do this effectively. As I postulated at the beginning of this book, past and present are not always neatly categorised separately in the mind, particularly where events are emotionally charged and meaningful. Even if it becomes difficult to determine the dynamics of current events, the knowledge that they are influenced and nuanced by personal histories is important.

Stern's notion of early affective experiences being laid down as emotional templates with their own powerful and enduring psychic force has parallels with the concept of 'transference' in psychoanalytic literature and practice. Both concepts are important in understanding interpersonal life as both can function wherever one person is engaged in influencing, or being influenced by, another. Because the concept of transference has its own particular definitions and controversies, particularly within psychoanalysis, for the purposes of this book, I will use the term 'emotional templates' to indicate the influence of early-life experiences on current intra-psychic, interpersonal engagements.

Intra-psychic engagements are the thoughts and feelings that come into play as you try to make an important decision, for example, or as you reflect upon your ambivalent reactions to a situation. Because we are all influenced in our psychic development by significant others in our life – parents, siblings, teachers, friends – we carry around in our heads things we have been told by them, as well as the emotional aura of the telling.

Of course, prior to the development of a reflective capacity, an infant or young child has no control over the kind of template laid down in the brain. Experiences will be recorded as primarily affective and unconscious, and therefore, largely undifferentiated. It is possible to see how an infant's sense of well-being and ultimately sense of self-worth can be positively influenced by the emotional responsiveness of others. The infant who sees the mother's joyful look feels good inside because that look stimulates pleasurable physiological reactions. Likewise, a look of distress from a mother, or other, evokes discomfort inside. If the mother notices the infant's expression of discomfort in response to her expression of distress, she may respond empathically and soothe the discomfort by talking reassuringly.

The mother's empathic responsiveness is helping the infant's coding of affects, and at the same time, is creating certain meanings for the infant. It is not the case that the mother always mirrors back the infant's affects. She makes decisions about responding and sometimes wisely invalidates an infant's particular response. For example, the baby might squeal with delight at the sight of a deadly spider, at which the mother might gasp with fright and grab the infant. The mother's function is not merely to empathically validate the infant's emotional reactions; sometimes it is to educate through her own reasoned reactions. She modulates the infant's affects and behaviour by mirroring, soothing or intensifying them. Later the child engages with others and with toys that can also function as self-soothing or exciting objects.

Clearly, empathy continues to be important in the development of interrelatedness, but as the child develops physically, cognitively, linguistically, socially and self-reflectively, other people, events and experiences can serve subjective and cognitive needs. Since the mother's empathic responsiveness in the first nine months or so is crucial in the development of the core self, it is easy to imagine that significant (albeit unconscious) empathic responsiveness from adults and socialisation experiences are closely aligned in children's minds. Of particular relevance here is the child's internalised sense of self as a competent learner.

Assuming a 'good enough' (Winicott 1965) job has been done in promoting a child's sense of emotional well-being and psychic development, we can assume that memory traces, or RIGS, are laid down in our psyches. They will reflect the powerfully affective contexts in which early learning occurred.

Kohut warned that empathy is not just an intuitive capacity:

> I do not write about empathy as being always correct and accurate ... empathy is a value-neutral mode of observation ... attuned to the inner life of man (sic) [which should be] examined and evaluated in an empirical context as a mental activity (1982, pp. 396–397).

Needless to say, in engaging with an infant in an empathic way, or engaging with a student later in life, parents and educators essentially need to be sufficiently well adjusted themselves to be able to attend sensitively to the child's and student's needs. In collaboration with the child or student, they need to be somewhat self-sacrificing and capable of introspection in order to determine appropriate reactions. Significantly, infants and children are well able to signal their needs, well beyond the early phases of spontaneously crying to attract attention. In all kinds of symbolic and linguistic ways, psychic states, intentions and needs are signalled, as well as readiness to learn and be challenged.

Although Stern's work derives from studies of infants and Kohut's from his psychotherapeutic work, their concepts are helpful to educators wishing to understand the role and nature of empathy in education. In educational settings the teacher's empathic awareness is an important precursor to understanding, explaining, question-asking and reinforcement of students' efforts, as well as to the scaffolding of challenging tasks and the establishment of a conducive learning environment. While educators might feel daunted by the prospect of responding empathically to a room full of energetic, or even disaffected, individuals, empathy can be a powerful learning tool and a source of satisfaction for the educators who employ it.

Part of learning in normal development involves modifications of those generalised interactions laid down unconsciously and consciously throughout early childhood and life as a learner. The Piagetian notion therefore, that learning is a process of increased cognitive differentiation, ideally needs to be subsumed within a concept of learning that incorporates a dynamic between cognitive and affective processes for increased differentiation in both. It is this dynamism that underpins empathic pedagogy.

Effectiveness in this mode depends on the capacity of teachers to suspend self-needs in the interests of the students, while simultaneously using their introspective awareness of their own emotional states as an empathic tool. Because this is a demanding, focused role for the teacher, certain safeguards must be built into the empathic classroom or community. These will be outlined in due course, but suffice to say here that educators need to be accorded a quality of empathic attunement from their colleagues and the systems in which they work in order for them to function empathically and constructively. As we have seen from mother-infant interactions, empathy is a mutually responsive system of engagement. It is responsible for promoting the intra-personal and inter-personal responsiveness from which empathic intelligence can develop.

EMPATHY IN EARLY LANGUAGE DEVELOPMENT

The linguist Michael Halliday (1975) theorised that early language development occurs, in part, because infants recognise what language does for them in inducting them into human society. It is timely to theorise now that the empathic attunement of significant others to the infant's efforts to speak is also an important trigger for language development. From Halliday's perspective, the empathic attunement of significant others to infants' efforts to speak may well be as important a trigger for such development, as infants' recognition of what language does for them.

Empathically attuned others function in a very practical and developmental way. They extend the infant's phrases to full sentences, thereby modelling or scaffolding the appropriate language forms: 'Oh, so you want the large teddy not the small one?' Better than that, the attuned others respond with enthusiasm, even exaggerated enthusiasm, to the infant's efforts. When it is done well, with full attention to the infant, it exemplifies pedagogy at its best. It is also pedagogy in a one-to-one context, with focused attention, expertise, care and attunement in perfect pitch. That context is markedly different to more public educational contexts such as classrooms or lecture halls with all their distractions and challenges.

If we identify imaginatively with an infant, it is conceivable that language development itself is prompted, in part, by a need to express feelings in a more differentiated way than by crying, effective as that often is. With the development of language and cognition, the developing infant's affective coding of experience can be expressed and made conscious to a greater or lesser extent. Prior to that development, and the development of impulse control, the infant might well be regarded as dominated by affects and the need to soothe or amplify them.

Language, play, symbolic interactions and fantasy create possibilities for rehearsals of life, the codifying of experience and the expression of inter-subjective/intra-subjective experiences. Empathic pedagogy attempts to synthesise and valorise certain democratic, student-centred principles of pedagogy. Many of these principles, particularly mentoring and learning through experience, have informed enduring educational practices, at least since Socrates.

Language fulfils a further function in the symbiotic relationship between the development of affect and cognition. It reflects or mirrors understanding and feeling, coding experience in ways that make it available for further differentiation and development. In finding a word to match the experience of certain affect states, the feeling can be encapsulated and managed better.

Included in language are forms of symbolisation broader than verbal language, such as algebra, music, dance and sculpture. In sophisticated ways, these symbolic forms encapsulate thought and feeling too. Arguably, written and spoken language has the broadest capacity of symbolic systems to differentiate and express experience in ways that can be communicated to wide audiences. High order computer programs and mathematical formulae operate in realms beyond normal language. But although they have the advantage of symbolising complex concepts to their initiates, they have the disadvantage of being understood only by these initiates. In spoken and written language the metaphors of poetic language come closest to synthesising thought and feeling in complex forms and have the advantage that they can resonate with feeling, as well as symbolise thought. Meaningful experiences are perceived and coded in both thought and feeling.

Imagine what it might be like for an infant who discovers pleasure in making random sounds, such as those made by pushing a sound through nearly closed, pursed lips. An observant, attuned mother might well notice what she thinks is a precise address to her. She might well be hoping that her infant will start to talk and could be alert to early signals of meaningful sounds. She might, for example, catch the infant's eye gaze, smile with delight and say 'Mumma' in response to this effort. The infant may well have had no intention to communicate a meaning, but since this exchange is mutually pleasurable, and the infant ready to learn language, both the word, 'mumma' and the behaviour required to utter it, are likely to be affectively charged for the infant.

Tuning in
SOURCE **Picture Partnership**

The mother might also be so pleased with what seems like a spontaneous affirmation of her worth that she picks up the infant and hugs it, thereby providing the infant with visual, aural and tactile reinforcement of this event. In such a scenario, both mother and child mirror each other's worth in a moment of mutual admiration and physical bonding.

If you were that infant and could understand the mother's later conversation with others, you might hear her report that her offspring has just uttered its first word, which was, of course, 'Mumma'. Not only are you smiled at and hugged, and that feels good inside, but you would also feel as if you had accomplished something special. Later, as you begin to string words together, you would discover that attentive others accept what you try to say as if it makes sense. Even more surprisingly, those empathic others kindly model for you the form of the sentence you are trying to utter.

Fortunately there are no rules that say that you mustn't speak until you can utter complete sentences. Nor does anyone ask whether you can name the parts of speech you are using. On the contrary, everyone behaves as if you are brilliant and able to make very good sense. In a finely attuned empathic response to your needs, others seem to know intuitively how to raise their expectations of your language development just within your range of capabilities. Attuned others even model for you elaborated forms of language that you can internalise in your repertoire of language forms to use when required. You can enjoy both the challenge and the achievement.

In the event that an infant's speech efforts are not responded to, s/he might repeat her efforts until someone notices, or give up and seek some other behaviour to gain attention. This 'acting out' behaviour is well known to parents and educators, and attests, even in its negative way, to the need for positive mirroring in the processes of learning. When language development (and other kinds of development) proceed in ways that enhance the infant with experiences of mirroring and modelling, a positive sense of self as an effective learner is embedded in the child's memory. Depending on the nature of other learning experiences, this positive sense of self as a learner and communicator can be stimulated, or it may lie dormant.

While I have simplified here the extremely complex processes of language development, it is clear that infants in a positive and enabling environment do experience empathic approaches that enhance their development. Empathic listeners often intuitively elaborate children's utterances and reply to them in a way that both affirms their efforts and scaffolds new learning. For example, a child might say 'Wanna biscuit!' The listener might reply 'Do you want a plain biscuit or a sweet biscuit?' thereby affirming that the communication has been understood but also that it needs to be differentiated. The listener might also want to suggest that demands are best modulated with the social tag, 'please', thereby modelling important social conventions as well. Exchanges such as this can move across the interface between mirroring and scaffolding. Mirroring reflects and affirms the effective parts of the communicative utterance, while scaffolding indicates how it might be improved. I explore the importance of mirroring more fully in the next chapter.

EMPATHY IN ONGOING LEARNING

Given that empathy functions so effectively and intuitively in early language development, it is surprising that it is so often ignored in formal learning. Arguably, emotional and cognitive templates for effective learning are laid down within any child who learns to speak. We can simplify the challenges of long-term education by understanding more about those learning experiences that children have enjoyed, and the masteries they have achieved in early childhood, long before they enter formal schooling.

If we know how to tap into students' tacit abilities and affective templates, and understand their concepts of themselves as learners, we can create a pleasing continuity in their development as learners. While it can be difficult to hypothesise about what infants and children experience as they learn and master skills, their emotional responses can often be understood by imaginatively identifying with them or reading their body language and tone of voice. Such responses are data for intelligent curriculum development across the spectrum.

The influence of past highly affective experiences on our lives, even decades after the event, is becoming well recognised. It was reported for example, that American war veterans' groups set up toll-free counselling lines for old soldiers for whom Steven Spielberg's film *Saving Private Ryan* might re-awaken traumatic memories (McCarthy, 1998. p. 19). The film graphically, even brutally, confronts viewers with unforgettable, unbearable images and sounds of the battlefields. While regular, civilian cinema-goers can cover their ears and close their eyes, denying the reality of events, former soldiers viewing the film lacked that option and had the emotional force of their own internalised terror to contend with as well. Our internalised experiences are not necessarily fixed or unchangeable; they are dynamic and susceptible to reactivation and introspection. In most cases these embodied experiences have their own fluidity and permeability that can surface positively or negatively on our meaning-making capacities.

When a cultural form such as art, literature, drama or film engages both moral imagination and aesthetic sensibilities, it has the capacity to influence our thinking and soothe or excite our feelings. It is that realisation which drives experienced educators to select for close study with their students, examples of cultural forms that offer possibilities of enhanced moral, aesthetic and creative sensibilities. The so-called classics in art, literature and music are not the only desirable choices for contemporary students, but they survive largely because they embody particular qualities and have met the criteria suggested here. Empathic educators are skilled in knowing how to capture students' imaginations in ways that connect them with profound insights from the past in order to better manage the complexities of the present. In that sense, such an educator creates the educative, poetic illusion that the past and present can enjoy some seamless continuities.

When read with empathic intelligence, such texts gain depth and power. This is evident in considering the role of a literary editor or an art or museum curator. Their brief is to present works to their audiences as advantageously and sensitively as possible. To do so effectively requires an empathic intelligence as well as particular literacy of the form. In such circumstances, empathic intelligence helps the editor or curator to anticipate and guide audience responses. Barristers or attorneys in court cases might also benefit from such intelligence in assessing the appropriate balance between rationality and emotion desirable in winning an argument, if not of contributing to the exercise of justice.

Parenting behaviour is notoriously influenced by the patterns laid down by the previous generation. It can be difficult, particularly under the pressure of managing a difficult child, to replace a punitive style with a more constructive one. It takes confidence in the long-term benefits of appropriate goal-setting, positive reinforcement and empathic understanding, along with endurance in the periods when progress seems paralysed. In such periods, parents need sustained support too.

EMPATHIC INTELLIGENCE IN PROFESSIONAL LIFE

There are other broad social arenas in which empathic intelligence is relevant as well. It has often intrigued and challenged university fundraisers in Australia, for example, that universities in the United States are astonishingly successful in securing donations and bequests from their alumni, even after students have paid fees much higher than those required in Australia. Notwithstanding the different attitudes to benefactions in the culture of the United States, and the particular tax structures in that country, a significant variable seems to be the sense of belonging and care experienced during their college/university years by those who eventually donate to university foundations (Ashburner, 1998). Undoubtedly, such feelings of identification and warmth towards an educative institution may endure for several decades, and conceivably, account for some measure of the career success enjoyed by these benefactors.

By understanding the nature of empathic intelligence and its relationship to other kinds of intelligence, we can formulate positions to assist the development of human resources, policies and practices in a wide variety of occupations, and professional roles. Undoubtedly many people have developed empathic intelligence without formal education in the field, but if a nation or corporation is seeking to gain an edge in an information-saturated environment, it is clear that this field offers ethically defensible human and material advantages. People who work in dynamically charged environments – people such as doctors, lawyers, educators, parents, performers, flight attendants, all positions requiring fairly constant engagement with relative strangers – know only too well how quickly and frequently interactions switch focus and emotional tenor, often moment by moment. In workplace situations emotionally charged moments can occur suddenly. For example, someone attempts to board the plane with a huge teddy bear as part of their 'hand' luggage, or a non English speaking tourist wants to pay for a bus fare with a one hundred dollar note, or a parent unexpectedly refuses permission for a planned school outing, and so on.

At the most testing moments in professional life, we are often alone, even among others. There are times when it is largely our responsibility to influence the outcome of such moments. Whatever we do, or say, will intensify or soothe the emotional tenor and either mobilise others to constructive action, or create stress or even havoc. How can a theory help? A good, functional theory acknowledges the important influences that impact upon such moments and helps to provide a framework for the fluidity that is integral to them. In that sense, theory can compose our thoughts and feelings, giving them shape and purpose. When theory functions constructively, it increases our sense of competence. When experience is named and thought about, it can be managed, bounded and put into perspective. One of the difficult parts of an emotionally charged moment is the feeling of confusion it can create.

If a nervous student teacher has never seen the group before, he sees thirty pairs of challenging eyes staring at him. But if he has had a chance to relate to the students in some personalised way, even through a brief conversation, he sees at least a couple of individuals among the eyes. It is important in such situations that theory serves to explain the ways in which depersonalised interactions can sustain anxiety, so that appropriately professional alternative strategies can be considered. It is a fact of perception that we see first and most clearly what we know and feel emotionally connected to. Advertisers exploit this fact ruthlessly and effectively.

By incorporating into a theoretical framework various significant interactive qualities such as enthusiasm, commitment, expertise and personal values, there is broad scope for analysis of the dynamics of interactions and thinking and feeling states. Influential individuals attracted to the model begin to develop a sense of community. It is common practice to affiliate with groups whom we perceive to 'speak the same language'. That affiliation gives us the confidence and context to discuss the experiences relevant to that group affiliation. We define ourselves through our affiliations and commit emotionally and rationally to such groups. That sense of belonging personalises our working experiences in meaningful ways. The more we use the language of the group, the more likely we are to affirm for ourselves the worth of the concepts we discuss. And the more likely we are to see evidence of those concepts in action. If the match between theory and practice fits, the concept will deepen in significance and is likely to become further refined.

A theory that seeks to explain the dynamism of developmental professional practice should itself be dynamic and developmental. It should act as a kind of scaffold for further professional development, and function within what psychologist Lev Vygotsky called the zone of proximal development. This is a space within the psyche that I visualise as vibrating with the potential for growth.

In order to hold and critique the connection between the theory and practice it is helpful to focus on one or two concepts. It is useful, for example, to explore the differences between sympathy and empathy, or the role of mirroring or the nature of enthusiasm, and to focus on their presence in professional or private life. Reflective journal writing assists this kind of qualitative research and becomes both a record and reflection of a developing synthesis between theory and practice.

INTELLIGENT CARING IN EDUCATION: SOME RESEARCH FINDINGS

It is important to establish appropriate boundaries around the notion of intelligent caring because caring can function along a continuum of functional to dysfunctional, depending upon the motivations and effectiveness of those engaged in giving and receiving care. Care, or discernment, needs to be exercised to ensure that caring of another is an enabling, dignified process that models an appropriate continuum between dependence and independence. The needs of the other must be paramount so that caring is functional for the one being cared for, rather than self-serving for the carer. To care about another, suggests holding their needs and interests paramount. The intelligent part of caring is to identify the right balance between dependency and independence. Effective health carers develop this expertise in order to know how much and what kind of help to offer a sick or infirm person, lest the caring becomes demeaning or dehumanising.

This raises the important issue of what is meant by caring. It is a concept that is open to different interpretation and different use. It is also a central concept underpinning empathic intelligence and it is therefore important to clarify its meaning. The concept of care can be used to express a view or a position – for example, I care about refugees, or I care about the results of the next election. In this sense, care is used to identify and signal what matters to me. Used in this way, the idea of care does not necessarily embody high order values or thought. It can simply indicate preferences – for example, I care about my hair, so I always go to such and such salon.

Care is also used in a general sense to mean looking after, as in child-care, home-care or in advertising: car care, skin care, laundry care. Some professions, namely teaching, social work and health work, are sometimes referred to as the caring professions. And certainly, many people who do this type of work say that their care and affinity with people was the motivation for choosing their career.

Intelligent caring:

- It embodies within it attention, engagement, an awareness of possible outcomes and the possibility of unforeseen events;

- positions the welfare (emotional readiness/learning/experience) of the other as the focus of attention and the purpose of engagement; and

- harnesses the psychic energy of engagement to modulate decision-making and action in functional ways.

Educator Franziska Vogt (2002) refers to an ethic of care in teaching and also attempts to describe what this actually means. And it is important that we do engage in such reflection for two major reasons. The first is that both students and their teachers identify care as the very feature of the teaching encounter or exchange that can make it exceptional (Hayes et al. 1994). The second is that value systems which hold caring as centrally important can readily be devalued in any contemporary society that places high value on competition and winning. It is important therefore, that we can differentiate intelligent caring and articulate its value for educational practice.

Given the emphasis on cognitive development in education, it is perhaps not surprising that research on the relational aspects of teaching and learning, and on affective development, is relatively sparse. The education discipline borrows widely from philosophy, sociology, linguistics and psychology, and is slow to assert its own fundamental principles and practices.

Educational practice foregrounds the essentially interactional, interrelational nature of teaching and learning as well as incorporating other complex factors that impact on pedagogy. The transfer of research findings from other disciplines, therefore, needs to be tempered by an awareness of the lived reality of actual classrooms, schools and learning centres. A fundamentally important aspect of this reality is the subjectivities (attitudes, motivations, enthusiasms, abilities) of the teachers and students engaged in learning processes.

There is plenty of educational literature that describes the importance of child-centred learning and widespread recognition that meaningful learning is more likely to occur if it is relevant, interactive and grounded in experience for the learner. This approach has had enormous impact, especially for the early years of schooling. What has not yet been researched adequately, however, is the scope and quality of what it is that constitutes relevance and meaningful experience – especially in the psychic and psychological domain.

If, for example, a student is passionately interested in animals, it is relatively easy for a teacher to incorporate this interest into curriculum activity. Linking a student's interest to an aspect of the curriculum is an important thing to do, but this does not necessarily mean that it encapsulates the qualities of empathic intelligence that are being explored here. For example, the teacher concerned may have no sense at all of what that student's emotional connection to animals encompasses, or what it feels like. We cannot assume that empathic intelligence has been in play simply because relevance has been considered – even though it certainly helps!

Empathic intelligence asks for something more than this, something located in the inter-personal character of the caring encounter. It takes place in what Vygotsky (1986) referred to as the 'zone of proximal development' discussed earlier. He asserts that 'A true and full understanding of another's thought is possible only when we understand its affective-volitional basis' (p. 252). What he means by this is that thoughts do not think themselves. They are not, as he puts it, 'separated from all the fullness of real life, from the living motives, interests and attractions of the thinking human' (cited in Wertsch 1985, p. 189).

A highly attuned awareness of self and the other in the interpersonal exchange – both cognitively and relationally – is what characterises empathic intelligence. It is this idea that Goldstein (1999) draws on to enhance our understanding of the construction of knowledge in the teaching process. Clearly the quality of focus and attunement required for such an exchange is not ever-present in all classroom interactions. But ideally it should be a basis of the teacher's relationship and connection with each student. In practice this means that each student will have experienced the teacher being totally present and engaged with their thinking and emotional processes. It is this experience that will mark that teacher as exceptional.

Indeed, so important is this affective area of teachers' impact, that some argue it should inform the recruitment and placement of teachers who have these qualities (Hayes Ryan et al. 1994). Interestingly this idea has been taken up in some contexts primarily because, when students' feel met in these caring ways, their resistance to schooling decreases, as does their challenging behaviour (Fox et al. 2003).

Other researchers have also revealed that if schools can develop a culture of caring, it develops students' capacity to take this approach into their homes and communities (Doyle and Doyle 2003). It is not surprising that educators involved in this approach become passionately committed to it. Not only can it transform the learning experience but it also holds the potential for transformative inter- and intra-psychological growth. Noddings exemplifies this sort of commitment in her claim that:

> Caring is the bedrock of all successful education and … contemporary schooling can be revitalised in its light…schools should be committed to a great moral purpose: to care for children so that they, too, will be prepared to care (cited in White, 2003, p. 301).

A research project undertaken by the educator Deborah Eyre and colleagues (2002) had the objective of identifying good teachers in order to examine their strategies. The particular context in which they were working was with teachers of 'able' (gifted) students. In particular, they wanted to work with teachers who were known to 'have something extra' (p. 160). Their research revealed that all of the teachers who fitted this description generally had the same educational philosophy, a fundamental point of which was having empathy with the learner. Other shared values included having humour, effective management and high expectations of students.

Teachers who work with culturally diverse students often assume that empathy is intrinsic to their work. The educator Gretchen McAllister and colleagues (2002) highlight this aspect of teachers' beliefs in their research and conclude that teacher education programs ideally should develop these dispositions if teachers are to become skilled in diverse contexts. Interestingly, in this work, empathy is argued as a social justice issue, that is, as a necessary component of ensuring that academic success is available to all students. Educator Sonia Nieto (2003) takes this idea even further in suggesting that the teachers most gifted in these ways should be placed with the poorest and most ethnically diverse students. Such teachers, it is argued, can, 'make the single greatest difference between a life of hope and one of despair' (p. 15).

Formal research work in the field of empathic intelligence as it relates to classroom pedagogy is relatively recent, yet it is reasonable to draw some key conclusions from it. Perhaps the most compelling is that students feel emotionally met and able to perform at their optimum levels of ability when teachers care about them and are able to communicate this care during the process of the teaching interaction. This significant finding has implications that extend far beyond the classroom. The integration of learning to include affective, inter- and intra-personal abilities has the potential to develop well-integrated people who are equipped to actively contribute to the world in which they live.

Empathy has been studied by philosophers, psychologists and social scientists, but importantly, it is now receiving attention from neuroscientists as functional magnetic resonance imaging and sophisticated brain scanning techniques open up new research possibilities. At University College of London, neuroscientist Tania Singer and colleagues (Singer et al. 2004) argue that our ability to have an experience of another's pain is characteristic of empathy. They used functional imaging to assess brain activity while volunteers experienced a painful stimulus and compared it to that elicited when they observed a signal indicating that their loved one, present in the same room, was receiving a similar pain stimulus. They concluded from their research that 'only that part of the pain network associated with its affective qualities, but not its sensory qualities, mediates empathy' (p. 1157). Furthermore, they showed 'a relation between empathy-related brain activity and individual difference in empathy as assessed by commonly used empathy scales' (p. 1158). In contrast to accounts of emotional contagion, the researchers demonstrated 'that empathic responses can be elicited automatically in the absence of an emotional cue (such as facial emotional expressions) through mere presentation of an arbitrary cue that signals the feeling state of another person' (p. 1158). The scientific study of empathy is not without controversy about whether or not it requires a specialised brain area (Keysers, 2004; Ramnani, 2004, p. 335). Notwithstanding differences about aspects of its nature and origins, there is fundamental agreement about the significance of empathy in creating in-depth relationships. In-depth research on brain-based activity and empathy opens up promising avenues for understanding more deeply the nature of relationships and the dynamics of pedagogy.

The studies mentioned in this section indicate that empathy merits further consideration as an important human quality. It can function at its most basic level as a simple appreciation of the feelings and perspectives of others. But it also has enormous potential to develop at a more complex level as empathic pedagogy, where empathically intelligent educators plan their work to develop these capacities in their students.

HYPOTHETICALS

- It is a common practice for marks to be awarded collectively for work done in a group. Sometimes good students feel resentful because either the collective mark brings down their expected grade, or they feel they contributed more than others and the collective mark gives insufficient reward. How can an intelligently caring teacher best manage this issue?

- You are a recently graduated teacher in a school. You are sensitive, caring, enthusiastic and well-prepared for your professional responsibilities. Shortly after you settle into your school, you realise that the qualities and attributes you demonstrate are threatening to some of your colleagues. Students value highly the way you relate to and work with them, but the effects of others' professional envy begin to erode your self-confidence. What strategies do you develop to manage the situation?

- A good student, disappointed with an examination result, shows you an essay question graded by one of your colleagues. You realise that the colleague has badly misinterpreted the question and penalised the student unfairly. As an intelligently caring adult, what do you do?

FURTHER READING

Costin, SE & Jones, DC (1992) Friendship as a facilitator of emotional responsiveness and prosocial interventions among young children, *Developmental Psychology*, 28: 941–947.

Moore, T (1994) *Soul Mates: Honouring the Mysteries of Love and Relationship*, HarperPerennial, New York.

Morris,V, & Morris, C (2002) Caring – the missing C in teacher education; Lessons learning from a segregated African-American school, *Journal of Teacher Education*, 53(2): 120-122.

Pinker, S (1997) *How the Mind Works*, WW Norton & Company, New York, London.

Sadler, TD (2002) *Socioscientific Issues and the Affective Domain: Scientific Literacy's Missing Link*, Paper presented at the Annual Meeting of the Southeastern Association for the Education of Teachers in Science, Kennesaw, GA.

Schwartz, JM & Begley S (2002) *The Mind and The Brain*, HarperCollins Publishers, New York, NY.

Smith, D (1980) *The Circle of Acquaintance: Perception, Consciousness and Empathy*, Kluwer Academic Publishers, Hardbound, Dordrecht.

CHAPTER THREE

EMPATHY, NARRATIVE AND THE IMAGINATION

DEVELOPING EMPATHY THROUGH NARRATIVE

To establish a context for the kinds of thinking and feeling which characterise empathic intelligence, I begin this chapter with a focus on narratives and their function in our inner world. This is purposely done to evoke readers' memories of oral or written stories in their own life and education. Such stories might have stimulated you to engage in imagined worlds and to identify with the thoughts, feelings, values and views of narrators. They may have evoked your capacity to engage in fantasy or in reality testing. I argue here that such experiences lay a foundation for an empathic approach to experience.

Once upon a time is an enticing opening for a story, and embedded in the culture of English storytelling. It was the opening of the first book I read by myself as a child. I recall being intrigued by the idea of *Once upon a time* and also puzzled by its ambiguity and seeming contradiction. I recall vividly that on the very first page, the initial letter **O** was enlarged so that it ran beside the first four lines of the story. It was such a prominent letter, that I stared at it for some time. So long, in fact, I assumed from its shape and size that it represented the whole world. Decades later as I reflect upon that experience, I know that in an important sense I was right. Through the experience of reading stories, particularly in childhood, we learn much of importance. And children may make sense of their experiences without adult intervention, especially if they have been encouraged to be imaginative.

Sometimes children enter the world of the imagination cuddled up to a trusted adult reading them stories. At other times they enter that world alone, with books and fantasies as companions on this delightful journey. With experience, children learn that stories reveal more than meets the eye – that, for example, stories of the past may illuminate the present. Stories may carry the wisdom of other cultures and provide comfort in the universality and timelessness of their contexts. They invite their listeners and readers, young and old, to enter a fabulous world in which feelings can be aroused, characters understood and events explored, all within the safe boundaries of the beginning and the ending. Children learn that even threatening experiences can be explored though imagination, safe in the knowledge that there will always be a resolution to a good story.

Howard Gardner argues that a story is not merely a 'message' or a 'vision'.

> It is a full-fledged drama, one that grows naturally out of the life experiences of the Influencer, and one that seeks to envelop the audience in the same quest. One might say that such a narrative marshals 'existential intelligence' – the capacity to address issues of being and meaning about which individuals care most profoundly. Individuals are prompted to change when they identify with an inspirational figure and an inspirational message; for human beings, compelling narratives are more likely to stimulate such identification (1997, p. 108).

Part of the attraction of narrative is that as the drama unfolds and readers engage with the characters, language and events of the narrative, they can discover an imagined role for themselves in the story. The sense of agency, choice and optional role-taking creates greater enthusiasm for identification, reflection upon existential issues and the imagined consideration of alternative endings than occurs through didactic communications.

The phrase *Once upon a time* encapsulates many aspects of the theme of this book. Empathic intelligence thrives upon curiosity about the world, a reflective disposition, a capacity to make analogies between experiences, and ready access to memories of significant emotional and learning experiences. However, empathic intelligence involves more than those abilities, important as they are. For example, a concern for others is fundamental to empathic intelligence. I discuss this in more detail later.

Many children learn more from reading than we expect or realise at the time. They make interpretations beyond the literal. The primitive theorising of children faced with the wonders of the world and seeking to understand such wonders, illustrates a capacity to observe, deduct and generalise that is characteristic of intellectual life (Bruner, 1986, 1990). In the early stages of intellectual development, myths and narratives can serve an important function of making sense of the world, particularly if that sense is fuelled by imagination and fantasy (Chukovsky, 1963; Hardy 1977; Meek, 1977). In time, logical thinking demands that generalisations and hypotheses be tested against reality, unless of course there is a willing suspension of disbelief. In the meantime, stories invite children to match their own experiences against those in the story. Just as importantly, when children compose their own stories, they can explore possibilities and transcend the boundaries of time and place – which must be powerfully liberating. This ability also allows them to relate to the feelings of others, a precursor to empathy. Arguably, imagination not only liberates, it also humanises. The American educational philosopher Martha Nussbaum (1997) argues that three capacities, above all, are essential for the cultivation of humanity in today's world:

> First is the capacity for critical examination of oneself and one's traditions – for living what, following Socrates, we may call 'the examined life' … [Second] Citizens who cultivate their humanity need … an ability to see themselves not simply as citizens of some local region or group but also, and above all, as human beings bound to all other human beings by ties of recognition and concern … The third ability of the citizen, closely related to the other two, can be called the narrative imagination. This means the ability to think what it might be like to be in the shoes of a person different from oneself, to be an intelligent reader of that person's story, and to understand the emotions and wishes and desires that someone so placed might have (pp. 9–11).

There can be a special intimacy and trust created between a storyteller and a listener. To hear another's story is to share something personal and revealing. The phenomena of individual experiences can be encapsulated in personal narratives that resonate beyond the telling. I am reminded of an encounter with an elderly woman in a long checkout queue in a supermarket. I engaged in a desultory conversation with this stranger with a strong Irish accent. I assumed, wrongly, from her accent that she was a recent arrival. I asked her what had brought her to Australia. She laughed and said:

> You'll think I am mad if I tell you. I have been here fifty years but I came here because of an experience in primary school. We were asked in a test to draw from memory the map of a country in the world. I always liked the shape of Australia so I drew that. Most of the others drew Ireland. I won the prize and that's why I decided years later to come to Australia.

At one level it seems remarkable that a simple experience in primary school might have such a significant outcome, yet if you are sensitive to the impact of personal experiences on decision-making, that outcome is not so remarkable (Stern, 1985). If that story engages you and makes you wonder about significant moments in life and how we learn, behave, make choices, think and feel, this book invites you to cherish and understand such moments. It invites you to think about them and consider education as a process of leadership – of encouraging others to experience the phenomena of existence in order to develop a mindful, meaningful life. In that model, educators engage in a lifelong, dynamic process of developing and transforming themselves, and model for others how to do likewise.

The cultivation of humanity, according to Nussbaum (1997) means 'learning how to be a human being capable of love and imagination' (p. 14). Further, she argues that when a child and a parent learn to tell stories together, and share a sense of wonder:

> ... the child is acquiring essential moral capacities ... stories interact with [children's] own attempts to explain the world and their own actions in it. A child deprived of stories is deprived, as well, of certain ways of viewing other people. For the insides of people, like the insides of stars, are not open to view ... The habits of wonder promoted by storytelling thus define the other person as spacious and deep, with qualitative differences from oneself and hidden places worthy of respect (pp. 89–90).

Professor of English Literature, Barbara Hardy, (1977) famously argued:

> ... narrative, like lyric or dance, is not to be regarded as an aesthetic invention used by artists to control, manipulate, and order experience, but as a primary act of mind transferred to art from life. The novel merely heightens, isolates, and analyses the narrative motions of human consciousness (p. 12).

The idea that narrative might be a 'primary act of mind' caught the imagination of educators in the late 1970s, increasing confidence in a centuries-old method of acculturating citizens and stimulating imaginations. Untestable though the idea is, it suggests something of the mystery and importance of narrative in human consciousness. Perhaps even more importantly, it accords with the intuition and life experience of reflective people, motivating scholarship and research into what is now a respected discipline – narratology. Interestingly, Hardy did not elaborate upon the affective aspects of narrative as a primary act of mind. However, she does acknowledge that she 'take[s] for granted the ways in which storytelling engages our interests, curiosity, fear, tension, expectation, and sense of order' (pp. 12–13).

It is that imaginative aspect of narrative that reflects its analogical function. Whether as spectators of events in stories, or as participants in their creation, we can use narratives to match, expand or create templates of reality against which to consider our own existence. There is a natural relationship between empathy and narrative. Through the function of imaginative, empathic engagements with stories and their characters, we can project vicariously beyond the known and transparent. Arguably, our sense of self and our sense of others grow through engagements with cultural and social life, modulated by a capacity for reflection, imagination and vicarious experience.

Complex stories, including fairytales, do not separate human experience into discrete either/or categories but, democratically, give parity of esteem to the varieties of ways humans process, evaluate and make sense of life's experiences (Bettleheim, 1978). Rarely do two people interpret a story the same way or respond with the same thoughts and feelings all the way through. Rather, the story engages us, or not, according to current emotional predispositions or concerns. Fundamental to the reading and viewing act is a commitment to living vicariously within a world created by another.

THE DYNAMICS OF QUALITY PEDAGOGY

In the past decade the development of qualitative research methods has begun to address the need for in-depth understanding of the complexity of learning contexts. The better we understand how students feel and think about their learning experiences, the better able we will be to construct effective pedagogies. The concept of empathic intelligence which I develop in this book attempts to encompass the most important qualities of effective teachers – empathy, enthusiasm, capacity to engage others and expertise. Fundamental to its effectiveness in practice is respect for, and understanding of one's own and others' inner worlds.

The educative worth of mentoring others, building communities of scholars, engaging in dialogue and modelling good practices which build upon students' interests and abilities is not necessarily a new phenomenon. From the time of Socrates, through the apprenticeships of the Middle Ages and the learning communities developed within monasteries, there has been tacit understanding of the role that parents and tutors can play in educating the young. Nonetheless, it takes time, commitment and resources to educate the whole student, a responsibility undertaken and regulated for the most part by public or independent education authorities. While information technology can provide access to vast sources of information well beyond what was available to scholars in the past, it is timely now to re-formulate the roles of educators to allow them to focus not only on developing students' skills and understanding, but also their social and emotional maturity and their capacity for informed judgment. It takes empathic intelligence, sensitive, attuned listening and ongoing classroom-based phenomenological research to determine how best to achieve that goal.

THE ROLE OF IMAGINATION

The role of imagination in education is currently something of a Cinderella figure (though if you follow through that analogy, the negative image transforms to a positive one). Elementary or primary schooling proudly attests to the importance of imagination in learning. Walk into most modern kindergarten or junior classrooms and your spirits are uplifted. The room is decorated with students' art work and formal project work, alongside charts and displays of important information designed by the teacher. Colours, shapes, textiles, sounds, and dedicated work spaces provide imaginative and aesthetic stimulation. The children can move, talk, share, read and research in flexible ways because there is a clear theory, structure and purpose underpinning the curriculum. Most parents and teachers in these environments are not mystified by the learning process because they can observe its nature and outcomes first hand. Imagination, creativity, exploration, problem solving, information-gathering, storytelling and story writing, dance and drama form part of an educative continuum which is confident about the diversity of ways children learn about themselves and the world. I'm painting a somewhat idealised picture to make the point, but the general point stands up to scrutiny.

Move up the education system and things change dramatically. Classrooms are dull, students are nervous about sharing their work, partly for competitive reasons and partly because it is not 'cool' to excel academically, or worse, artistically. Fifteen years ago, I asked a gifted Grade Six girl what she expected to happen when she moved from primary/elementary school into high school. With disarming insight and quiet authority she told me: 'You leave imagination and creativity behind and deal only with facts'. She was trying hard to prepare herself for that ordeal. It is mainly arts educators (those in drama, music and art departments) and sometimes English, history and social science educators, who are authorised by official documents like syllabuses, to teach imaginatively. There is a nervousness that imaginative or lateral thinking is removed from the serious business of accumulating knowledge. This holds, even in the face of the ready access to vast quantities of information through the Internet. Never have we been in a better position to let information technology take the drudgery out of teaching and thereby free us to engage in the kinds of educative interactions which technology cannot provide.

It is metaphor and creativity in the expressive, performative and communicative arts that can interpret and articulate individuality and uniqueness. Each highly-skilled performer – for example, an Olympic sprinter, an acclaimed actor, artist or singer – exceeds certain quantifiable benchmarks, then adds individual style or interpretation to the performance. An excellent education or leadership system seeks to aspire to that additional component of performance. You have to be able to imagine its possibility to aspire to it.

Maxine Greene (1995), the eminent professor of philosophy and education and past president of the American Educational Research Association, argues passionately and persuasively for the role of imagination in education. She says:

> One of the reasons I have come to concentrate on imagination as a means through which we can assemble a coherent world is that imagination is what, above all, makes empathy possible. It is what enables us to cross the empty spaces between ourselves and those we teachers have called 'other' over the years … .of all our cognitive capacities, imagination is the one that permits us to give credence to alternative realities (p. 3).

There it is, imagination cited as a cognitive capacity, essential to empathy. I want to suggest that imagination works best as a cognitive capacity when it is underpinned by curious anticipation, whether that be pleasurable or anxious. Curiosity derives from both thinking and feeling. For example, when a child wants to look at a dead animal, s/he is curious, or anxious to know what deadness looks like. There might be multiple reasons why the child is so curious but you can be sure that the curiosity won't be satisfied until direct observation is made. Imagination, curiosity, the need to know and to experience life both directly and vicariously, fundamentally enhance intellectual and emotional growth. As a child, or adult, you won't reach out easily to satisfy curiosity if an authority figure forbids exploration or risk-taking. Metaphorically speaking, if you think you have to keep strictly within the outlines when colouring in a picture, you'll be intimidated by structures. If you know the difference in importance between colouring in the picture and keeping to the lines on a pedestrian crossing, you'll be wise and flexible (and probably safe!). I am choosing to ignore the fact that the world is full of people who never keep to the lines and those who always keep to the lines. I guess what we really want is those who can choose wisely when or when not to.

At the top of the scale of cognitive development is speculative thought – the capacity to think beyond the known to imagine what might be. We can observe, gather data, hypothesise what might be happening in a certain scientific experiment or site of human behaviour, but at the end of the research, it is the researcher's capacity to generate new hypotheses, or better still high level speculations, which will matter. Students with empathic intelligence, insatiable curiosity, lively and constructive imaginations, comfortable with ambiguity and familiar with the joy of conjuring up possibilities, are graduates of an excellent education system. It is to be hoped that they are found as readily among the graduating classes of tertiary institutions, including business, law, science and medical schools, as among those graduating from primary schools! It would be sad if education were progressively a disappointing process.

NARRATIVE AS VICARIOUS EXPERIENCE

Narratives serve a psychic organising function in emotional development (Bettleheim, 1978) and they reflect a need to think by analogy. By structuring events and observations on life within a narrative framework, a perspective is created with which readers (or listeners/viewers) can connect and compare their own points of view. Sometimes the narrative (or other symbolic work) can be absorbed or internalised so strongly it becomes part of the reader's or viewer's identification and perspective. Metaphors and artistic works can function for their spectators (and their creators) as an affective and cognitive analogy – a way of expanding one's psychic boundaries. An ongoing process of integrating experiences and developing a sense of an individual self that is functioning coherently in a purposeful, though challenging world is one part of life's education. An outcome of that process is the increased sense of life's complexities and ambiguities, and a confidence in the capacity to function within such parameters. Increased differentiation of thought and feeling as a measure of intellectual development can be promoted through analogic processing of experience.

When readers or listeners engage deeply with narrative, what is familiar in the narrative reinforces the known, while what is new, or beyond immediate mapping with existing templates of experience, is reached for tacitly. In that sense, narratives (and metaphors/symbolic experiences) can function to differentiate or develop thought and feeling. It is important to hypothesise connections between narrative as analogic experiencing and empathic intelligence as high order analogical processing because it is a promising route to understanding holistic cognitive, emotional, social and moral development.

In telling our own stories, we feel an affinity with our past and in hearing the stories of others we can feel an affinity with them. Storylines connect individuals across time and space. They can inspire the young and affirm the old, providing imagined role models for all kinds of endeavours, while reminding us that experience endures beyond our own mortality.

The surface meanings and deeper meanings of stories can co-exist in pleasurable, contradictory tension, sometimes oscillating between reason and fantasy. Stories, gossip, anecdotes and reflections create a pattern to human experience. We know too that past experiences could happen again and this knowledge can inform our present decisions and our view of the way the world functions. That knowledge is comforting. That's why we want to listen to stories or turn the page and read on, even if the story does not have a traditionally happy ending. For some deeply engaged readers, stories herald moments of private intimacy, and from such experience in our inner world grows the capacity for empathy, imagination, creativity, playful and moral conjecturing about it. 'I wonder what it would be like to be the strongest girl in the world?' 'What would I do if I were held captive in a castle surrounded by fire-breathing dragons?' Or more realistically: 'How would I respond if I were tempted with fame and fortune as reward for a favour or some secret information?'

Through the stories of real and imagined life we become aware of ourselves as feeling and thinking beings who belong in a world potentially richer than, or very different from, our own everyday existence. The culture of narratives experienced through reading, viewing and even participating in dramas can forever stimulate our minds and hearts. Heroes, gods, fairy queens, tyrants, angels, monsters, devils, supermen and their partners, superwomen, will always exist to inspire, threaten, challenge or protect us. Stories, myths and dramas of the human condition survive in literature, mass media and computer games because boardrooms, families, playgrounds, classrooms and offices are filled with their descendants. As engaged participants in reading or viewing stories and dramas, we can choose our own identifications with characters and events, guessing or hypothesising what we would feel like in this or that role.

This book invites you to recognise the roles you play, to reflect on their nature and purpose so that you can choose the stage on which you play out your life. Whether you lead or follow, and mostly we do both in life, it helps to know our own life histories and to respect those of others. It is challenging psychically to extend the boundaries of our known selves by imaginatively engaging with vicarious possibilities. Even very young children meet that challenge when they role-play imaginative or lived experiences.

The good storyteller, whether in prose, verse or conversation, demonstrates a quality of empathic intelligence – the ability to create the affecting mood which will best resonate with readers and listeners and to select from observation and reflection the appropriate information. We engage with stories to the extent that they seem to connect with or enhance our lives. The connection might be tenuous, unconscious or blindingly apparent. The experience can be psychically and aesthetically pleasurable. Some stories draw us back into the past; others project us into the future. Some illuminate the day; others take us into the darkness of human behaviour. The best storytellers lighten and enlighten the paradoxes and ambiguities of life.

EMPATHY IN LITERATURE AND THE ARTS

Good literature is a rich source of examples of writers' empathic intelligence in action. Shakespeare's plays are prime exemplars of the art of empathic intelligence embodied in blueprints for action. His understanding of the dynamic between thinking, feeling, words and action meets all the criteria for excellence, inspiration and imaginative, person-centred pedagogy. Drama educators realise this. So do those students in schools who are introduced to the plays by empathic teachers – teachers who are skilled in engaging students with the texts, confident that the author's spirit, insight and intelligence will eventually resonate strongly for them, possibly in many different ways.

Constructing Emma

Jane Austen's classic novel *Emma* can be read as an example of an author's empathic intelligence in action. A central theme in the novel, Emma's misguided but well-meant matchmaking efforts for her young protégée, Harriet, can be read as Emma's psychological journey towards empathic intelligence. The novel famously opens:

> Emma Woodhouse, handsome, clever, and rich, with a comfortable home and happy disposition, seemed to unite some of the best blessings of existence: and had lived nearly twenty-one years in the world with very little to distress or vex her ... The real evils indeed of Emma's situation were the power of having rather too much her own way, and a disposition to think a little too well of herself ... (p. 1).

As the novel unfolds, Emma's confidence in her ability to judge what is best for others, Harriet in particular, is sorely tested. She discourages Harriet from accepting a suitable proposal from one suitor and then is surprised when Harriet, under her influence but also misguided in her aspiration, gradually raises her marital expectations to include Mr Knightley, the man who eventually proposes to Emma. Within the framework of a social comedy of errors, a genre richly exploited in the soap operas of contemporary mass media, is revealed Jane Austen's serious moral purpose and her understanding of the ways in which empathic intelligence can be developed. Through her capacity to take responsibility for her actions, through ruthless self-scrutiny and reflection, Emma comes to recognise that her desire to arrange everybody's destiny is 'unpardonable arrogance' and damaging not only to Harriet and Mr Knightley, but also to herself. She takes responsibility for Harriet's growing vanity and embarks on a road from compassion and empathy to empathic intelligence.

> ... the only source whence anything like consolation or composure could be drawn, was in the resolution of her own better conduct, and the hope that, however inferior in spirit and gaiety might be the following and every future winter of her life to the past, it would yet find her more rational, more acquainted with herself, and leave her less to regret when it were gone (p. 373).

In her characterisation of Emma, Jane Austen reveals a finely nuanced, deeply wise understanding of the nature of empathic intelligence and the complexities of psychic development and interpersonal relationships. She understood all too well how rarely humans function successfully as wholly rational or wholly emotional beings. The inevitable imbalances between these two major sources of psychic existence might best be tolerated with wry humour and forbearance – 'Seldom, very seldom, does complete truth belong to any human disclosure' (p. 381). Austen almost certainly would not have warmed to the term 'empathic intelligence' – it lacks the texture and grace of her own subtle prose. However, the ability has always existed in the conduct of human affairs and the arts and sciences owe much to its dynamics.

Wilde and the compassion of others

Oscar Wilde's moving account of his intrapersonal life while a prisoner in Reading Gaol (*De Profundis* 1905) and his compassionate understanding of fellow prisoners evidenced in *The Ballad of Reading Gaol* (1925), offer insights into the nature of his empathic intelligence. The story of Wilde's homosexuality and imprisonment barely needs retelling. What does warrant telling is his account of his self-reflections and poignant appreciation of the compassion of others in his plight. He cites one particular incident that profoundly moved him:

> When I was brought down from prison to the Court of Bankruptcy, between two policemen, [Wilde omits the name] waited in the long dreary corridor that, before the whole crowd, whom an action so sweet and simple hushed into silence, he might gravely raise his hat to me, as, handcuffed and with bowed head, I passed him by. Men have gone to heaven for smaller things than that ... I have never said one single word to him about what he did. I do not know to the present moment whether he is

aware that I was even conscious of his action. It is not a thing for which one can render formal thanks in formal words. I store it in the treasure-house of my heart. I keep it there as a secret debt that I am glad to think I can never possibly repay ... that little, lovely, silent act of love has unsealed for me all the wells of pity: made the desert blossom like a rose and brought me out of the bitterness of lonely exile into harmony with the wounded, broken, and great heart of the world (1920 ed. pp. 16–19).

In restoring Wilde's sense of dignity through a symbolic gesture, another compassionate human mirrored back to him his self-worth. It took little more than a perfectly-timed, imaginative and courageous gesture. Such empathic communications, whether in words, symbols or through gestures, illustrate the function of empathy at the heart of moral imagination. Sometimes, as in the incident above, such gestures arise in contexts where prevailing mores might easily silence or paralyse them.

Central to an understanding of the role and function of empathy is the recognition that one might come to understand how another acts and feels without necessarily making a moral judgment about it. This is because empathy seeks to understand prior to evaluating the consequences of behaviours that might derive from such thoughts and feelings. To that end, literature, art and films can provide opportunities to engage in identification and reflection upon a whole range of human feelings, thoughts and behaviours. Whether the issues portrayed be those associated with the Holocaust, or current terrorism concerns, or the plight of refugees in Australia and elsewhere, many sensitive humans find themselves engaged in reflection upon them. Literature, art, film and conversations with others can provide a rehearsal ground for the expression, elaboration and modulation of values, feelings and thoughts.

Reading the Holocaust

In her book *Reading the Holocaust* (1998), author Inga Clendinnen cites as an example of the disruption of normal moral codes during the Nazi regime, an incident when German soldiers broke into the children's hospital of the Warsaw ghetto to seize the children for deportation to Treblinka – one of the notorious concentration camps. Knowing the unspeakable fate awaiting them, the woman doctor in the ward quickly administered poison to the children. The survivor and others regarded the doctor as a hero, an estimation with which Clendinnen agrees, but she insightfully questions whether that doctor:

... could be confident that men and women who knew nothing of the ghetto or the history of anti-Jewish actions by the German army would have the moral imagination to recognise her action as the heroic act of compassion it was? (pp. 43–44)

As you play out in your mind the horror of that situation and the ethical dilemmas which that doctor had to face, with little time for advice from others or for deep reflection, and as you weigh up what you might have done in the circumstances, and whether she should have acted as she did, you are empathically engaged in an experience of moral imagination. If you struggle to make sense of atrocities, and of heroic gestures, in the past and present, and find that struggle almost overwhelming for the claims it makes on your empathic intelligence, you will recognise the complexity of that intelligence. Discerning judgments about human behaviour defy easy analysis and resolution, as the educated heart knows. Compassion sometimes makes the strongest call on that perceptive heart, ensuring that compassion itself survives the worst catastrophes. Or you might be hearing in your inner voice an admonition that killing is never acceptable, which might well drown out other calls on your decision-making strategies.

No matter what decisions you reach about that appalling situation, they may well be provisional because empathy at the heart of moral imagination is relentlessly dynamic and demanding. The empathy that informs a structured empathic intelligence takes law and morality into account. Its adherents are as rational as they are sensitive. They recognise and respect the critical function of morality and law in human societies. But empathy in moral imagination doesn't work in absolutes. Nor does it offer easy options. It cannot necessarily soothe the existential anguish of ethical dilemmas because it reflects the complexities of the human condition. Empathy, even the sophisticated version which engages a dynamic between thinking and feeling, should help us come closer to understanding the mysteries of the human condition, but it will not necessarily yield up completely the secrets of that mystery. It is simply a more promising method than its closest competitor, and part ally – rational analysis. Nonetheless, when rational analysis and informed, imaginative sensitivity cooperate in the service of understanding, the rewards are embedded in the processes. Those who willingly and painstakingly engage in the pursuit of meaning through acts of moral imagination add their 'grain of sand' (to echo William Blake) to the shore of human evolution. In a hierarchy of significance, engagement in the pursuit may be a greater measure of success than the outcome of the pursuit.

Is life beautiful?

Once one is alert to the concept of empathy in its shaping of educated individuals, one can read or perceive cultural artefacts in a variety of innovative ways. The issue of empathy and culture is raised by academic and social commentator, Robert Manne, in an article on Roberto Benigni's movie *Life is Beautiful*. In the movie, set in Tuscany during the fascist era, Guido, a Jew, and his beloved son, Joshua are transported to a death camp when Tuscany falls to the Nazis. Guido is determined to maintain his son's spirits and defences against the real horror of their situation. To that end he convinces Joshua that everything happening to them is part of a game. Just as the camp is being evacuated by the Germans, ahead of the arrival of the Americans, Guido is led to his death. Ever mindful of his commitment to his son's emotional well-being even in his own last moments of life, he clown-walks to his death.

A film as affecting and evocative as this one, stirs passionate responses. Childhood, parental love, altruism, hope, despair, play, reality, horror and beauty are passionate themes in life and art. Whether this film encompasses fully enough the complexities of the themes it touches upon, is debatable. Nonetheless, the evocative story line and the film's themes moved many movie-goers to reflection. Robert Manne's analysis of the message of the film is poignantly influenced by the personal history he discloses of his own Jewish background and his discovery as a child of the facts of the Holocaust:

> I do not know what kind of person I might have become if I had not discovered in my early years these facts about my family's and my people's recent past. What I do know is that after discovering facts such as these my sense of the world would never be quite the same again.
>
> I understood something now about the nature of political evil and about the human capacity for savagery. I had lost the capacity to say, in any uninflected way, that life is beautiful ... In Benigni's concentration camp none of this radical assault on the human person is conveyed ... As it turns out, then, there is no way in which the aesthetic requirements of the fairytale and the ethical duty to remember the Holocaust truthfully can be reconciled ... Benigni is, I suppose, aware that if at the end of this terrible century he is to convince us that life, is, indeed, beautiful, he cannot avoid taking us to the heart of humankind's darkest experience. Yet once he has led us there, because it is a sunny fairytale he has to tell, he finds

no alternative but to avert his eyes from its reality and dissemble ... Is not the story of the Holocaust unadorned simply too stark and desolate for human beings to bear? (1999, p. 13).

Good art, and good writing such as Manne's, entices us to ask important questions. There are any number of interpretations and questions arising from this film and Manne's response to it. Once you shift out of the framework of the film, reality intrudes with reflective questions about how long Joshua would have sustained his faith in the beauty of life once the reality of his father's death broke through his defences. Is it the function of art to confront us with the unspeakable horrors of the Holocaust or is its function to enrich us in ways that sustain hope in the indestructible nature of beauty in life? Faced with death, torture, unbearable psychic and physical pain, can anyone reflect upon the meaning of life? Doesn't functional human life cease when we are so self-absorbed with terror and agony that thought, sense of purpose and feeling are paralysed?

I actually did not interpret the film as essentially being about the Holocaust. That event seemed to me rather like an operatic background to the film. I read the film as being about a relationship between a boy and his father, and between that father and his wife. While I can appreciate Manne's disappointment in what he sees as the film's shortcomings, its satisfactions and shortcomings were different for me. I am mindful too that art fulfils a very different function to reality. For a start, there is an aesthetic filter in art which reality usually lacks. We can act as spectators in art but reality asks us to participate. And so on. Were we really to endure the truth of the Holocaust, or Bosnia, or Kosova, or Iraq, we could hardly function in normal ways. The despair and suffering on the faces of the Kosova refugees and those tortured in Iraq begs the question about the limited extent of empathic intelligence in international affairs.

This observation is underscored by Robert S. McNamara, former United States Secretary of Defense in the Kennedy and Johnson administrations. In Errol Morris' Oscar winning documentary *Fog of War* (2003), McNamara offers some candid, and at times chilling, reflections on the US, and his own, involvement in the Cuban missile crisis and the Vietnam War. Despite some elements of self-justification, McNamara's reflections (structured in the film as eleven lessons) provide some deeply insightful and cautionary advice about the paradoxical 'ethics' of war and wartime foreign policy. His first three lessons are:

1   empathise with your enemy;
2   rationality will not save us; and
3   there is something beyond one's self.

He elaborates the first lesson as follows:

> If we are to deal effectively with terrorists across the globe, we must develop a sense of empathy – I don't mean 'sympathy', but rather 'understanding' – to counter their attacks on us and the Western world.

While McNamara's empathy is clearly underpinned by a strong streak of pragmatism and nationalistic self-interest, his comments are nonetheless remarkable, in international affairs, for both their candour and their introspection. It is difficult to imagine George W. Bush subjecting the US war against Iraq to such scrutiny. Can you imagine Donald Rumsfeld asking whether he should have tried to understand or empathise with the Iraqi people?

The Holocaust, Bosnia, the Gulag, and Hiroshima could stain the twentieth century with indelible and seductive despair. Unlike their victims who had no realistic defences against despair, and who, in the case of those entering Auschwitz were instructed to abandon hope upon entry, we have to mobilise hope, even when confronted with unspeakable horrors. And we can do so precisely because there is a difference between reality and art, between history and art, between the experiences of others, however empathically attuned we are to them, and our own experiences. To sustain hope sometimes we have to exercise an option not available to the godforsaken souls of the Holocaust, namely, to fantasise things could be different or were not as bad as they seem. This is not to dishonour the truth of the Holocaust. Its truths will endure as long as humankind is capable of atrocities and redemption. Rather, it is to seek in art, myths and fairytales, and heroic human actions, the sustainability of moral imagination. Perhaps the counterpoising of messages in a film such as *Life is Beautiful* carries the more significant message: life is beautiful as much as it can be appalling. The relationship between the father and son, and the parents, *was* beautiful, even if filtered through a selective cinematic lens.

With the grace bestowed by empathy, moral imagination and creativity, we can sometimes soothe our passage between the extremes of existence. The best art and literature inevitably raise profoundly important questions in the minds of reflective people. For some, a particular film such as *Life is Beautiful* can fulfil that function. For others, it might be another cultural form such as literature, sculpture, music, drama, opera or art. As we now talk about 'literacies' as various symbolic and expressive systems that need to be read and understood in their own terms, we are well placed to enlarge the parameters of empathic intelligence to encompass those systems.

Biographical relationships

In a feature article on the biographer Richard Holmes '[who] has been called the greatest biographer', journalist Luke Slattery (1998) analyses the art in Holmes's writing and comments on his capacity to transport himself across time by a feat of imaginative sympathy. Holmes himself elucidated this when he wrote:

> You're studying someone, following their tracks and footsteps for a long period of time, and that's how you build up a biographical relationship with them. They need to become very vivid to you. But of course the trick is that at the same time you must remain as objective as you can (Slattery, 1998).

This sounds convincing to an empathic leader or educator, as it describes that skill of merging with the subject in a form of imaginative identification, and detaching from the subject with equal passion, in order to illuminate the truth in all its complexities and mystery. This is not to claim that such methods can reveal absolute truths but rather to suggest that in the eyes of discerning researchers (or truth-seekers) such methods promise compelling approximations to truth, at the very least. However, some would categorically dismiss such possibilities in biographical writing. Germaine Greer, for example, famously characterised biographers as 'bloody leeches' – a perception almost certainly fuelled by the imminent publication of an unwelcome and unauthorised biography about herself.

Monstrous imaginings

While it is possible to understand how empathy and a psychodynamic attitude can deepen the art of biographical writing, there are times when even such illuminating approaches can defy the best intentions of writers. For example, understanding the Holocaust and the rise of Hitler still challenges scholars and writers. Gitta Sereny's (1995) acclaimed analysis of Hitler's architect in her book *Albert Speer – His Battle with Truth* contributes much to the search for such understanding. Sereny makes it possible to identify with Speer's early childhood experiences and to imagine how he was so taken with Hitler's vision and personal power. Sereny describes how Speer lived and worked in the hope of gaining Hitler's approval, while Hitler, in a cruel abuse of empathic understanding, knew exactly how to tantalise his lackeys to keep them in a state of thrall. Towards the end of her massive analysis of Albert Speer's life and his role in the Third Reich, Sereny writes:

> Pity, compassion, sympathy and empathy were not part of his emotional vocabulary. He could feel deeply but only indirectly – through music, through landscapes, through art, eventually through visual hyperbole, often in settings of his own creation: his Cathedral of Light, the flags, the thousands of men at attention motionless like pillars, the blond children ... This became beauty to him and, another substitute for love, allowed him to feel.
>
> This was an erudite and solitary man who, recognising his deficiencies in human relations, had read five thousand books in prison to try to understand the universe and human beings, an effort he succeeded in with his mind but failed in with his heart. Empathy is finally a gift, and cannot be learned, so, essentially, returning into the world after twenty years, he remained alone ... Unforgiven by so many for having served Hitler, he elected to spend the rest of his life in confrontation with this past, unforgiving of himself for having so nearly loved a monster (p. 719).

This powerful, painful reminder of the limits of Speer's empathy might well serve to inspire us to educate the heart, together with the mind, ideally long before the quest is hopeless. Perhaps Speer had to deny his culpability right to the end. To accept responsibility for his role in a moral and human catastrophe would require faith in the power of forgiveness, and he had sold his soul to a system that murdered compassion. The Holocaust functioned on systematic, pitiless brutality. How could Speer hope to access the redemptive quality he seemingly lacked in his early life and denied in his professional life? Nor could he find in his imprisonment a sustained relationship with someone willing to provide mentoring for what would be a very traumatic painful journey of self-discovery. (A benign pastor did fill such a role for a time, however).

Sereny herself demonstrates the educative capacity of empathy through this biography. It is imaginable that had someone worked with Speer in a therapeutic capacity, a kind of work that in itself can engender hope, he might have been able to forgive himself, a form of self-empathising. In this biography, Sereny succeeds in extending our empathic attunement to a man we might imagine to be utterly contemptible. Her belief that empathy cannot be taught, but is a gift, is acceptable in the circumstances, but contestable. More than ever, her work on Albert Speer reminds us that empathy lies at the heart of moral development, and in its most sophisticated form can inspire virtues of the highest spiritual order.

But as painstaking, objective, empathic and insightful as Sereny is, and as extensive as my own reading on the subject is, the Holocaust defeats my capacities to imagine or to understand its perpetrators. Even to contemplate identifying with the monsters of history is a terrifying experience, leading us to a chasm of self-understanding with its engulfing possibility that there but for the grace of a mystery go I.

In a world as pitiless as that of the Holocaust, to truly empathise with its perpetrators risks imagined self-annihilation. Paradoxically, and painfully, that state defeats empathic attunement, predicated as it is on a healthy sense of self. Perhaps too, the point of that apparent failure of empathy resides precisely in its capacity to defeat hubris, or intellectual pride. Ultimately it is the quest for understanding that defines human excellence, rather than the plateaus of achievement. The footholds on the rock climb are reassuring and safe, but the leaps between them can be terrifying.

For all the excitement of the new millennium with its apparent opportunities to start with a new white-black board, the shadow of the Holocaust, that unimaginable man-made catastrophe, has cast its darkness across the dawn. When empathy and imagination fail to dispel that darkness, inspiration has to come from a primitive hope in the durability of a mysterious life force. Maybe that acceptance of mystery is a hallmark of empathy and imagination at their most elusive.

Back to the future

In narratives, the past and present exist in a seemingly timeless realm in which human characters confront physical challenges, emotional and moral dilemmas in some form, and implicitly suggest to us as readers how we might best choose to conduct our lives. The past is a tacitly known country. It is the geography and the architecture of our present. It can be cultivated and structured to enhance our understanding of the present. Even as we read or tell stories, we indulge in the hope of learning how to control the future. While not even narratives can achieve the impossible and foretell the future, the imaginative engagements they encourage promote speculative thinking and belief in the ineffable.

So we return to *Once upon a time* – a phrase that is timelessly evocative and paradoxical, a phrase which connects the past, present and future: memory, time and hope. Through time, memory and hope it hints at a coherence between physical, mental and emotional aspects of being. It functions like an algebra of human life. In an important sense *Once upon a time* has to be the opening phrase of a book concerned with empathic intelligence. The phrase hints at the challenge embedded within a statement of fact – namely, that even the certainties of apparent facts can prove illusory when tested against reality and influenced by feelings. Those who are excited by that challenge are likely to find empathic intelligence a welcome concept. They are also likely to function in empathically intelligent ways, even though their professional or personal orientations might move across a continuum of scientific and poetic ways of functioning.

Further, I argue here that when empathic intelligence functions well, it can inspire excellence through the quality of its processes and outcomes. That quality relies on relationships, imagination and creativity to energise the theory, planning and implementation involved in most significant enterprises. Such enterprises will be those involving people working together in mutually dependent and beneficial ways, whether on a small or large scale.

REFLECTIONS ON PROFESSIONAL PRACTICE

Often it is significant moments in a career that shape professional identity and practice more sharply than the slow accumulation of mediocre memories. By reflecting on such significant moments in my professional practice, I can discern reasons why I think as I do now. I did not start teaching as a result of a long-term commitment to that career. I had very little idea of what was involved in becoming a teacher, other than what I could extrapolate from having been a school student. Like many novice teachers, I had no idea I wanted to teach until I did my first practice teaching. Mine was in a rough inner-city boys' school in a major city. While the school building seeped its own history of despair, I resolutely tripped along in high heels to teach, improbably, fourteen-year-old boys about the Roundheads and the Cavaliers in British History. The concept of relevance was not then part of teacher education courses and I was as mystified as the students about the purpose of the lessons.

The next topic on the syllabus was the Renaissance and I had the bright idea of setting a project on religious art to liven things up a bit.

Mindful of the need to clarify expectations, I set out very clearly what the students had to do. They had to write about religious art and provide illustrations. Anxious to please, they followed the spirit of the instructions. On the due date they handed in thick, illustrated, text-rich projects. Each page of 35 projects was filled with clear text and shiny pictures of saints and cherubs, dutifully and guilelessly cut with razor blades from all the best art books in all the best libraries in the neighbourhood and city! To this day I have complete recall of my conflicting feelings – panic that the desecration for which I was responsible would be discovered and amazement that the students would go to such lengths to please.

The irony embedded in this story is that those students actually enjoyed doing their illicit projects. They knew how to steal books by concealing them in their shirts or elsewhere. They were experts in defacement and expected me to be impressed with their efforts. Much like the family dog that offers you a gift of the next door neighbour's squawking prize rooster, they were expecting to be rewarded. 'But Miss, no one even reads these books. They've never been opened'. I began to question the nature of education that widens rather than narrows the gap between its ideals and the readiness of its students. My Renaissance art students in that grimy slum school had aspirations and hopes, albeit unorthodox ones. Some things had to close or widen to match these students with the prevailing systems. While I was not particularly aware of it then, out of curiosity I was formulating my own meaningful research questions out of reflection upon practice.

Later I thought hard about the relational aspects of education, supported through reading the humanist philosophers Martin Buber and Teilhard de Chardin. Their complex views of education as an existential, relational experience were inspiring. Notwithstanding that the popular scientific writer Richard Dawkins (1998, p. 184) now discredits Teilhard de Chardin's (1955) notions of science while admitting that he too was once inspired by his writings, I thought teachers could help students to reach for the stars. Perhaps the unconscious mentoring and vision offered by inspirational writers is more important at times than their scientific credibility. Such unconscious mentoring can create a sense of hope in those who have idealistic fantasies about improving the world.

Another seminal experience in the development of this research interest was that of teaching English to a gifted group of students for the four years prior to their final examinations in secondary school. In direct contrast to the first experience in an inner-city school, this school had a history of academic excellence and high student achievement. The teachers were highly professional and their teaching exemplified outstanding pedagogy. The focus of the school was on enabling its gifted students to develop their full potential. Teachers had to model excellence in knowledge of their subject and know how to create educational processes that would effectively encourage the students' prodigious potential. It was not such a hard call because the environment was unequivocally affirming in its student-centred focus, long before this became orthodoxy. We enjoyed our professional dedication, firm in the belief that these gifted students needed mentors just as much as less able students. For contrary to popular myth, giftedness does not offer protection from self-esteem issues. Both envy and high expectations are factors that can create difficulties for gifted individuals.

Although this was my first full-time experience of teaching, I recognised from their writing in Year 8 (age 13) that we had an unusually talented group of English students in that year. I seized the opportunity I was offered to stay at the school and see this group through to completion of their secondary school education. In retrospect, I now see that I was curious then about the nature of effective pedagogy. I had been taught by three exceptional teachers myself and had a strong recall of those moments as a learner when puzzles or challenges were resolved through the teacher's explanations or empathic understanding of how to sustain motivation. I wondered how particular peer group dynamics influenced students' development. In an intuitive way, I was confident that students needed to develop their individual writing voices and I wanted that to distinguish this class. One particular student was outstanding even in a group of remarkable peers. I could not imagine that anyone would be more accomplished at her age. However, my inexperience in teaching for public examinations meant that I was unprepared for the outstanding results to come. In all, eight students from that class were included in the top 20 positions for English, including first, second and sixth position, in the state-wide examination of more than 30 000 students.

My task then was to reflect on what it was about the group dynamics of this class that had produced these results. And could it be replicated, even to some extent? I was able to identify some themes. These included: long-term shared commitment; peer mentoring; shared enthusiasm for literature and language; parity of esteem for different writing styles; and the teacher's unrelenting confidence in the students' abilities, verging on awe on occasions. While my enthusiasm and empathy were evident then, I think my expertise was moderate.

The third significant extended experience of reflection on the questions that interested me about effective pedagogy was my doctoral research. That involved teaching two groups of junior school students from two different areas of Sydney for a four-year period, using various student-centred methods to develop their writing abilities. The study demonstrated that at the end of four years, the experimental students in this longitudinal study were better writers than their peers in the control group. Writing ability was judged on thinking ability; effective use of language; ability to write to a particular audience; and creativity. Clearly something about the experimental program made a significant difference (Arnold, 1991).

But challenging questions remained. What makes a significant difference to students' learning across the age/stage spectrum? How do they tacitly support each other? What influence does the teacher exert? What really happens below the surface in learning situations? I felt that I could not fully explain what happened in the space between myself and my students unless I first tried to formulate the internalised theory of pedagogy which was informing my own practice. I knew that empathy was central to this. The following statement is an attempt to encapsulate the term as I understand it:

> Empathy is an ability to understand your own thoughts and feelings and by analogy, apply your self-understanding to the service of others. It is a sophisticated ability involving attunement, de-centring, conjecture and introspection: an act of thoughtful, heartfelt imagination.

To achieve the necessary objectivity for such understanding, complex cognitive and affective functioning, including self-understanding, is required. While even small children can demonstrate empathic attunement to the feelings of others, empathic intelligence, as it is discussed here, is a well-structured, mature, patterned and consistent way of functioning cognitively, socially and emotionally.

BEYOND SYMPATHY

People commonly think sympathy and empathy are the same thing. Although empathy shares some characteristics with sympathy, it is a very much more sophisticated and complex concept than sympathy.

Empathy, narrative and the imagination 87

Enthusiasm is timeless: 1957
SOURCE Frank Burke, Fairfax photos

Enthusiasm is timeless: 2000
SOURCE Quentin Jones, Fairfax photos

The latter is an ability to feel something akin to what you might imagine another person is feeling, usually when you witness some distress in them. You might feel sorry for their plight and spontaneously express your sorrow in a comforting way. Such expressions of sympathy acknowledge a human kinship that may be soothing to the person in distress. Certainly, expressions of sympathy at appropriate times are an important ritual in our lives and in our social communities. To this extent the person expressing sympathy may well also be in an empathic mode, but where the two concepts begin to part might best be illustrated in the following scenario.

Imagine you are feeling distress because, for example, a much loved pet has just had to be 'put down', as we say euphemistically. As you leave the veterinary surgeon's office, feeling extremely sad because that pet has been a much-loved companion and an important part of your life, let's imagine you encounter a friend. You feel a bit foolish because you don't want to explain your grief, but it is obvious that you feel distressed and she notices your state. She offers her sympathy. She might express some of the following sentiments:

> How very distressing for you ... I remember when we had to put down our cat it was just dreadful ... I couldn't stop crying ... and my husband wouldn't come with me to the vet and I had to go all alone ... I don't think I have ever quite forgiven him for that ... I don't know how they always manage to avoid the difficult things in life ... you poor thing ... you had to do this all alone too ... let's have a cup of coffee and talk about it ... you look dreadful.

And so on. As you read that, could you hear how the speaker's emotional sensitivity at the beginning shifted from sympathy for her friend to self-pity as she remembered her own similar experience? You were probably adopting the stance of an empathic reader as you imagined that conversation above. You might even have recalled a similar encounter yourself. You might have identified with one of the roles more than the other, even though I invited you to be the distressed person in the encounter. Or you might have switched between both.

However you related to the piece, it is very likely that you were engaged in a way that I call dynamic. That is, your mind shifted almost simultaneously between a felt response and a thoughtful response. You were thinking and feeling at the same time, engaging both your emotional and reflective abilities to make sense of that imagined encounter.

Because the encounter is fairly commonplace, you probably don't need to know much more about the participants to make sense of the event and their motivations. Our generalised understandings of human dynamics help us to flesh out the picture.

A number of relevant issues are embedded in that small vignette. For a start, the speaker did share a feeling of commonality with her distressed friend, and appropriately began to express her genuine regret for her friend's emotional state. However, in expressing that feeling, her recall of her own past experience of the death of a pet, that very same experience which gave her some insight into her friend's plight, overcame her initial intention and assumed primary importance in her mind. She was not sufficiently aware, or perhaps did not care enough, to resist the temptation to re-visit her own concerns, and was unable to remain focused on her friend's pressing issue. The encounter became too good an opportunity to miss, and she became absorbed in her own distracting memories. Her friend, presumably, felt worse after that encounter, rather than better. In the tacit understanding governing social interactions, we tend to think that the person with the greatest need has first call on our empathy. In the encounter above, the speaker, quite possibly, only had to give her friend a couple more minutes of quiet, empathic listening before they both might have been ready to move onto more generalised issues about the nature of support and the management of grief.

The truly empathic listener would have checked the impulse to shift the conversation to her own concerns and allowed the friend to occupy the space in the encounter. In order to check that impulse the listener would have exercised a sensitive thinking, or cognitive, capacity. That ability to check feelings and impulses against rational thought is a prime characteristic of empathy. You use imagination and 'gut response' to feel as if you know what the other person is experiencing; then you check the situation with observation, reflection and sensitivity. You might pause and seek clarification from your friend. You might look and listen more closely. All this can happen in a couple of seconds, but those seconds make all the difference. Had our ultimately self-centred listener above taken one second to imagine what role she might have liked her friend to play, were the current roles reversed, she might have known that a truly supportive role often requires silence and attuned listening. The air does not have to be filled with chatter in times of sadness. Ironically, of course, the listener reveals that she experienced disappointment when her husband failed to support her. So by exercising our own empathy we might conclude that, understandably, she lacks an internalised model of appropriate support for others in grief. Hence her behaviour now. She actually needs to work through her own issues before she can be truly empathic.

Further embedded in this illustration is the role of past experience in the development of empathy. The unempathic listener revealed unconsciously both the pressure of her own past disappointment and her lack of an appropriate response. The issue of past experiences and how these might be utilised and possibly re-shaped, will be elaborated later.

One further point needs to be made now about the illustration of the two friends' meeting. I hope it is clear from the brief analysis I have given that the development of empathy requires, and indeed helps us to develop, a non-judgmental stance in our responses to human behaviour. You might have noticed how your own feelings towards the listener above shifted from irritation at her response to something like acceptance when it was suggested that she might have lacked an internalised model of an appropriately empathic response. Sympathy suggests we can share common experiences with others. Empathy encourages us to decentre, to see things from another's point of view, to experience layers of thought and feeling, beyond what might be immediately accessible.

Empathy seeks to understand human behaviour, not to judge it. In achieving that idealistic outcome, it also reveals itself as the heart of moral imagination. The metaphor of the heart here suggests both the traditional emotional connotation, and the functional notion of the heart as a pump, sending life-sustaining blood around the body. Empathy as the heart of moral imagination helps us to judge how our actions might affect others, recalling the golden mean: 'Do unto others as you would have them do to you'. It also generates exquisitely difficult moral dilemmas. Reflect for a moment on how easy it is to adopt an unequivocal ethical or moral position on an issue, until you have to confront personally the circumstances giving rise to the issue, or until you develop a personal relationship with someone involved in those circumstances. Black and white merge to grey the closer we have to look at them. Fortunately, an excellent education, the arts, and a functional family, social and professional life can all enhance the life-long process of seeing and experiencing the world in increasingly more complex, differentiated and integrated ways.

HYPOTHETICALS

- For a group discussion on empathic intelligence, select ahead of time a novel, play or movie as a shared experience and focus for the discussion. It will help if you choose examples rich in significance, with a strong story line and complex characters. Ask participants to note:

  a   those parts which they find most engaging or most moving;
  b   ethical or perplexing questions raised in the example;
  c   examples of empathic intelligence in action; and
  d   aspects of one's own empathic intelligence that come into play in engaging with the examples, and in working with the group.

- Use topical ethical and political issues for group discussion, illustrated with pictures or other visuals if possible. As group leader, carefully invite participants to reflect on the reasons and feelings which support or influence their perceptions and point of view. Encourage the group to seek understanding above judgment.

FURTHER READING
Arnold, R (1991) Drama in the round: The centrality of drama in learning. In *Drama in Education: The State of the Art* Hughes, J (ed.) Educational Drama Association, Leichardt, NSW.
—— (2004) *Empathic Intelligence: The Phenomenon of Intersubjective Engagement*, Paper presented at the Global Conference on Excellence in Education and Training, Singapore Polytechnic, May.
Chukovsky, K (1963) *From Two to Five* (transl. M.Morton), University of California Press, Berkeley.
Coles, R (1989) *The Call of Stories: Teaching and the Moral Imagination*, A Peter Davison Book – Houghton Mifflin Co, Boston.
Diamond, M & Hopson, JL (1999) *Magic Trees of the Mind: How to Nurture Your Child's Intelligence, Creativity, and Healthy Emotions From Birth Through Adolescence*, Penguin, USA.
Harris, PL (2000) *The Work of the Imagination: Understanding Children's Worlds*, Blackwell Publications, Oxford.
Lovesy, S (2004) *Drama Education: Secondary School Playbuilding: Enhancing Imagination and Creativity in Group Playbuilding Through Kinaesthetic Teaching and Learning*, Unpublished PHD Thesis, University of Western Sydney.

CHAPTER FOUR

THEORETICAL ANTECEDENTS OF EMPATHIC PEDAGOGY

As I have said earlier in this book, the development of empathic intelligence has been influenced by research and scholarship over a long period of time and in several domains, particularly those of pedagogy, psychology, philosophy and arts education. Some of these influences are outlined below.

A HOLISTIC THEORY

Since evidence has accumulated of the complex nature and influence of cultural and social settings on students' learning, issues such as self-concept, self-esteem and self-constructs (Bannister and Fransella, 1980) have attracted attention. The role of emotions in organisations, including schools (Fineman, 1993) and personal life (Goleman, 1996; Steiner, 1997) is now well established, but it is timely to seek an integration of the apparent divide between affective and cognitive development and to understand the potential energy released when thinking and feeling work together. In this book I use a theory of empathic intelligence to postulate that this energy, or dynamic, increases learning and informs understanding and insight. It goes beyond the purely rational or purely intuitive, guiding the outcomes of the processes of reason and intuition. These outcomes are coloured by feeling and informed by rational evidence and are greater than what can be achieved by either reason or intuition alone.

While arguing for the worth of encouraging the natural dynamic between complementary ways of experiencing, I feel it is important to encourage reflection upon the essentially interdependent nature of personal and professional lives. Just as there is a dynamic between thinking and feeling states, there is also an essential dynamic between our individual, unique existence as human beings, and our existence within a group, society and culture. How we develop constructs of ourselves as individual and collective beings is part of the challenge of each individual's life. The philosophy underpinning empathic pedagogy values enrichment of individual lives in the belief that well integrated people wish to contribute to society because from such contributions develops further personal and community growth.

It becomes pointless to develop your own artistic, intellectual, emotional or imaginative abilities if the enterprise is secretive, solitary and self-absorbed. This is not to deny that at times you might have to retreat in order to work undistracted, but eventually your work has to reach out to others. If there is no audience to value your products, affirm your uniqueness or mirror back to individuals the collective benefits of your enterprises, it can become difficult to continue. It is just not in our human nature to work forever alone. We are both independent and interdependent in the life-long processes of complex psychic and personal development. We create our own meanings of experience as we shift between states of private reflection and public conversation. Obviously, private thoughts are not shared indiscriminately but generally with intimates. But we tend to know what we think and feel, even if we can't always put words to those states. If education, social and cultural life, work, imagination and reflection engage us in experiences that enable us to communicate and express those thoughts and feelings, we begin to both integrate and differentiate our unique existence.

If that sounds paradoxical, it might be because for too long we have fragmented experiences into separate subject domains. Certainly, there are specialised areas of the brain responsible for particular motor skills, language, thinking and feeling, but the brain's capacity to compensate for damage to specialised areas and to integrate experience in holistic ways (Damasio, 1994) should encourage us to be more confident, holistic and visionary in our spheres of influence. Educational programs built on hope and realistic expectation can succeed against all odds, partly because they activate hope, that essential constituent of human development (Arnold, 1991; Nicolson, 1997).

To contextualise this theory it is helpful to summarise some of its theoretical antecedents.

RESEARCH ON THE EMOTIONS

Human emotional responses and their expression have been researched from many angles for many years. A number of researchers have considered issues surrounding the universality of emotional expression. In the 1860s, Charles Darwin (1965) noted the expression of universally recognisable affects in human beings. He argued that while there are idiosyncratic variations in the physiological expression of those feelings, it is possible to recognise in humans the expression of basic affects such as fear, anger, surprise, anguish, shame, excitement, disgust and joy. These affects he regarded as universal, physiological phenomena. The basic emotions are believed to be experienced across cultures and races and expressed in recognisable facial forms, notwithstanding cultural and social pressures to repress or mask some feelings (Horowitz, Marmar and Wilner, 1979).

Psychologist Paul Ekman (2003) concurred with Darwin's views about the universality of facial expressions after studying people from an isolated area of Papua New Guinea in the 1960s. He also noted that studies undertaken with congenitally blind people support this theory, especially for those expressions that are spontaneous. However, Ekman also suggested that while anger, disgust, happiness and sadness appear to be universal human expressions, the ways in which they are triggered and given meaning, may be culturally specific. For example, while some people will be adversely affected by the death of a family pet, others will be more circumspect. Ekman explains this is partly because of our cultural background and partly due to the fact that we are all different and therefore react differently to any given circumstance (p. 18).

Ekman also suggests that we can learn, and sometimes heighten, our emotional responsiveness by witnessing others' emotional responses. However, he observes that we won't feel empathic emotions unless we care and identify with the person involved (p. 34). In discussing sadness, he explains that we may not fully experience the agony of a bereavement until we are with family and friends 'who can and do share our loss' (p. 86). 'We are constructed to respond with emotion to emotion; we usually feel the message' he writes, but this 'does not always mean we feel the emotion that is being signalled to us'. When viewing a person who is extremely sad 'empathic reactions are common'. Furthermore, 'they are a means by which we establish bonds with others, even with total strangers' (p. 96).

While we may not always share others' anger or surprise or fear, we can often understand these emotions and Ekman suggests that this is a considerable skill. For example, he writes 'it requires a well-developed capacity for compassion to respect, feel sympathetic toward, and patiently reassure someone who is afraid of something of which we are not afraid' (p. 153).

Empathy can heighten or temper emotional responses. For example, while we may be disgusted or repelled by an unknown person's blood or physical injuries, we respond differently when people close to us are injured and our primary response is likely to be the desire to reduce their suffering. Ekman suggests that the desire to remove ourselves from the suffering of strangers and from sights that disgust us, reduces 'our capacity for empathy and compassion, which can be very useful in building community' (p. 180).

Ekman identifies three types of empathy. He describes these as 'cognitive empathy' when we are aware of and identify another person's feeling; 'emotional empathy' when we can physically feel the other person's emotion; and 'compassionate empathy' when we are driven to assist the person emotionally and help them to cope with the situation they find themselves in (Ekman, 2003, p. 180). Ekman argues that as both empathy and compassion are 'reactions to another person's emotions' neither of them are themselves emotions.

RESEARCH ON TEACHER EXCELLENCE

Educator John Hattie's recent work helps us to understand the value of expertise in empathic intelligence in the teaching profession. His research studies have shown that what the student brings with him/her to the school accounts for about 50% of the variance influencing student achievement, teachers account for approximately 30% variance and factors such as peer effects, principals, schools and home account for 5–10% of the achievement variance (Hattie, 2003, p. 2).

Hattie argues that while educationalists have focused on spending more money on education and school buildings, reducing class sizes, introducing new testing methods, encouraging parental assistance in the school and focusing on problem students, that it is excellence in teaching that is 'the single most powerful influence on achievement'. Within the teaching profession we should therefore be directing our attention at 'higher quality teaching, and higher expectations that students can meet appropriate challenges' (p. 3). We need to 'identify, esteem, and grow those who have powerful influences on student learning' (p. 4).

Hattie identified five major dimensions of excellent teachers. Expert teachers:

1 can identify essential representations of their subject;
2 can guide learning through classroom interactions;
3 can monitor learning and provide feedback;
4 can attend to affective attributes; and
5 can influence student outcomes (p. 5).

Hattie explains that expert teachers are capable of attending to students 'affective attributes' (the fourth dimension) by having 'high respect for students' (p. 8). The ways in which teachers treat their students, respect them as learners and show care and commitment towards them, are all qualities of their expertise. Expert teachers are involved with and care about their students, and show the capacity to be receptive to their students' needs. They do not attempt 'to dominate the situation' (p. 8).but on the contrary, work to lessen the physical and psychological distance between themselves and their students. They are also noted to be 'passionate about teaching and learning' and have more emotion invested in whether they succeed or fail at work (p. 8). Hattie concludes, however, that while many professions recognise and esteem excellence, 'in teaching we reward primarily by experience irrespective of excellence' (p. 16).

Student perspectives

An American study that was designed to 'address the relative lack of information related to students' perspectives on class management' (Cothran, Hodges Kulinna and Garrahy, 2003, p. 436) helps to illuminate classroom dynamics from the students' perspectives. The researchers wanted to know how students describe effective (and ineffective) class managers in order to produce 'more successful and enjoyable learning environments' (p. 436).

The study involved 182 grade 6–12 physical education students from 14 schools. It was shown that 'students reported more positive students' behaviour in classes where the teachers set early, clear expectations and consequences, and developed caring, respectful relationships with students' (p. 437). The students perceived that it was the teachers who were responsible for initiating positive or negative relationships with their students, and that in order for the teacher to be treated well they needed to treat the students well (p. 439).

Care was another key word used by the students. It was explained: 'when teachers didn't care, neither did the students' (p. 439). 'Teachers demonstrated care by communicating and getting to know their students' and 'caring teachers also listened' (p. 439). The students and the teachers should 'get to know each other' (p. 440). Respect for both teachers and students was considered to be equally important. 'The students saw themselves as equals and expected to be treated as such' (p. 440).

PIAGET AND AFFECTIVE DEVELOPMENT

Educational psychology has focused on cognitive development for decades, profoundly influencing curriculum development and assessment procedures in educational institutions. Psychologist Jean Piaget's research and writing over a lifetime of research and scholarship from 1918 to 1969 identified four major stages of cognitive development from childhood to adulthood. Piaget pointed out that the behaviour patterns characteristic of the different stages do not succeed each other in a linear way but 'in the manner of the layers of a pyramid (upright, or upside down), the new behaviour patterns simply being added to the old ones to complete, correct, or combine with them' (Piaget, 1952, p. 329). The concept of a spiral of development postulated later in this chapter is consistent with Piaget's concepts of development, with additional dimensions. Primarily, these are the dynamic nature of engagements which individuals experience with others which facilitate development or temporary regressions, and the dynamic influence of feeling on thought and vice versa.

Psychologist Barry Wadsworth (1989) notes that psychologists and educators have focused primarily on Piaget's work on cognitive development and overlooked the role of affective development in intellectual growth. He suggests that because Piaget gave most attention to determining what knowledge is and how it is constructed by children:

> ... many came to Piaget's work believing that the cognitive aspects of intelligence must be the most important. Piaget's earliest works speak to the major role of affect in intellectual development. Because this was less emphasised (in a quantitative sense), affect, until recently, has taken a back seat to cognition (p. 29).

It is also well known that affective aspects of intellectual development create particular difficulties for those working with others' affects. Whether it be parents coping with two-year-old temper tantrums or adolescent risk-taking behaviour, or educators helping students who are disaffected with learning, the intersubjective nature of such work is complex and demanding. You may experience feelings of frustration, guilt and impatience, coupled often with a sense of mystification at the sources of the behaviour, and this can make it difficult to shape the situation constructively. Scholarship and research that illuminate the interconnection between cognitive and affective development in intellectual growth are much needed.

It is refreshing to re-visit Piaget's work and to discover his prescience on this subject:

> It is impossible to find behaviour arising from affectivity alone without any cognitive elements. It is equally impossible to find behaviour composed only of cognitive elements ... It is obvious that affective factors are involved even in the most abstract forms of intelligence. For students to solve an algebra problem or a mathematician to discover a theorem, there must be intrinsic interest, extrinsic interest, or a need at the beginning. While working, states of pleasure, disappointment, eagerness, as well as feelings of fatigue, effort, boredom, etc. come into play. At the end of the work, feelings of success or failure may occur; and finally, the student may experience aesthetic feelings stemming from the coherence of his solution (1981, pp. 2–3).

However, Piaget's argument (1981b) that all behaviour has both cognitive and affective elements ends with a contentious qualification:

> ... even if affectivity can cause behaviour, even if it is constantly involved in the functioning of intelligence, and even if it can speed up or slow down

intellectual development, it nevertheless does not, itself, generate structures of behaviour and does not modify the structures in whose functioning it intervenes (p. 6).

While Piaget believed that there are important parallels between cognitive and affective aspects of intellectual development, he ultimately privileged the cognitive. This becomes particularly evident when you consider children's reasoning about moral issues – an aspect of social, emotional and cognitive development that resonates with affective life. I contend that it is probable that children internalise or assimilate affective experiences in the same way that they assimilate experiences into cognitive structures. The child who can reason that bullying behaviour hurts individuals and creates an environment that has a negative effect on everyone, is capable of abstract cognitive and affective functioning. However much a child can reason altruistically, that same child might well prefer to deal with feelings of personal inadequacy, or feelings of personal entitlement, by inflicting pain on others. This dysfunctional response may manifest not only in physical bullying but also in more subtle forms of emotional bullying such as offensive name-calling or inciting a group to reject an individual. In such a case some method, such as withdrawal from social contact, needs to be found to combat the child's dysfunctional response option.

I suggest therefore that Piaget's statement above that affectivity does not modify structures, needs careful scrutiny. It is clear that both Piaget and Vygotsky *did* pay attention to the function of affectivity in thinking. However, for reasons beyond my scope here, that aspect of their work was less influential than their work on cognition.

THE WORK OF ANTONIO DAMASIO

There are challenges in undertaking scholarship in a field like empathy, which traverses several established disciplines such as psychology, philosophy, neurophysiology, education and the arts. At best such challenges fuel debate and interest in the subject. At the same time they sharpen the scholar's scepticism, because work in an imprecise area of interpersonal and intrapersonal dynamics means that scientific evidence is particularly helpful in the search for professional credibility.

The work of Antonio Damasio (1994, 2000, 2003) has provided a strong impetus to theories about the complementary nature of thought and feelings and influenced my work immeasurably. As a neurophysiologist his three books, *Descartes' Error: Emotion, Reason and the Human Brain* (1994); *The Feeling of What Happens: Body, Emotion and the Making of Consciousness* (2000); and *Looking for Spinoza: Joy, Sorrow, and the Feeling Brain* (2003) show how consciousness arises from the development of emotion and how human consciousness is actually consciousness of the feeling and experiencing of self. His case studies make compelling reading and offer deep reassurance to those who believe in the complementarity of emotion and cognition in intellectual development. He demonstrates persuasively that emotion and feeling 'provide the bridge between rational and non-rational processes, between cortical and subcortical structures' (1994, p. 128).

A summary of Damasio's work cannot do justice to the power of the insights expressed in his own prose. What follows is merely illustrative.

Damasio's Case Studies

Phineas Gage

Damasio (1994) recounts the dramatic story of the effects of damage to the frontal lobe of a man, Phineas Gage, who worked building the railroads of the United States in the middle of the nineteenth century. His job was to pack the dynamite prior to blasting the ground. In a freak accident in 1848, the iron rod he used to pack the dynamite was blasted through Gage's head. He made a good physical recovery from the accident but was reportedly affected in important ways. His attention, perception and memory were intact but he lacked respect for social conventions, he violated ethical concerns, had no concern for the future and no capacity for forethought. Careful investigation of Gage's preserved skull by Hanna Damasio has established the exact part of Gage's brain damaged by the accident. The Gage story gives credence to the view that reasoning needs to be modulated by affect, sited in the frontal lobe, to assist humans to make subtle but crucial social and emotional judgments. Two further accounts by Damasio add to this view.

Elliot

Elliot suffered a brain tumour that was successfully operated upon. Like Gage, he seemed to make a full recovery from surgery until it was observed that his normal capacity to sustain personal relationships was impaired, along with his decision-making capacity. This outcome is described by Damasio (1994) as the 'ineffable effects of reasoning without feeling'.

> Elliot had a normal ability to generate response options to social situations and to consider spontaneously the consequences of particular response options. He also had a capacity to conceptualise means to achieve social objectives, to predict the likely outcome of social situations, and to perform moral reasoning at an advanced developmental level. While [this] was consonant with his superior scoring on conventional tests of memory and intellect, it contrasted sharply with the defective decision-making he exhibited in real life (pp. 48–49).

> I began to think that the cold-bloodedness of Elliot's reasoning prevented him from assigning different values to different options, and made his decision-making landscape hopelessly flat (p. 51).

David

Perhaps Damasio's most compelling case study is that of David (Damasio 2000), one of the most severely brain-damaged patients Damasio has encountered. David barely scored at all on all the standard tests for brain functioning. Nonetheless, it was observed that he seemed to exhibit preferences for certain people who cared for him. Damasio designed an intriguing study, called the good guy/bad guy experiment that involved David in engaging with three different people who related to him in either a warm, neutral or cold way. Although David could not recall ever meeting those who engaged with him in these ways, in 80% of choices he was able to select from a wide sample of photographs the person who had related to him warmly. In an added twist to the experiment, the 'bad guy' was actually a very pleasant female, similar to one whom he was earlier observed to show some interest in. Seemingly, the overriding factor in David's choice of companion from the photographs was a person who behaved warmly and encouragingly towards him. This is in spite of the fact that he seemed unable to consciously recall meeting the experimenters. Damasio demonstrated how a man with limited psychic functioning could detect emotional response in others and recall his own emotional responses to them when selecting from photographs.

Damasio's research has shown that emotion is integral to the processes of reasoning and decision-making. He puts to rest the debate (*Descartes' Error*) about the separateness of cognition and feelings, arguing that feelings are 'just as cognitive as other percepts' and that they 'form the base for what humans have described for millennia as the human soul or spirit' (1994, p. xvii and xviii).

THE EMPATHIC STANCE OF THE RESEARCHER

Damasio's own philosophical and ethical commitment to both understanding and enhancing the lives of his patients, even those whose mental functioning is demonstrably very minimal, merits discussion, along with his use of narratives to illustrate his insights and their contexts. He said of Elliot's case:

> I found myself suffering more when listening to Elliot's stories than Elliot himself seemed to be suffering. In fact, I felt that I suffered more than he did just by thinking of those stories (1994, p. 44).

His empathic remarks about his responsiveness to Elliot's stories suggest a quality of commitment and care in his own engagements with patients. And he is not afraid to reveal that concern in his scientific reports. Those interested in student-centred pedagogy or client-centred professional practices could well find Damasio's work illuminating, even enthralling. Arguably, his scientific work is more accessible to lay readers through his case study presentations. Importantly, he provides strong scientific support for the worth of pursuing the development of a concept of empathic intelligence.

VIEWS FROM OTHER DISCIPLINES

It is pertinent to note the remarks of Steven Rose, a practising scientist working at the forefront of medical research. In his book, *The Making of Memory* (1993) he describes his experience of discovering that his feelings interfered with his game of chess, a game that he previously believed involved 'purely cognitive and logical skills' (p. 36). From his scientific work and his reflections upon his own learning experiences, he argues that 'cognition cannot be divorced from affect, try as one might'. He continues:

> ... the problems that it illuminates are fundamental to my research strategy, just as much as their resolution However, even today I find myself frequently in danger of forgetting that lesson, though it ought to be fundamental to a strategy for living.

In a similar vein, but from an aesthetic perspective, the critic Michael Heyward (1994), writing about the well-known Australian artist Donald Friend, remarks:

> What Friend thought, saw and felt was swept up by his enormous gift for telling stories. He knew, better than most people, that feeling is the source of all knowledge, and he put into his diary most of what he knew (p. 3).

One wonders whether it was Friend's painting or his writing, or the combination of both which best met his expressive needs.

In arguing for a more complex view of intelligence(s) than commonly prevails psychologist Howard Gardner (1985) comments:

> ... the roots of a sense of self lie in the individual's exploration of his own feelings and in his emerging ability to view his own feelings and experiences in terms of the interpretative schemes and symbol systems provided by the culture (p. 294).

The work of philosopher Michael Polanyi (1983) on tacit abilities and psychologist, Jerome Bruner's (1986) work on 'scaffolding' in cognitive development have contributed to the multidisciplinary traditions out of which empathic pedagogy developed.

In his book *Extraordinary Minds* (1997), Howard Gardner reminds us that:

> From psychology, we have learned that human beings possess many different intellectual faculties and that these have considerable independence from one another. Any attempt to isolate a unitary intelligence is fraught with measurement problems; and even so-called pure measures of intelligence are actually contaminated with effects of practice and context.
>
> From anthropology, we have learned that other cultures (like Japan's) make strikingly different assumptions about human learning and motivation. Such cultures have achieved educational success that would be impossible if one were to adhere to the 'unchangeable intellect' views of most psychometricians (p. 35).

Poetry and theory can share a common purpose in symbolising experience in ways that plausibly and creatively represent experience – even if the first encounter with that poetry or theory has the emotional colour of an acquaintanceship rather than a reunion. If such poetry and theory are affectively charged, they will tacitly, if not overtly, stimulate newly-imagined possibilities. It is a curious phenomenon that empathic pedagogy seems to embody the dynamism of its own genesis. In recognising the function in pedagogy of enthusiasm, attunement, engagement, reflection and imagination, and its role in their own practice, educators become more enthusiastic, engaged, imaginative and reflective themselves. It is as if this theory about the spiralling nature of development propels its adherents along that dynamic. Potential energy is transformed into actual energy. Maybe this is the meeting point of science and metaphor – in the poetic fusion of actual and potential energy articulated through language or symbolisation.

VISUALISING EMPATHIC DEVELOPMENT

Needless to say, this theory is continually evolving. Some years ago I conceptualised the development of writing abilities as a metaphor spiral – an image that was described in and appeared on the front cover of my book *Writing Development – Magic in the Brain* (1991). Since then I have applied the spiral image more widely to the development articulated in empathic pedagogy. It is possible to describe the principles of the spiral in words, but a three-dimensional model would be truer to the symbol, and to the concepts it is meant to represent. The reason for using a symbol alongside words is to provide an encapsulated visual image that has its own particular resonances. Were I to brief a designer, engineer, artist or computer graphics artist to build the spiral, these would be the instructions:

- The base point has to be firmly on the ground ('feet on the ground', 'grounded', 'plausible', 'real,' 'concrete'). But the base point represents infinite possibility ('human potential development') so it has to look vibrant, expectant, dynamic (affectively charged but reasonable).
- The base point is composed of two connected, but individual, strands that can move in tandem around a spiral trajectory according to stimulation from the environment. The path of that trajectory is a cone shaped spiral moving up and out.
- The spiral can regress to the base point, but after each regression it progresses further up and out. Because the spiral represents development it must never reduce in size permanently; it has to enlarge. It can become stuck but it cannot revert permanently to base point (each experience is potentially developmental, even apparently negative ones).
- The trajectory of the spiral is surrounded by a mirrored cone (empathic other/significant experiences) that assumes the shape of the spiral

and matches its movements. The mirroring others serve the function of providing attunement but they also have the capacity to develop in tune with the focus of their attention. It is possible that the learner can replace the mirroring others with his/her own internalised sense of confidence but the process of development must offer mirroring of some kind. Without such mirroring the process stagnates.

- The two connected, but individual, strands representing affective and cognitive can merge with each other sometimes, and remain close but separable at others times (rarely). They are mutually dynamic, perhaps magnetised. They could be coloured separately to signal their individuality, but their complementary, even symbiotic relationship in learning needs to be clearly symbolised.
- The spiral is open-ended at the top to suggest that development is infinite.

Finally, the image of the spiral needs to be aesthetically pleasing since we are talking about development within the art of pedagogy. Even if it requires time and effort to understand the symbolisation, there should be sufficient inherent attraction in the model for it to resonate even in subliminal ways. Then it should become increasingly more pleasing as one engages with it to create a personal and embodied meaning. While I have suggested that this spiral might be a three-dimensional, architectural model, it could also be symbolised through dance and movement.

The reason for conceptualising development in a psychodynamic model in this way is to provide a visualised image to focus the attention of those who work in this model. Difficult as it is to represent the essential dynamism and complexity of development in either words or visual image, it can help to have one's methods and aspirations or goals symbolised in a visual form. Under the pressure of engaging empathically with another, or when reflecting upon complex events, it is easy to lose focus. A visually internalised image of experience, such as the spiral, can provide shape and form to a mass of data being processed psychically, while you work through its meaning and significance. In that sense, the visualised image can act as a support to tacit abilities while they move towards greater clarity. You might think of a runner mobilising greater speed by visualising crossing the finishing line first.

In itself, development is too abstract a notion to be either attractive or inspiring. Yet if educators are to underpin their practice with an enabling theory, an easily accessible version of that theory can be both

The spiral of development

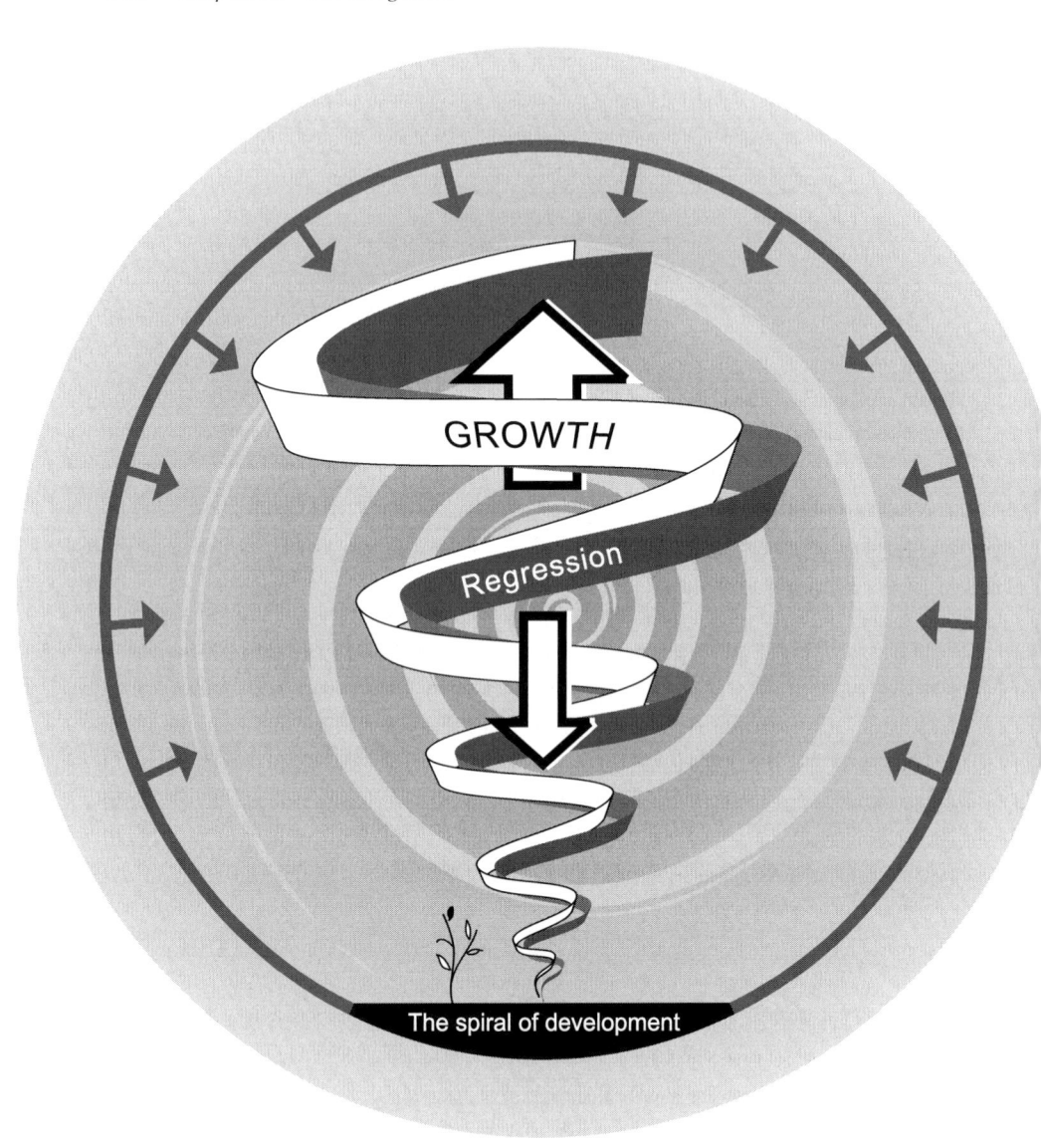

supportive and informative. This symbol of development is just one form of conceptualisation. It is instructive to ask those attracted to this model of pedagogy to draw their own images of teaching and learning. Not only does the exercise assist the development of consciousness and meta-awareness of pedagogy, it provides evidence of the various, idiosyncratic and embodied experiences from which reflective individuals develop personally meaningful theories to guide their lives. Educators sometimes invite students at different stages of education to draw or model their symbolisations of learning and its processes. Teacher Moira Sullivan (1998) gives an example:

> The class began with a discussion about the fact that learning was a two-way process (I learnt from them and they learnt from me) and that in order for me to teach them effectively, I needed to understand what learning meant to them. So I asked them to represent their individual ideas about learning through visual means i.e. draw or create a model – the boys then each explained their symbol to the class so that we could combine their ideas into how we could all best learn in the classroom. We then created a mutual symbol, which became our class logo (the students placed this logo on all their work) that made them feel proud, special and accomplished.

The individualised expressions which result can be revealing and thought-provoking, for both the students and their teachers. Put to the test, most students do have embryonic notions, if not well-constructed ones, of what learning means to them. Sometimes they cannot articulate this in words, but they can draw or otherwise symbolise their learning constructs, including the place of the teacher and themselves in such constructs. The processes of reflection, selection, visualisation and symbolisation involved in this exercise, are more important than the product. For many students, it is important that different forms of expression and composition, including drama improvisations, are encouraged as part of their concept development. Forms involving art, music, bodily movement and voice work allow them to access different communicative abilities to those traditionally favoured in classrooms. Feeling and thought can be communicated through multiple literacies.

Consistent with the student-centred nature of pedagogy espoused here, students as learners need to feel centred in the process. This applies at all stages of life. That feeling of centredness offers poise and balance that focuses the learner's tacit abilities in a state of psychological readiness. Excellent performers in all kinds of endeavours can access that feeling of centredness with its sense of equilibrium and expectation. It is more than just a state of concentration, which sometimes sounds rather forced and cognitive. It is a pleasurable state in which the individual might be symbolised as positioned deeply within the cone of the spiral with the surrounding mirrors reflecting poise, balance, and potential, as they have always done. The expectation of success and the reality of the challenge provide a tension that mobilises resources.

In this spiral model, failure is not an appropriate construct because regressions can be construed as sources of growth, depending upon their integration within the centred experience. That is, we need to analyse why a student is lacking some skill or ability. How important is the lack? Does it impede progress in related abilities? Do other students succeed without that skill? Is it worth giving some particular attention to the teaching of that ability/skill if it is so important? The detail here is not as important as the mindset that practises the habit of evaluating professional methods against graduated outcomes. Some outcomes are essential, others are peripheral. Some underpin later development, others reflect social biases or political agendas of a particular time.

NAVIGATING IMPASSES

An example in the literacy area comes to mind here. Much is made of students whose spelling is imperfect. Traditionally, spelling has been regarded as an important measure of literacy development, partly because until the past three decades or so we didn't know how else to measure literacy. Spelling and neat handwriting featured on report cards under 'English'. Even today some people hold negative images of their composing or writing ability because in childhood someone commented adversely on their handwriting or spelling. It is facile and ill-informed to reference spelling mistakes as evidence of a decline in educational standards. Now that we understand better the principles and theories of literacy development, particularly the time and effort it takes to develop students' writing abilities, teaching methods and assessment practices can reflect that understanding.

To experts in the field of literacy development, the failure to grasp how very much more complex literacy is than any measure of spelling can determine, is every bit as annoying and frustrating as spelling mistakes are to those who persist in targeting them. The fact that people cite their own school experiences as evidence to support the worth of their arguments says more about the influence of schooling on thinking and logic than it does about desirable literacy methods. Sure, it is irritating to encounter poor spelling in public writing, often because it reminds us of all those admonitions about correct spelling in our own school life. 'Here's someone who escaped those admonitions about correct spelling, or here's someone with the gall to not care about spelling. They can't be let off the hook lightly.' And so on. In actual fact, incorrect spelling rarely interferes with meaning. We can usually guess from context what the writer means. However, writers who feel proud of their work are highly motivated to present that work as well as possible. They don't want the humiliation of being exposed by spelling mistakes and that is a compelling reason to learn to proofread or use spelling programs on computers. What is more of a problem is the writer who can't engage the reader, or the writer who is overly repetitive, or inelegant, or confused. Some world-class performers make mistakes – pianists hit the wrong note sometimes. Professionals in the field can assess the significance of such mistakes against the quality of the overall performance.

I am not arguing here for spelling being ignored: I am arguing for an appropriate assessment of the relative worth of sub-skills in the overall picture of development. Such development might be in mathematics, or art or science or drama or something else. Within the spiral model, educators need to be able to determine what abilities students have developed, which ones need to be mobilised, and the quality of their overall progression. This prevails whether a student is gifted and performing consistent with that giftedness, or particularly under-talented in a certain area but performing well given certain limitations. Added to that analysis should always be the factor of surprise – some talented students peak early and fail to maintain their momentum; other students gather momentum under the influence of certain enabling conditions such as gifted, inspiring teachers or a constructive, generative peer group. We need to be guided by testing procedures and conceptual theorising, not constrained by them. Unexpected shifts can occur in learning patterns – witness the large number of people who discover interests, abilities and new careers at different stages in life. If we build that possibility overtly into our educational planning, it will reinforce the flexible thinking needed for complex civic and professional life. Our understanding of the processes of human development are far from complete. Psychic abilities far exceed our capacities to describe or harness them. Since imagination sparks on hope, there is benefit in imagining surprises are possible. So-called hopeless students are just that! Depressed by lack of someone to believe in them, their spirits are crushed. Overworked educators depressed by unrealistic expectations can suffer the same sense of defeat. Empathic leaders can sometimes break the impasse.

In the model of excellence outlined earlier, failure to achieve a goal can be a precursor to a different kind of success. Commonsense

You don't measure up
SOURCE **Craig Golding, Fairfax photos**

dictates that the truly excellent performer has been tested by episodes of frustration and disappointment. Even winning brings its own stress and challenge, notwithstanding that it feels infinitely better than losing. This is not to suggest that failure will be easily rationalised, nor to deny that feelings of failure can dog the defeated. Personal constructs of self-worth vacillate relative to the achievement of desires and established goals. Perceived failures can be accompanied by deep feelings of frustration and disappointment, temporarily assuaged by self-blame or projected blame. The depth of these feelings might reflect the very level of commitment, effort and drive that characterised the endeavour. To deny the source or depth of these feelings can be destructive, but it is a painful reality of life that those who can endure the pain of failure or frustration are well positioned to meet life's inevitable challenges. It is always difficult to establish a timeframe for experiencing intensities of feeling. Elation and depression can seem to last longer than is the case, and boredom is known to be interminable! Some students respond well to the hint that it is worth timing the periods of intensity, just as a reality check. The act of addressing one's feeling states in this way acts to change the feeling anyway, bringing a sense of purpose to the experience.

The empathic mentor is never more necessary than when a striving individual meets a seemingly unmovable obstacle. While we may not be able to move the obstacle, we can alter our thoughts and feelings about it, and about our relationship to it. In due course, the thoughts and feelings aroused by pinnacles of achievement or troughs of defeat can be remobilised to underpin continued developmental processes. They can work with reflective analysis to determine the factors influencing past and future outcomes. Much will depend upon the empathic attunement of the significant others who act as reflectors or mirrors for the striving learner. Needless to say, the empathic others will be of most help to the learner if such attunement is informed by an understanding of the skills, attitudes and rehearsal experiences likely to achieve success. Some experts in a field of endeavour are excellent educators, mentors or coaches because they are well aware of the complex factors influencing success and they know how to structure or scaffold experiences in developmental ways. Other experts can find exasperating and bewildering the apparent inability of others to reach a similar level of excellence to their own. Needless to say, they are rarely effective as mentors or educators, although they can still model excellence in their particular field of achievement.

EMPATHY IN THE ZONE OF PROXIMAL DEVELOPMENT

One of the most helpful concepts for educators wishing to attune to students' readiness to learn is Vygotsky's concept of the zone of proximal development, or *zo-ped*. (Vygotsky, 1978). Vygotsky argued that one cannot understand a child's developmental level unless one considers two aspects of it: the *actual* developmental level and the *potential* developmental level. He explained the zone of proximal development as:

> The place at which a child's empirically rich but disorganised spontaneous concepts 'meet' the systematicity and logic of adult reasoning. As a result

of such a 'meeting,' the weaknesses of spontaneous reasoning are compensated by the strengths of scientific logic (1978, p. xxxv).

Psychologist Jerome Bruner developed the notion of scaffolding as a way of explaining the role of the teacher (or the capable peer) in helping the child achieve his/her potential developmental level. The metaphor suggests an adjustable support that can be removed when no longer needed. According to Bruner's *Actual Minds, Possible Worlds* (1986, pp. 74–76) scaffolding involves the adult entering into the dialogue with the child in a fashion that provides the child with hints and props, to assist him/her through the zone of proximal development – clearly a description of empathic expertise in action.

The empathic educator has to judge sensitively the right amount of challenge to set the student, and must allow the student to experience the pleasure of meeting that challenge. The challenge can be both intellectual and emotional, for both student and teacher. Sometimes it can mean that the teacher needs to conceal her ability to do the task, lest that thwart the student. At other times it can mean the teacher has to structure the task in measured ways so that it can be accomplished by the student. This ability to recognise a student's zone of proximal development is part of a competent and professional educator's repertoire. In literacy development, it can mean knowing that young writers need to be able to see that they can write words on a page which another can read back sensibly (even if some words have to be guessed at) prior to writing complete and accurately spelled sentences.

The empathic and informed educator knows the power of autonomous composition for the young writer's self-concept as an effective communicator. Once that concept is in place, and it is essential that the reader confirms that the text communicates, then the writer is ready to begin to construct writing which more consistently accords to social conventions. For adult writers the issues are just the same. They too need to be encouraged to keep writing, preferably in private and with empathic teachers, even when there are flaws in spelling and construction. Once writers and speakers are confident they will not be humiliated by mistakes in their language, or they know how to deal with negative feedback, they can afford to take the very risks inherent in development. In that difficult emotional space where the learner struggles with the fear of failure and the allure of the rewards of success, the attuned educator has to support the students to be ready for either outcome.

I witnessed an excellent example of an attuned educator working in sympathy with Vygotsky's zone of proximal development in a literacy development centre attached to a university. Screened behind a one-way mirror, I was observing a literacy teacher helping a ten-year-old boy read a story. As the boy encountered difficulties, she provided appropriate prompts but on one occasion he could not decode the text, in spite of various helpful strategies, and simply stopped trying. Tears filled his eyes and it seemed to me that he needed a break. However, the teacher urged him to persevere and ignored his tears. He persisted with the tears. She refused to allow him to give up. After a few seconds of silent 'tug-of war' with the teacher, the boy persevered with reading the text and suddenly made a breakthrough. Smiles all round! In discussion with the teacher afterwards, I was interested to know why she chose to persist in spite of the boy's tears. She explained that because she was essentially tuned into the boy's needs and had worked with him for a long time, she knew to interpret the tears as a response to frustration rather than as a signal of real distress. With empathic intelligence, she judged that he could tolerate the temporary frustration in the interests of imminent development. As it happened, she was accurate in her judgment that together she and her student were working within the boy's zone of proximal development. In other words, she knew he was nearly there. It was worth persevering.

For many professionals in the middle of their careers, the extent to which they have had to keep developing their professional and pedagogical expertise is probably surprising. In my own profession of education, teachers in all sectors of the profession, but particularly those in primary and secondary education, have had rapid and increasing demands upon their knowledge and responsibilities as teachers. In taking seriously their professional responsibilities to develop the whole student – that is, emotionally, cognitively, socially and ethically – they have accepted a role that requires considerable structural and community support. Few graduates of the past twenty years would have imagined the intensity and complexity of the profession they entered. This suggests all the more reason for realistic assessments of what is professionally possible and appropriate. It is a feature of the professionalism of many of the most committed and expert educators that they demand much of themselves. It is important within communities or groups of intelligently caring professionals, that there is co-responsibility for appropriate professional development and support.

THE BOUNDARIES OF EMPATHY

The work of philosophers Allison Barnes and Paul Thagard (1997) provides insights into the complex phenomenon by which intellectual development is promoted. In a journal article 'Empathy and Analogy', Barnes and Thagard present a conceptual study of empathy that shows that it is a cognitive process that is fundamentally analogical. By that they mean that empathy always involves simulation (comparisons with known experiences) but it might also include the application of a theory about how minds work. They specify the analogical processes of empathy and the constraints on these processes, and show how this is determined:

> Empathy is independent of theory application when an analogue of the other's mental state is easily retrieved from memory. Processes of rule-based reasoning are required when empathy is achieved by constructing an analogue. The constraints of analogical mapping determine when an analogue is likely to be retrieved and when it is likely to be constructed ... empathy can be difficult to achieve, but ... it can be possible between people of different backgrounds ... (p. 706).

Interestingly, having defined 'empathy' as a cognitive act, the authors then suggest that 'centrality of feeling distinguishes empathy and sympathy from other kinds of interpersonal acts' (p. 707). They argue:

> ... achieving empathic understanding involves making a comparison of emotions ... the process of 'feeling into' is essentially analogical ... In addition to mapping between structures, analogical thinking involves stages of selection, evaluation and learning ...(pp. 708–9).

While the central purpose of Barnes and Thagard's work is to determine the balance of simulation and theory application in empathic understanding, their arguments contribute to an understanding of empathic intelligence as it is postulated here. Their concept of empathy as analogical thinking connects with my argument that empathic intelligence involves the capacity to understand one's own thinking and feeling processes and the dynamic between them. While Barnes and Thagard argue for empathy as a cognitive process, their example of the processes and psychic procedures involved in understanding, for example, Hamlet, seem to suggest that feeling and thinking are actually complementarily involved in that process. Knowing what we feel about

Hamlet, and what we feel as we watch or read the play, and conjecturing (through analogising) what Hamlet might be feeling and thinking, can engage us in complex cognitive/affective processes.

Those processes can be mapped, structured, analysed and constructed algebraically as formulae, as Barnes and Thagard demonstrate. However, in real time such processes are infinitely more complex and dynamic than fixed formulae might suggest, inclusive as such formulae might seem to be. For example, you might feel a different level of identification with Hamlet according to your present psychic preoccupations. The energy committed to making an analogy between his behaviour and motivations and your own will be a factor of engagement. Put simply, if you don't care about the play, you won't bother engaging with it. There has to be some resonance between the stage and the audience. Nonetheless, Barnes and Thagard's work provides important data for the development of a concept of empathic intelligence, supporting the idea that analogy is essential to empathy. The difference in emphasis in my own theorising is the premise that analogical processing is both cognitive and affective.

On the limits of empathy as analogic processing, Barnes and Thagard suggest that empathy can fail 'either because the source analogue does not correspond to the goals, situation, and emotions of the other person, or because a retrieved source does not correspond well' (p. 713). They cite as support for their point an unfortunate incident during the 1992 Canadian election when the Prime Minister Kim Campbell told the residents of a shelter in Vancouver's Skid Row that she, too, had known loss and disappointment – she had been thwarted in her ambition to be a concert cellist. Visualising the audience for her speech, it takes little empathy to see that this remark was the antithesis of empathic intelligence in action. It sounds more like an opportunistic and insensitive attempt to exploit fellow-feeling. The mistake probably derived from the primacy of Campbell's political agenda. Notoriously, such agendas can paralyse compassion.

Barnes and Thagard analyse failures in empathy. They postulate that empathy will be weak to the extent that the source analogue of the empathiser:

1. has disparate goals, situations, and emotions from those in the target analogue;
2. has causal relations with a different structure than those in the target analogue;
3. does not contribute to the cognitive purposes of the empathiser (p. 713).

This differentiation of the causes of failures in empathy serves a number of purposes. In the above Skid Row example, the plight of the people on skid row was the source analogue of the Prime Minister but her goals (to win their support) and situation (a very successful middle-class professional) did not match theirs. Unfortunately for her purposes, there was a mismatch between her idea of plight, namely failure as a concert cellist, and their idea of plight, presumably, hunger, poverty and homelessness. Her failure to perceive this mismatch was a failure to exercise empathic intelligence. Her failure in judgment, tact and sensitivity signals by default the underlying emotional and cognitive attributes of empathic intelligence. It further suggests that empathic intelligence requires an ethical or altruistic choice in the third attribute highlighted by Barnes and Thagard: the match or mismatch between the cognitive purposes of the would-be empathiser and the person with whom they are wishing to empathise.

As the example above indicates, an attempt at empathy can be potentially exploitative. Empathy and empathic intelligence can be engaged to serve destructive purposes. Hitler's understanding of others' fears, ambitions and vulnerabilities might be seen as empathy. However, I would argue that where empathy is so weak that the mismatches between goals, purposes and emotions of participants prohibit constructive outcomes, empathy has probably broken down.

An example of such a breakdown was observable in *Facing the Demons*, a television program shown in Australia (ABC television, 1999, 2000 and 2003) that filmed the reconciliation meeting between the perpetrators and victims of crime. Right up to the end of the program, the meeting could well have been described as an extraordinary example of empathy in action. Victims had an opportunity to ask the perpetrators for explanations, and the perpetrators could try to explain their motivations. Viewers had evidence and emotional responses to guide them to empathic understanding of the minds of both the perpetrators and the victims. In spite of the powerful emotional undercurrents in the meeting, there was a civilised commitment from all parties to understand rather than blame.

However, towards the end of the program that commitment was fractured. In a dramatic and unexpected symbolic gesture, a murdered boy's mother threw a plastic bag of ashes (possibly those of her son) towards one of the men convicted of the boy's murder, with a comment to the effect 'Here's your Christmas present'. Up to that point, empathic engagement with all the participants seemed possible. One could engage with intense feeling while simultaneously evaluating the motivations, causes and effects of the crime and its outcomes. For instance, there was one point where one of the convicted men, was asked for an explanation for his crime that involved the tragic shooting of a young boy. He replied to the effect that he now recognised that he had, at the time, lacked a moral code to inform his actions. The tenor of his response, its emotional colour and its content, made plausible (not necessarily excusable, but understandable) the nature of the crime.

With the mother's confronting gesture, the boundaries tacitly established for this especially difficult interpersonal meeting were transgressed. Up to this point, it had been possible to engage in an empathic engagement with the mother, in particular, but also with others affected by the crime, including the perpetrators. Her gesture was so emotionally forceful, and so shocking, that it broke the discipline required for such an engagement and probably shifted many viewers' responses back into a judgmental mode. The focus inevitably shifted to thoughts such as 'Should she have done that?' 'What purpose does it serve?' It was not that one lost sympathy for the mother: her plight and continued suffering and grief could not dissolve that. Rather, it become at least temporarily impossible to maintain the non-judgmental, evaluative, coherent interplay of dynamic thinking and feeling required to sustain an empathically intelligent stance.

Nonetheless, the exercise of attempting to reconcile victims and perpetrators of crimes can provide insight into the very complex, emotionally and cognitively demanding nature of sophisticated empathic intelligence in action. Among professionals working in a humanistic tradition, work continues to find ways to bring affected parties together in a spirit of reconciliation and personal growth through trauma (McDonald, 1996).

I hope you can see from the examples and comments above that an empathic stance is demanding but potentially rewarding. In seeking to understand others, we signal a wish to engage in constructive ways. Below the surface of our communications lie thoughts and feelings that shape our voice, stance and expressions. These can assist in the communication of messages beyond our immediate awareness. Hence the true spirit of engagement influences its outcomes, sometimes to surprising effect.

HYPOTHETICALS

- Imagine you are undertaking a self-development course to increase your self-awareness. Keep a log of the range of emotions you experience in a day. To do so, reflect upon and note down each two hours, on the hour, what you have felt in that time. See if you can find words to describe very precisely the intensity or blandness of your emotions. If need be refer to a thesaurus to find the words.

- You are auditioning for a role in a movie and want to develop observation skills. Sit and 'people watch' in a public space, such as on a bus, in a park, or a shopping mall. Unobtrusively, see if you can guess what others are thinking or feeling. In particular, notice people conversing and guess what they might be conversing about. Then consider whether your thoughts and feelings are shifting as you observe. Try to write a short story about your day 'people watching'.

- You are undertaking research into your family history. Look at photos of yourself and other family members at a younger age. What do you read into the photos now? Pair photos from different generations and imagine the dialogue that might occur between those whom you have paired.

FURTHER READING

Barnett, M & Thompson, S (1984) *The role of affective perspective-taking ability and empathic disposition in the child's machiavellianism, prosocial behaviour, and motive for helping*. Paper presented at the annual meeting of the Midwestern Psychological Association, Chicago, May. In Berliner, D & Calfee, R (eds) (1996) *Handbook of Educational Psychology,* Simon & Shuster Macmillan, New York.

Duan, C & Hill, D (1996) The current state of empathy research, *Journal of Counselling Psychology,* 43 (3): 261–274.

Johansson, E (2002) Morality in preschool interaction: Teachers strategies for working with children's morality, *Early Childhood Development and Care,* 172(2): 203–221.

Lazarus, RS (1991) *Emotion and Adaptation,* Oxford University Press, New York.

Mezirow, J & Associates (2000) *Learning As Transformation: Critical Perspectives on a Theory in Progress,* Jossey-Bass, John Wiley & Sons, San Francisco.

Nussbaum, MC (2003) *Upheavals of Thought: The Intelligence of Emotions,* Cambridge University Press.

Wentzell, KR (1991) Social competence at school: relation between social responsibility and academic achievement, *Review of Educational Research,* 61: 1–24.

—— (1993a) Does being good make the grade? Social behaviour and academic competence in middle school, *Journal of Educational Psychology,* 85: 357–364.

—— (1993b) Motivation and achievement in early adolescence: the role of multiple classroom goals *Journal of Early Adolescence,* 13: 14–20.

CHAPTER FIVE

EMPATHIC LITERACY FOR EFFECTIVE LEADERSHIP

In this chapter, I tease out the ways in which an applied theory of empathic intelligence can guide good professional decision-making in a range of situations. I explore what it is that constitutes professional expertise and examine the conditions necessary for intra- and intersubjective engagement. I suggest that through the introspection that is central to empathic intelligence it is possible to create dynamic psychic spaces in which we can manage and enjoy encounters with the ineffable. I examine the capacity of hope to transform despair and powerlessness. I consider the impact of theories of empathic intelligence on research methodology. Finally I explore the paradoxical ways in which leadership has been defined and argue for the necessity of empathy in effective leadership and consider the ways in which it contributes to the building of social capital. I discuss the values that underpin empathy and explore how empathic 'literacies' can be developed to transform personal and professional life and curricula.

A THEORY TO INFORM PROFESSIONAL EXPERTISE

The concept of empathic intelligence, with its attributes of expertise, enthusiasm, capacity to engage and to be empathic, is an attempt to provide a functional articulation of effective pedagogy. Effective pedagogy is, in practice, a deeply complex and dynamic interpersonal and intrapersonal engagement. While the mysteries of interpersonal dynamics will not yield insights easily, brain-based research (Damasio, 1994, 2000, 2003) and Hattie's (2003) extensive research on expert teachers [see Chapter 4] provide a rationale to re-conceptualise teacher education and professional development. Of major significance is that we are now able to honour the essential importance of creating a dynamic between affect and cognition in a climate of care in classrooms. To achieve that re-conceptualisation, many novice and experienced educators will need support to understand, develop and re-shape their own professional biographies, particularly when such biographies have been bereft of support for the affective and caring dimensions of intellectual development.

The concept of empathic intelligence can be relevant wherever people engage in interpersonal interactions. Whether the dynamic is operating in an interpersonal setting, for example, between two people, or in a public gathering, such as a meeting of leaders to resolve a conflict, the principles are the same. Hence the strategy here is to start with the particular and personal to engage people's tacit understandings. As those understandings become more overt and recognisable, they can be experienced richly, reflected upon and tested against reality. The outcome of that kind of process can be to reach beyond the known. Such striving for excellence can be demonstrated in diverse fields of endeavour but psychic cooperation between thinking and feeling can enhance that goal. Such psychic cooperation is at the core of empathic intelligence.

If you are curious about the concept of empathic intelligence, you might well want to reflect on the ways humans make sense of the flow of experiences that constitute life. Whether as leaders, educators, change agents, caring professionals, communicators or parents, it is usual for us to seek understanding by talking, reading, viewing, creating, reflecting or symbolising. Through such activities we can signal a need to know, to enjoy, to pattern and share our individual experiences of life. Thus we engage in an interface between personal and public life.

To shape that interface, and give it coherence, we do well to seek to understand our past and its relationship with the present. With its respect for the complementary nature of thinking and feeling, empathic intelligence can mobilise the development of insight, vision and even wisdom. If we strive to make sense of our own personal and professional lives we can develop ourselves and inspire others to engage in constructive, mutually beneficial enterprises. By modelling strategies such as close observation, personal and informed reflection and imaginative problem-solving, we help ourselves and those whom we influence, to become effective life-long learners, responsible adults and caring citizens.

Educators, business leaders, health care professionals and parents sometimes have a significant influence upon others for a relatively brief time, but that time and the opportunities it offers are profoundly important. Influential people meet others' complex needs, physical, emotional or educative. If such needs are met at a time when feelings are intense, the influence tends to be greater. Conversely, if the needs are ignored, connectedness and influence are minimal. The teacher or mentor who models successful learning strategies at a time of critical needs is influential. The world leader who promises solutions and delivers on that promise is influential. The nature of such influence is relevant to the concept of empathic intelligence where it describes the kind of interpersonal influence frequently characterised by mothers, fathers, educators, and world leaders such as Gandhi, Mother Teresa and Nelson Mandela.

Many readers will be people of influence in terms of the criteria outlined here. They may be involved in professional work that is highly interpersonal and dynamic. While such people are engaged in influential ways with others, the script they deliver in their theatre of influence deserves to be informed, eloquent and memorable. Often that script has to be improvised from embodied experience and philosophy. Hence the need for such influential people to be well-integrated, flexible and consistent.

Empathic intelligence is not just about planning strategies to implement change, to educate others or to mobilise them to perform. It is about developing a personal, intelligent theory of professional life to guide decisions and reactions in challenging, often surprising situations. It is also about knowing how to find from within the culture the understandings that others may well have discovered earlier. Such predecessors might be educators, artists, composers, writers, scientists or thinkers.

Most of us have vivid memories of a time when a few significant words had a remarkable effect upon us. Poets are particularly gifted at structuring emotional and insightful ideas in evocative language. The agony of making difficult choices and gambling on the future is part of the human condition. How often we wish we could have it all. Robert Frost's famous poem *The Road Not Taken* emphasises the powerful effects of our choices in life. It is the nature of choice to evoke regret and concern about alternatives. Ultimately, we know we have to take responsibility for our choices and live with their consequences. But although that rational thought doesn't soothe the anxiety of the process, Frost's imagery and empathic understanding of the problem softens the impact of an existential reality. Poets remind us we are not alone in the terrain of affective life.

Just as powerful in life as choices taken or rejected, are the spaces filled with words of empathic insight or eloquent stillness. In a poetic sense, this book might be a companion to those of us who are called upon metaphorically to fill spaces, create futures, build roads, light paths. Such endeavours can be lonely, though awesome. The companion you might find in these pages is your own inspirational self. Put simply, those who influence others might want to know why they are successful or how they can be more successful. They might seek a meta-awareness of their strategies.

With empathic intelligence one builds upon an individual life story, researching the past and present, seeking data to create patterns and coherence. In a sense this lives within a grounded theoretical model (Strauss and Corbin, 1990) but it involves more than developing theory as an objective reality. It creates an embodied sense of theory for its participants and therefore grounds the theory in the phenomenon of the researcher. To develop a sense of empathic intelligence, one needs to identify the extent to which one relates to the theoretical attributes and then observe how that theory informs practice and experience. To the extent that one calls upon the reflective capacity within empathic intelligence to connect the disparate data of experience, one can strengthen that intelligence and the purposefulness of individual experience.

While parts of this book will convey information, much of the book might evoke your own memories of certain significant experiences, in the expectation that such evocations will serve your own purposes in reading for understanding, enjoyment and even delight in your own reflections. As you engage dynamically with the book and your own experiences, you might be prompted to think more deeply and feel more acutely. Ambitious as it may sound, reading which engages thought, feeling, reflection and discussion, may serve such purposes.

Empathic intelligence is likely to be functioning wherever one person influences another in interactive, psychological ways. While emotional blackmail or manipulation involves psychological forms of influence, it ceases to be empathic once the needs of the other are ignored or exploited for self-interest. More than the information imparted by influential people, the dynamic, or interpersonal energy created in interpersonal interactions will mutually influence feelings, thoughts and behaviour, often in ways beyond ready awareness. Ideally, informing that dynamic will be a mutually beneficial, affectionate and caring relationship. The better we understand the characteristics of the dynamics governing our engagements with others, the better we can understand and evaluate our influence, and create optimum leadership situations. Every encounter offers ample evidence of its surface and covert dynamics. It just takes time, patience and skill to observe, collect and analyse that often fleeting but richly informative data. It takes even more time to pattern such data and make sense of it. Empathic intelligence works with such evidence, and from it a theory of empathic pedagogy has been developed.

CREATING THE CONDITIONS FOR ENGAGEMENT

When two individuals engage in attending to each other by maintaining eye contact or listening or speaking together within their established roles and relationships, the space between them can become charged with significance. When a speaker stands before an audience, a musician plays a solo in a concert hall or a child gazes at its mother, the elastic space between them can fill with potential energy. While we cannot see that energy it is easy for empathically intelligent people to feel its presence.

Consider for a moment the following scene. A concert pianist plays one of the most evocative, stirring pieces of music ever composed for the piano. She is an expert in the particular composer's work and plays like an angel, bringing tears to the eyes of expert music lovers in the audience. The concert hall fills with the energy generated by this excellence. Everyone waits for that final note at the climax. Silence fills the concert hall as that final note dies away. No one wants to break the spell. There is an attenuated pause, then thunderous sounds of applause fill the air. The performance has been resolved. Everyone breathes deeply again.

What I would like you to think about is that couple of seconds between the dying of the final note and the start of the applause. The audience sits stunned, the pause is silent but explosive with possibilities. These seconds contain the fusion of the whole performance – the pianist's playing, the audience's reactions, the movement of the free-floating radicals in the air. What fills the metaphoric vacuum in those seconds? What is the nature of that space? How does it relate to the preceding seconds and those that follow? Why are those few seconds worthy of intense speculation?

I don't have an answer to my own rhetorical questions here. They are truly rhetorical, which is unusual in writing. Those two seconds of silence I have described are a condensed form of the space that is shared, framed, and possibly enlarged when meaning is created in significant engagements between individuals. That space is shaped, articulated, energised and coloured by the metaphorical energy composed by the engaged individuals and expressed through the particular air they share.

If you are not sure about the function or importance of space between mutually engaged people, try conducting a heartfelt conversation with someone who turns his/her back to you. Try declaring your love to a person who avoids your eye contact. Have you ever seen a proposal on stage or screen where the couple ignores each other? Have you ever tried to sustain an argument or conversation with an indifferent opponent? Notice how painful it feels if you express your delight, excitement or enthusiasm to someone who stares blankly at you. Engagement is socially constructed, psychologically driven and essentially mutual.

Merging and emerging

It is surprising how little we know about the spaces between us, and within us. We commonly talk about being 'swamped with information' or feeling we 'can't take any more in' or needing 'time out' or 'space to breathe'. Sometimes another's personality can leave us feeling 'overwhelmed' or, more positively, 'liberated'. When we are aware of these feelings, we are aware of the signals from our body and its physiological responses to engagements with others.

The nature of eye contact, voices and smiles readily influences such responses. In love-making the space between individuals is closed by mutual, physical embodiment and the bliss of temporary self-abandonment can ensue. Whether the inevitable separation that follows engenders existential sadness or sustained fulfilment, depends very much on the psychic embodiment of the relationship. It does not have to be that in separation lies existential angst. The capacity for empathic imagination and pleasure in the embodied experiences of another can soothe the loneliness of existential sadness.

The phenomenon I am trying to describe belongs to empathy and is created by those with empathic intelligence. It can be created when two strangers establish eye contact across a room. It happens in a meeting when two empathic people feel each other's responses to events – even though they might choose to avoid eye contact because it could break social masking and decorum. It is familiar to lovers who truly love and to those who feel bonded with another. It takes many shapes and intensities. Few can live happily without it. Those who experience it and value it often choose to live and work in ways that allow them to compose it themselves through the engagements of their life and work.

In making a choice to commit to such ways of being, individuals may transform themselves and others. That intersubjective space between individuals and the intrasubjective space within the functioning of the brain and mind, with all the affective and cognitive interplays therein, compose a psychic harmony just as worthy of our attuned attention as the greatest symphonies of the world.

That claim is ambitious and grandiose – deliberately so. The greatest composers heard the silence of that space and filled it with their compositions. Poets, dancers, writers, sculptors, architects and painters perform the same feats in symbolic forms that are different in shape and content but similar in function. Physicists and astronomers compose their truths by the light of the stars. All these explorers of truth are committed to a quest of bounding space and articulating mysteries through symbols energised within the space of our intelligences.

As those intelligences expand in response to deeper wisdoms, the quests continue to evolve. The intuitions that drive the quest become intelligences when these researchers and explorers articulate their findings in ways that allow them to be transformed through their recognition within the culture. No matter how we choose to symbolise our discoveries or creations, eventually many creative people seek to communicate with an audience to test the worth or robustness of their creations. Mirroring for such people often has to occur through audience affirmation. Some need affirmation, some can manage without it and others can be seduced and distracted by it.

Would Vincent Van Gogh's life have been different had he experienced some of the adulation his work has received since his death? Would his art have been positively or negatively influenced? When I read a wonderfully composed, heartfelt obituary, I often wonder whether the subject of that piece of prose ever enjoyed the acclaim expressed in it? Would we dare to express such acclaim face to face?

CREATING DYNAMIC PSYCHIC SPACES

By definition, it is difficult to describe the ineffable. The Pocket Oxford Dictionary barely even tries. It defines 'ineffable' as 'too great for words'. The matter cannot rest there however, because much of the challenge of empathic intelligence is to develop the articulations and concepts that inform and inspire influential people in their groundbreaking work.

One concept of importance for such people is that of dynamic psychic space. It is an ineffable concept, in many respects, because it relates to a deeply introspective experience close to the affective states of awe, wonder and personal spirituality. People with empathic intelligence are not overawed when they introspect in such psychic spaces. They can manage and enjoy the intimacy of encounters with the ineffable. If the word 'erotic' were not so debased by its unfortunate connotations, I would align it with other words used here because deep introspection is very much an embodied experience.

When engagements with the world of work and responsibilities wear us out, we seek the solace of 'time out' to 'recharge the batteries' as it is commonly described. For highly functioning individuals, such 'time out' is generally spent redirecting the balance between public and private life, between existing for others' benefit and managing our own personal development through introspection and self-enhancing activities. In knowing how to seek such personal, exploratory development, we create the kind of dynamic psychic spaces that make the ineffable achievable.

I will explore these concepts further with a personal example from some experiences involved in writing part of this book. Upon reflecting on the process of writing about psychic space and empathic intelligence, I realise that I started writing this section without knowing how the white spaces on the page would be filled. I had not worked out what I would say before I began. I had to just start and see what emerged. I had to move into my own psychic space. I was confident that there was much to write about the concepts I had in mind because I can viscerally experience that space and feel its force as I write. If you want to relate this to your own experiences, think of someone whom you really love or something which you love doing. As you pause to follow that directive, you will notice a change in your physiological state. You will feel a lift in spirits and a kind of centredness. That is your dynamic psychic space seeking your attention.

In order to focus on the meaning of this ineffable concept of psychic space, and the challenge of communicating its nature, I have to recall the embodied experience of standing before an audience waiting to hear me speak. I search to think of the audiences who will be reading this book. What will I communicate to each of those individuals? I find myself recalling what it felt like to gaze at an infant and even what it felt like to be gazed at in my own infancy. I don't consciously pull up all these memories in order to write, but they live within me guiding the words. When I read back the words, I test them against the tacit feelings driving the composition. I don't know whether I sculpt or draw but I know I compose. The old fashioned notion in school, of writing as 'English Composition', contains the culture's corporate wisdom in this case. Words have a timbre, harmony and rhythm – if not a score – with all its fortunate and unfortunate connotations.

THE FUNCTION OF HOPE

Mentors and leaders in corporate and human resources management, cultural activities, educational contexts and professional development programs share many challenges. One shared challenge is that of mobilising individuals to perform at a certain level, either for individual benefit or the benefit of the group. Obviously there is overlap possible between the beneficiaries.

A theme I develop in this book is that effective leaders and mentors tend to understand something important about the nature of their own achievements. This gives them a certain credibility in the work place. They have the authority of experience and that can speak volumes to those aspiring to emulate or exceed their achievements. By a quirk of human nature, the aspirants often expect their mentors to be able to short-cut the process of development by passing on handy tips and foolproof agendas. Mentors and leaders are expected to be able to scaffold progress and indeed, often they meet this expectation very well. The greatest challenge lies in dealing with the unexpected, or even the expected – those periods of fallow when nothing seems to be happening or when hopes have been defeated.

Even in an optimistic state of mind, few aspirants to excellence want to hear the truth about coping with disappointment and relentless struggles. The sorts of growth, insight and experience that I speak of are not simple or formulaic (despite what the self-help books may tell us!).

In a defeated frame of mind, the truth is even more unpalatable. Leaders are expected to engender hope and resilience. The phrase 'grin and bear it' is one of the culture's more hostile clichés. How helpful is the truth to those needing to sustain hope? Hope is a vulnerable affect susceptible to change. What replaces it when it ceases to sustain expectation and performance? Utter despair and paralysis.

I surprise myself in finding an answer to this question. As I wrote about loss of hope, I began to feel the effects of my own rhetoric. My spirits began to drop, then suddenly a thought came to mind. Professionals do not rely solely on feelings. They practise their performances so that they can rely on habit, routine, skill and a range of cognitive, affective and performance-based embodiments to help them through. They can select from a range of strategies developed over a long period of time to inform and motivate their performance. Obviously, hope can play its part, but a true professional would never rely on it alone. I think that is what happened when I was writing about the function of hope above. I found myself in a psychic space that I actually began to dislike. I wanted to leave the subject and cease writing. Fortunately, what came into play was my buried knowledge that writing through resistances can often resolve them. I learned that from my own writing habits and from working on a writing development project with resistant writers (Arnold, 1991). I discovered that free association writing can dry up, but if a writer keeps writing through the writing block, it can inform further writing. Young writers found it worked for them too and they told their peers about it.

In earlier days this quality of endurance might well have been called 'discipline'. No wonder no one wanted a bar of it. It sounds too unattractive and even painful. But when practice is understood and experienced as rewarding and self-serving, it takes on a wholesome allure.

Deeper than the description of this exercise is my tacit theory that endurance works because it integrates resistance with progression, rather than isolating it in some psychic space where it continues to create mischief. It files itself in a psychic space labelled 'too hard' or 'hateful personal failures' or 'ignore at all costs'. We are familiar with the common practice of encouraging trauma victims to re-visit the scene of the trauma as part of a healing process. The purpose is not to deepen the effects of the trauma, but to allow these effects to be integrated within the now recovering psyche. Those with particular experience in certain fields can share their experience and let others know what to expect in the process of development. A respected, plausible expert in the field can help both high level and resistant performers to accept the peaks and troughs of development as an inevitable part of the whole.

How you convey that point as a leader or mentor depends very much on the contexts in which it arises. Empathic intelligence has to come into play in resolving the challenges that are raised here about performance and the role of hope. It takes skilled judgment to read interpersonal signs accurately, and even then the best leaders can miscue. They too have to accept the reality of their own wisdom that success is hard won.

As a parent, or committed mentor, or devoted coach or team leader, it hurts to stand beside a defeated aspirant. Your own defeats can surface in sympathy and they can be a big distraction. Learned patterns of emotional response are not always functional, even though they seem to protect us (Stern, 1985). With maturity, we know to re-shape, where possible, those learned responses that are dysfunctional, interfering with our intentions and even thwarting them. Nonetheless, they are the mind's way of organising experience and they spare us the impossible task of learning everything anew. With experience we can learn to expect our emotional templates to influence our behaviour, and we can learn to modify those templates, just as medical officers and others can learn to overcome feelings of disgust at sights, smells and sounds which normally provoke revulsion.

The temptation to deny pain, both physical and emotional, or to talk it away, is enormous. I have watched with admiration, and even envy, the doctors, nurses and paramedics who manage to attend to physical injuries with commendable professional detachment. They can actually do something to resolve a crisis and in doing so, feel competent as well. It is absolutely appropriate that they act efficiently and skilfully. No one wants empathy alone while bleeding to death! What then is the intelligent empathic equivalent to physical resuscitation when a person is feeling like death? The question exaggerates the plight of the disappointed or the humiliated but it makes the point about intensity of feelings in defeat.

What are the appropriate defence mechanisms a mentor needs to bring into play? It is a hard truth to accept but many excellent individuals do not receive the recognition and affirmation they deserve, particularly not in societies that place enormous emphasis on winning at all costs. It defies logic that those who come second in a competition between peers lose a sense of their excellence because winning is all. Smart societies would think of a way around an attitude that works against their best interests. Again, how do you continue to mobilise the abilities of those high achievers who miss the gold medal by a nanosecond? Do we advocate keeping them on a treadmill with promises of next time? As a mentor, coach or leader do you believe in the infallibility of winning as a measure of excellence? Without wishing to blame the media for focusing on winners rather than losers, public accolades and sponsorships do follow the winners. It is hard to comfort the vanquished without seeming to reinforce their situation, yet positive mental attitudes are a significant factor in developing excellence and in winning.

Schools struggle to resolve the issue by awarding prizes for contribution as well as for achievement. But the most highly-desired prizes are still those for achievement. I don't pretend to have an answer to the complex issue of rewarding and sustaining motivation, and I certainly would not want to suggest for one second that high achievement should go unrewarded for the sake of sparing others some discomfort. However, it is important to continually assess those accomplishments that we acknowledge and reward. Such analysis could better encourage the development of qualities and skills that contribute to a healthy, productive, peaceful and stimulating society.

Oddly enough, when words fail in interpersonal crises calling for high levels of empathy, silence often works rather well. This is enshrined in the clichés 'silence is golden' or 'silence is eloquent'. Shakespeare modelled this strategy dramatically when Cordelia in *King Lear* resists her father's demands for public and effusive affirmation of his worth, by replying 'nothing'. She utters the most minimal word possible before choosing silence. Lear urges her to elaborate her response and she attempts to explain her position, but her refusal to mirror him falsely enrages Lear. Her sisters, Goneril and Regan, respond to King Lear's need for public adulation with hypocritical, competitive and meaningless speeches which serve the immediate purpose of gratifying their father but which ultimately diminish them and him.

Sometimes we are called upon to mirror others falsely and sometimes we see the folly of so doing. Empathy has to function within a framework of personal ethics and sense of interdependent responsibility for self and others. And, while wanting to affirm others, it is also important to sustain one's own authenticity and integrity. A commitment to an empathic form of interpersonal relationships is constantly challenging, for all its long-term rewards.

Having outlined aspects of excellence, leadership and empathic intelligence, it is time to look at how an interested reader might begin to extend existing spheres of influence so that the possibilities of relating, educating and transforming go beyond the limited sphere of one person. Management and leadership books are misleading when they promote a guru-cult or convey the message 'just be like me and all will be well'. Empathic leaders do not want to develop clones of themselves, even if such a feat were possible. They realise that individuals have to develop their abilities in their own particular ways.

THE ROLE OF THEORY IN EMPATHIC PEDAGOGY

Theory is often regarded as something working at such an abstract level of understanding that it is detached from experience. Such should not be the case with theories purporting to explain human developmental and social behaviour. You would expect that at their simplest level, at least, the theories would make some sense to the man and woman in the street, since they relate to aspects of their behaviour. The commonplace is used here, not to over-simplify the role of theory in the development of high order research and understanding, but to suggest that we all embody, over time, personal constructs of how we might best conduct our lives, based on personal theory-building.

The nature of living and common sense determine that we cannot make separate decisions about each action we take. We manage by behaving habitually in ways that suit our needs well enough, if not admirably. In other words, we embody layers of experience, along with our psychic templates. Upon meeting our man and woman in the street, a plausible theory of human behaviour should be greeted as an acquaintance, at least. For some the meeting is more powerful than that. There is a strong sense of immediate, heartfelt bonding.

One of the gratifying aspects of developing this theory of pedagogy over at least a decade has been the enthusiasm and relief of educators who have spent years in professional practice, working in ways that clearly articulate with empathic pedagogy – though they had lacked guidelines for articulating their practice. Once they discovered the theory and its principles, they experienced the relief that coherence brings to formerly tacit understandings. They saw themselves and their students in new ways and related their observations to their dynamic understanding of the theory, which they felt embodied their experience. It was as if the theory was mirroring their own professional life and validating it. From such a supported position, their professional development gathered its own momentum, provided there was access to other like-minded colleagues. Theory became an internalised mirror of their experience and informed practice, enlivening it and creating sense of it. The subjectivity of inner experience becomes objective when articulated in language or other symbolised forms such as art, dance, improvisation or music. In turn, the objectification creates further internalisation and a deeper level of embodied understanding. So it can be with theory building, testing and development.

Empathic intelligence and research methods

Thankfully, there have been significant developments in the past 20 years in ethnographic research methods. I see these developments enhancing research into something as complex as empathic intelligence and empathic pedagogy. At the same time, there is still every reason to quantify data if quantification, such as statistical measures, will increase the plausibility of an argument. In my own doctoral study of long-term student writing development (Arnold 1991), it was essential to know whether the pedagogy had increased the students' writing abilities. Empirical measures of students' writing and statistical data yielded that information, providing encouragement to analyse further the nature of the pedagogy that influenced the positive result. While participating in the teaching central to the study, I was mindful that there was a need for analyses of my interactions with the students. It has been possible to categorise those interactions through reflection, but what is missing is evidence to characterise how the students experienced those interactions.

In spite of the encouragement we give to the notion of the teacher-researcher, it is difficult to conduct research and teach simultaneously, such are the compelling demands of both roles. I had not worked out the nature of my interactions with the students, except to know that they were student-centred and grounded in certain theories of process-orientated literacy development. I focused mainly on a quantitative study, adding 'narratives to numbers' by writing several case studies too. Naturally, we revere what has served our purposes well, but I still feel it is advisable to be comfortable with a range of both quantitative and qualitative research methods in order to select what best serves the purposes of the questions informing research.

Extended reflective writing or case studies require particularly strong writing abilities and a commitment to iterative writing. Good qualitative research writing requires high level writing and thinking skills, including the logical structuring of arguments, the skilful selection of plausible data to inform the thesis, and imaginative identification with an expert audience of readers in order to judge what to include and what to exclude in the work. Perseverance as a writer is needed also to move from writing to determine thought and meaning, to writing to inform the examining/expert audience.

Ethnographic research borrows from the principles and practices of anthropological research and legitimates studies in which researchers can be either participants themselves in the research field, or observers of behaviours and interactions in particular fields of research. Research questions are developed from preliminary observations in the field, and methods are chosen to provide relevant data to be collected in order to answer the research questions. It is accepted that because researchers are necessarily engaged in some way with participants in the field of the research, inevitably the research influences the field. In ethnographic research, provided legitimate research data collection methods are followed, and the data yields rich evidence to support the researcher's field work descriptions and arguments, such influences are acknowledged as acceptable, and often illuminative.

Empathic pedagogy is beginning to inform practice and research in a number of social science areas. These include, for example, literacy development, drama in education, dance training and special education, as well as fields such as voice production/education (Cartwright 1999). It is likely, therefore, that both ethnographic and empirical research methods will be chosen, according to different research purposes. If you wanted to know whether students perceived a teacher as empathic (or enthusiastic, or expert) a questionnaire seeking such perceptions would provide empirical data. If, however, you were interested in whether a teacher's empathy (or enthusiasm, or expertise) fluctuates according to different dynamics among different cohorts of students, careful observations and interviews with the teacher would be necessary. Even then, the researcher could discover that empathic teachers are susceptible to anxiety about their performance, so that participation in the research alters their effectiveness. In which case, the researcher might well need to be empathic also, as well as aware of the influence of the research upon the field of study. It could well be that a study that sets out to understand the nature of empathic intelligence in action yields useful data on the research skills needed to understand it. The beauty of ethnographic research is that it can make good use of whatever relevant data the research reveals, because it can be designed to encompass, and even to encourage, the dynamism of human interaction. For example, it would be useful to research the practices of educators deemed to be enthusiastic, engaging, and expert, in order to determine how those qualities manifest themselves, and how students react to such educators.

As qualitative research methods become more highly differentiated and dissertation examiners become more skilled at assessing research written in genres that reflect creative models of research, we could expect to understand more about the nature of empathic pedagogy. Embedded in that expectation is respect for genres such as auto-ethnography, (Ellis and Bochner, 2000), personal narratives of professional practice (Beattie, 1997), visual methods (Harper, 1998, 2000), arts-based research (Saxton and Miller, 1998), and others outlined in Denzin and Lincoln (2000).

These approaches share in common a commitment to qualitative research as:

> ... an inquiry project, [which] is also a moral, allegorical, and therapeutic project,[characterised by] the avowed humanistic commitment to study the social world from the perspective of the interacting individual (Denzin and Lincoln, 2000, p. xvi).

Or, as educator Thomas Schwandt (2000) explains:

> ... the idea of acquiring an 'inside' understanding – the actors' definitions of the situation – is a powerful central concept for understanding the purpose of qualitative inquiry (p. 192).

The world of educator Mary Beattie (1997) will also resonate with researchers seeking to understand effective ways to research empathic intelligence.

There is considerable scope for research into empathy in education, and in other person-centred professions. We need to know more about the ways students experience empathic and non-empathic educators, how they learn to read and interpret facial expressions, vocal cues and body language. We also need to know how educators develop the important attributes of empathic teaching; enthusiasm, a capacity to engage, expertise and empathic attunement.

We also need to know how to sustain the long-term professional development of empathic educators. Since it is a holistic, dynamic commitment to a demanding, caring but rewarding professional orientation, it requires sustained mentoring. At the same time, it has a special quality in that theory and practice inextricably nurture each other in this model. Self- and other-awareness, imagination, critical thinking and deep reflection cooperate to enhance confidence and professionalism marked by its vitality. We need to hear educators' voices and stories about their engagements with empathic pedagogy.

START WITH INDIVIDUALS

The concepts can be modulated by practitioners through application to experience. In this way, they reflect a good match between theory and practice. In so doing, practitioners will discover examples of enthusiasm, engagement and so on, in action, and personalise these concepts, thereby embodying their own philosophy and practice in meaningful ways. It is important that a theory designed not only to explain interpersonal enactments, but also to influence them, has sufficient plausibility to be engaging, and sufficient flexibility for its application in a variety of appropriate contexts. One of the common responses to this theory, from those who have encountered and applied it, is its value in encouraging them to personalise, analyse and shape their own professional interactions (Maza, 1996; Nicolson, 1997; Kitson, 2001).

Let me make some suggestions to help you deepen your commitment to this way of being an influential person. As such, I expect that you hope to model an aspiration to excellence in yourself and in so doing, influence others to a similar pursuit. I hope it is clear by now that such a pursuit is essentially dynamic with all the progressions and regressions inherent in a dynamic model of development.

Underpinning such a life-long process will be the experience of emotional fluctuations across the gamut of feelings and across the different intensities of those feelings. Pleasure will be intense at times and mild at other times. Pain might fluctuate in intensity too. At best, it might manifest itself in irritation that things are not moving faster; at worst, as the agony of grief and emotional paralysis fuelled by despair. Fortunately, in the extremes of negative emotions, we sometimes find others to help us through such phases. It helps if someone can affirm the inevitable passing of emotional extremes, so that hope can be mobilised against the experience of compelling and contrary feelings. I introduce the extremes to assert the reality that in-depth human development is no soft option. Those who are drawn to complexity and ambiguity in life quickly lose trust in those who deny the existence and function of such complexity.

REFLECTION

The habit of observing closely your own thinking processes, your feelings and the dynamics of your relationships with others and the world around you is the data for reflection. The ability to continually wonder why things happen as they do is the science of this way of being. If you do not feel you have developed this reflective mode of being as well as you would like, try writing a personal dairy or journal of events in your life. Don't just record the event. Think about the memorable aspects of it. Noting that you attended a meeting or went to a movie is basically boring. But noting that something funny, amazing, disgusting, pleasurable, quirky or fearful, happened, is potentially interesting. Scan the pages of quality newspapers, even the television critics' columns, and note how good writers of particular genres are able to grab your attention and make an ordinary observation interesting. A good writer can make the act of putting a key in a door engaging and memorable. Imagination makes the difference.

For the kind of reflection needed to develop empathic intelligence, you don't need to start out as an imaginative writer. But you do need to develop the habit of observation and recording. Making a mental note is the first habit; writing it down is the next step. Over time, as the volume of recording begins to grow, it is worth re-reading what you have written and reflecting upon its significance. Gradually, insignificant details are dropped in favour of more important ones. You become more discriminating and less worried about small issues. By reviewing your observations and sorting out what really matters, you also develop the habit of discriminating prior to recording. Gradually, with practice and commitment, reflective writing influences the habit of reflective thinking. And reflective thinking is deepened by the habit of writing.

Conversations with like-minded, reflective people also develop a capacity for discrimination, provided the conversation involves empathic listening between equals. The equality does not have to be a factor of age, class or education. Empathic intelligence is very egalitarian. Watch how the very old and the very young share empathic moments. Notice how some leaders and their followers share rapport. Special bonds develop between people sharing certain experiences. Sometimes such bonds dissolve when the shared experience ceases (holiday friendships often meet such a fate). At other times, the bond extends across time and space. Much depends on the mutuality of emotional needs and rewards in the relationship.

BUILDING RESILIENCE THROUGH COMMUNICATION AND REFLECTION

Whether the capacity to be empathic is a gift or a developed ability is an issue raised in discussion about empathy and empathic intelligence. Certainly the latter is not simply a gift. Empathic intelligence builds on empathy but also integrates other cognitive abilities and affective sensitivities. What is crucial is a commitment to protecting that capacity whenever it is functioning effectively. Empathic educators and caregivers can attest to the wearing nature of empathic attunement, even though it can be a satisfying professional philosophy and method of working. It is clear from the responses I have had from people who function in empathic ways that it is a physically and emotionally demanding style of working and relating. It requires attunement to our own thoughts and feelings, attunement to others' thoughts and feelings, attention to the purposes of the meeting or lesson or encounter, along with on-going assessment of the shifting dynamics of that engagement. It requires considerable physical and emotional energy to maintain an empathically educative position. Like running a marathon race, it can be a satisfying but exhausting experience.

I sound this warning, not to deter anyone from this approach, but to suggest some ways to protect its practitioners from possible burnout. We need to understand better the nature of the demands of empathic attunement on our physiological states. At some point it may become of interest to medical researchers to investigate the issue, but in the meantime there is sufficient cause from the anecdotal evidence to date to indicate a need to reflect on some protective strategies.

I can recall the experience of conducting a two-hour teaching workshop for a group of educators whom I had never met. It involved the explanation of some aspects of empathic pedagogy, together with a demonstration of the theory implemented in practice. I had to:

- establish rapport with the group;
- explain the theory in an engaging way;
- explain purposes;
- assess the group's readiness for the implementation exercise;
- organise the group to undertake the implementation;
- judge whether my plan was working by monitoring the emotional climate of the group; and
- shift direction when necessary, keep an eye on the time, answer questions, bring the session to closure, clarify issues and so on – a fairly routine teaching experience.

It is exhausting to just think about it. And this was a group of mature, experienced and committed adults. Teachers in school classrooms could add another whole dimension of demands upon their energy levels. At the end of such an experience, it is essential to take time out to replenish your resources. It is impossible (and close to upsetting) to be called upon to maintain an empathic position when it is physiologically impossible.

Empathic parents can surely relate well to my claims here. A day spent meeting the incessant demands of small children is tolerable, provided there is relief in sight. Should that relief vanish, the risk of an acute emotional outburst is high. Even with informed planning and foresight, one can never completely anticipate how groups or individuals might react in dynamic situations. Empathically functioning professionals have to monitor their own energy levels to manage their effectiveness, but they have to be supported in appropriate ways as well. They tend to respond readily to requests for help, but they can rightfully resent being asked to give more and more, especially when they can observe their less empathic colleagues avoiding scrutiny. Even more importantly, an intrinsic reward of effective functioning derives from setting one's own agenda. Sensitive leaders recognise this and monitor their demands accordingly.

As with other concepts in empathic pedagogy, expertise is dynamic. It is not a fixed position marked by some rite of passage such as graduation from a school, training institution or university. The nature of contemporary life requires us to recognise that roles, responsibilities and skills need constant revision and further development. Even if it were not an attractive notion to many, the notion of 'life-long learning' is a contemporary reality. I recall a young man facing his first major academic hurdle, the Higher School Certificate (HSC), at the end of secondary education. He was dreading the final examinations and hating the blight they cast on his life. In the course of our meetings to discuss literature, he discovered that I too was facing a hurdle in the middle of my career. He looked aghast and said 'You mean to tell me this goes on all your life?' What can an empathic educator reply?

As I suggested in the earlier part of this book, we are storytelling, reality-testing human beings. We need to make sense of our experiences to satisfy our curiosity about the world and to enjoy feelings of agency, autonomy and self-worth. The child who fills a bucket with sand, pats it down, tips it up and creates a castle, is as proud and satisfied as the business tycoon who creates a company merger. The contexts are vastly different but the motivations and feelings are similar. Deprived of functional, imaginative play, both the child and the tycoon would feel bored and useless.

Once you become interested in a particular theory or topic, you feel compelled to test its significance in the 'real' world. It is surprising how often you discover references to it in literature, current affairs and the arts. This affirms the reality that if a subject is sufficiently engaging, inspiring and important, it will function in relationships, culture, education, work and leisure. With my own mindset attuned to empathic intelligence, I seem to discover it functioning prominently in my personal, professional and social life. I sometimes wonder why it has not featured more prominently, sooner. Perhaps it will be the discovery of the new millennium. I am also mindful that empathic intelligence is potentially an exciting and a challenging concept. As such, it can stir ambivalent responses even within scholarly communities. For example, there is ambivalence about whether to regard empathy as either a 'soft' or a 'hard' option.

The Director of the Australian Council of Educational Research (ACER), Dr Geoff Masters, reported that an Australian university sought the assistance of the ACER in devising a test to explore things like empathy and moral reasoning as part of its selection processes for medical students. According to the national newspaper story, as part of their extended reporting on the selection of medical students, ACER found that some of the ideas were too hard to test. 'There are real challenges trying to assess, reliably, some of the softer kinds of skills', Dr Masters said (*The Australian Magazine*, March 27–28, 1999, p. 26).

The language here of soft and hard, is revealing in itself. But more important is the recognition that empathy and moral reasoning are significant attributes for people whose role is to help vulnerable others. This would seem so self-evident that it is to be hoped that the challenges of measurement continue to be tackled. As has been outlined earlier in this book, cognitive and empathic intelligences are not mutually exclusive, or in competition with each other. We can have both-and should aspire to this outcome wherever it is relevant.

EMPATHIC INTELLIGENCE AS INSPIRING LEADERSHIP

Empathic intelligence can both exemplify inspirational leadership and motivate it. Hence the deliberate ambiguity in the heading above. At its most complex, empathic intelligence demands considerable psychic energy, focus and relational ability, but it is not the province only of highly experienced professionals. It can be observed in neophyte form among young people with leadership abilities and altruistic drives. It can be nurtured through mentoring and through opportunities to demonstrate its functioning and effects. It can both inspire leadership and reflect it.

Leadership here refers to those dispositions, behaviours and values that motivate others. This motivation may be applied to many things – engaging in teamwork, or striving for better performance, or more commitment or enthusiasm for personal or community goals or tasks. Sometimes in both organisations and families, leadership is assumed by those with more finely tuned political astuteness than real leadership quality. In organisations wishing to develop empathically intelligent practices, the nature of leadership supported in the organisation or group therefore needs to be assessed to determine its congruence with organisational values.

Empathic literacy for effective leadership 141

▲ Rapport speaks volumes SOURCE Associated Press
▼ It is very tiring staying empathically attuned to the joy of others.

EMPATHIC INTELLIGENCE IN LIFE-LONG LEARNING

There are many kinds of leadership that may involve empathic intelligence. Political leadership is one, but it may also manifest in the leadership demonstrated by a child who shares his/her lunch with another; the parent who sacrifices income and time for the welfare of children; the person who makes choices to forego personal rewards for a common good. Such actions attest to an ethic that acknowledges the needs of others and intuitively recognises a social benefit. While these demonstrations of altruism do not alone constitute empathic intelligence, they do demonstrate a contributory disposition that can be mentored and developed.

One of the most difficult aspects to manage, for both novices and those practised in empathic intelligence, is the realisation that your own self-interest is seemingly not always best served by a disposition focused on the care of others. However, in caring for others you must also be vigilant about self-caring. In striving for the essential balance between these two equally important priorities, you may find that others may express disappointment that their expectations are not being met promptly and fully. Adults need to protect children who are strongly compassionate or empathic because they can become victims of their own altruism. Such children need to be nurtured to become intelligently caring.

In this model of learning, a key objective is to model for others how they might develop their own empathic intelligence. It aims to inspire leadership for the sake of both individual and community enhancement. Such leadership is intrinsically inspirational because it is visionary. It is both idealistic and realistic, aware that human perfectibility is an impossible quest.

Empathic intelligence is a concept which values those human processes designed to nourish high levels of social, intellectual, emotional and creative experience. Inevitably, such transformative processes involve trust, mutual respect, participation in community life, tolerance of difference, equity and transparency in the management of resources, respect for human dignity and congruence between values and behaviour. Such values are affirmed when humans recognise and develop their potential, both to enhance their own lives and to contribute to the well-being of others as members of democratic communities. The sum of these values and behaviours is more than morality. As psychologist Howard Gardner (1998) notes, on standard tests of moral reasoning, altruists did not stand out. '…the capacity to behave in a caring way seems quite different than the capacity to reason acutely about moral dilemmas' (p. 132).

EMPATHY AND SOCIAL CAPACITY BUILDING

It is now recognised in well-functioning corporations and educational institutions that human beings are more productive and fulfilled when they are recognised for their efforts and have opportunities to demonstrate the range and diversity of their abilities. The renewed interest in emotional intelligence (Goleman, 1996; Mayer and Salovey, 1997) discussed in the previous chapter has reignited arguments about the role of feelings in intellectual and corporate life (Goleman, 1998; Little 1999).

Since information is now widely accessible it is possible for committed Internet users to develop some measures of expertise through access to that information. The fact that self-help books and videos are among the world's bestsellers attests to a desire to understand and manage our own lives through access to the knowledge, and sometimes the wisdom, of others. This wish to understand is apparent in many professional areas, such as medicine, where educated patients often choose to research their medical problems themselves and seek to consult widely with specialists, rather than rely on a single source of information such as their local doctor. Needless to say, while the wish to be self-managing has merit, information is rarely sufficient to inform us adequately about complex matters. Expertise is often needed to discern the merits of competing claims and to interpret information. In addition, the context in which the information is received and the emotional climate of that context, influence our reception of even the most clinical information. Try hearing that someone close to you has a brain tumour, and see if you can process that information without feeling, along with compassion for the patient, concern that you might have some hidden tumour too, or relief that you are not so blighted. Hence, the wisdom of consulting professionals who can manage the interplay between emotional and cognitive information and deliver astute, sensitive judgments.

Professionals engaged in disseminating information are now expected to be sensitive to contexts as well as skilled in offering sound judgment on the relative worth of information or research. To meet this need, the education of professionals needs to focus on developing abilities such as empathic intelligence. How else can you judge how much, how little, how complex, how simple the message should be? In traditional professions such as medicine, law, engineering and science, advances in technology have eliminated some of the drudgery of tasks such as making complex calculations by hand, and thereby opened up time and opportunities for the development of high-order communication and interpersonal skills

In this domain, artists, writers, actors and dancers have had a head start. Those who have become leaders in their fields have often done so because they have developed a range of intelligences, such as those researched by Howard Gardner (1983, 1993). It is evident that the function of imagination and empathy in creative problem solving and group dynamics is being increasingly acknowledged. Corporations now spend millions of dollars taking their executives or trainees on leadership retreats where they learn to access or develop certain abilities in the interests of more productive team outcomes. This suggests that employers are seeking to mobilise kinds of dynamic intelligence beyond the reach of formal examinations and beyond the ambit of current educational institutions.

Empathic intelligence is generative because it enables and stimulates emotional and intellectual growth. When that occurs in a climate perceived as caring, it tends to create social well-being, or social capital. That is, a climate that cares about personal growth and autonomy generates participation and a willingness to share and engage, because such processes are mutually beneficial. This philosophy is predicated on the belief that cooperation is more generative than competition, even though there are times when each could be purposeful. A principal purpose for an empathically intelligent approach is to generate both personal and social gains through the mobilisation of human potential. When progress stalls, or the benefits of the approach seem elusive, those with a deep understanding of the dynamics involved in the approach will be positioned to analyse how best to adapt, proceed and evaluate progress. Usually, regressions can be attributed to loss of vision, natural psychic fatigue, or obscurity of purpose. In such instances, participants could be helped to reflect upon their own feelings and thoughts about their practices and beliefs in order to identity inhibitors to well-being and commitment. Empathic intelligence can build capacity in organisations because it taps the intrinsic abilities of individuals who wish to contribute to a common good.

DEVELOPING EMPATHIC LITERACY

By acknowledging empathic intelligence as a particular ability dependent upon emotional and cognitive development, we accurately describe its character or nature, and we ascribe to it the status it merits. It is more complex than the interpersonal intelligence so helpfully differentiated by Gardner (1993) because it requires an 'intrapersonal' ability as well. That intrapersonal ability develops when we can engage in reflections upon our own thoughts and feelings (Arnold, 1993). Such dialogues can have a cast of many characters as we re-imagine the voices of those who have influenced us in the past, or we recall incidents that have been affecting.

For example, mindful of my reluctance to work collaboratively with a particular person, I managed to recall that he actually reminded me in his appearance of an unpleasant teacher I had once encountered. Once I recalled that unfortunate memory and connected it with the present, I was able to put things into perspective. The processes involved in making these connections involved the kind of intra/interpersonal intelligence that I am discussing here. Rather than just trusting instinct, I had to check my own life experience to better understand my responses. Without such scrutiny, my response might have been generated solely by unthinking prejudice. Sometimes, instincts, feelings or gut responses can be reliable guides to behaviour. At other times, however, they can be very misleading. Empathic intelligence can work to maximise the benefits of both affectivity and rationality. It can guide the educator, leader or parent in those moments of indecision about whether to intervene to help others or watch while they mobilise their own resources, mindful that inappropriate assistance can be patronising or imply that you think the other person is not capable.

Empathic intelligence is a super-ordinate intelligence requiring both interpersonal and intrapersonal intelligences. In its expression of these abilities it is dynamic in itself, and can create change in its practitioners and those within their sphere of influence. It is not limited to particular chronological frames or particular traditional subject boundaries. It can be promoted through artistic, creative, interpersonal, intrapersonal, musical and visual 'literacies', provided attention is given to both the affective and cognitive dimensions inherent in their development.

Moreover, it is important that the development of such 'literacies' includes 'composing' and 'reading' the symbolic systems particular to their form. For example, in the area of furniture design – a literacy in which I have no expertise – proficiency would require familiarity with the aesthetic qualities of raw materials, such as the weight, feel, grain, properties and colour of different woods. If I wanted to do more than simply follow a pattern for making a piece of furniture, and sought to design my own piece, I would need to learn how to work with different woods, how to 'read' the work of experts in the field, and so on. In involving myself in a process and product of learning, I would expect to learn how to 'compose' and 'read' in that particular symbolic system of furniture design. Several practical, aesthetic and affective abilities would come into play in such an enterprise. The responses of other people to my efforts might well influence the development of my ability. I would need to 'read' the responses of my 'audience' and evaluate their worth. It is in these ways that 'literacies' are discussed here.

The dual concepts of care and curiosity add to both cognitive and emotional intelligence, an important social and psychological dimension: that the development of persons is not solely self-interested. Philosopher Michel Foucault's (2000) comments on curiosity are pertinent here:

> I like the word (curiosity); it suggests something quite different to me. It evokes 'care'; it evokes the care one takes of what exists and what might exist: a sharpened sense of reality, but one that is never immobilized before it; a readiness to find what surrounds us strange and odd; … a passion for seizing what is happening now and what is disappearing; … I dream of a new age of curiosity (p. 325).

Foucault suggests something of the attention, focus and preparedness for risk-taking that can characterise the empathic stance. In that stance, there is a heightened awareness to possibilities and a willingness to move beyond the known. In that sense, too, the empathic stance is both self-caring and other-caring, since both parties are crucial to the dynamic. The curious educator is likely to evoke students' curiosity, in both the attuned and caring sense of the word as it is elaborated here. Further, it requires something of an imaginative and poetic frame of mind to accept the crossing of boundaries evoked by this discussion of care and curiosity; a suspension of literal meaning in favour of a figurative or provoked meaning.

In this book, I advocate promoting both cognitive and affective ways of interpreting experience, since each contributes shape and quality to the process of making sense of the world and relating effectively and affectively to others. The literal, quantifiable, scientific and linear are all valuable – in their place. Alongside these, however, there exist equally important mental strategies that are metaphoric, variously shaped and yet potentially quantifiable. What we now realise is that the boundaries between these broad distinctions are actually blurred. I suggest, therefore, that there is great benefit in encouraging people to accept broader, 'blurrier' definitions of intelligence, science, art, and education, than those that prevailed in the twentieth century.

As knowledge and understanding expands, words and concepts develop to reflect change. Sometimes such words and concepts work to promote change. In that sense, empathic intelligence could be thought of as the meeting place of science and poetry. In such a meeting place, empathic intelligence can seem paradoxical at first. It can be both confronting and liberating. The confronting part may require you to reflect on deeply held beliefs about education and interpersonal and professional life. The liberating part is the affirmation this concept may give to ideas that you know intuitively, even though the reasons are not yet clearly articulated or understood. For explanatory purposes, I ground empathic intelligence in a context of personal narratives or histories because they play a formative role in the development of personal, interpersonal and professional life. The nature of professional practice is patterned for each individual practitioner by the phenomenon of lived, professional experience. Like stories, reflective practitioners blend theory and idiosyncratic experience into meaningful structures to stabilise the flow of phenomena.

Empathic intelligence seeks to empower people with knowledge, skills and abilities so they can participate in democratic decision-making processes at both macro and micro political levels. It can demonstrate how care for others can actually have beneficial outcomes beyond the personal and immediate. It encourages transparency in decision making since such transparency both attests to the worth of others and encourages the taking of responsibility through principled debate and the sharing of information. Since care is fundamental in empathic intelligence, the consequences of fair care, or intelligent caring, encourage consideration of an appropriate balance between personal needs and common good. While some individuals might prefer sharing to be done in personally favourable ways, intelligent caring attests to the need for resource sharing to be fair, and transparently so.

EMPATHIC INTELLIGENCE AND CURRICULUM DEVELOPMENT

Empathic intelligence offers parity of esteem to different learning styles, to learning about the world through different symbolic systems and to communicating that meaning through different media. It privileges processes over products, but positions each as an important part of experiencing and communicating experience. It suggests curricula based on the best contemporary theories of intellectual, emotional, aesthetic and social development. However, such theories must allow for the possibility that enhancing experiences might well create unexpected outcomes in performance, behaviour, achievement and understanding.

Empathic intelligence favours curriculum development that maximises interpersonal relatedness, the development of emotional sensitivity, the development of self and other-awareness and sensitivity to the patterns, rhythms and complexities of natural and cultural worlds. It tolerates error making as part of the natural process of developing expertise and encourages reflection as a form of self-mirroring and self-development. Further, it encourages feelings and thoughts to be equally engaged in curriculum processes.

MOBILISING TRANSFORMATIVE LEARNING

Empathic intelligence resonates with the idea advanced by postmodern education that personalised experiences are central to deep learning, but it challenges postmodern educators to imbue their practices with well-chosen values. Values that enhance human and social functioning are fundamental in a civilised society educating autonomous, democratic individuals. The values underpinning empathic intelligence privilege important feelings such as hope, trust, and love of self and others. It is the dynamic link between personal and public values, thoughts and feelings that serves educative purposes in the theory outlined here. The link is dynamic because the psychic energy created by the interplay between values-driven behaviour, thought and feeling, mobilises transformative learning. Such energy helps to build resilience in learners who feel they can endure set-backs and await long-term gratification when the learning process itself is purposeful, even if difficult. Attentive, empathic others who can offer realistic, even silent support, also have an important role in building resilience.

As researchers, Deborah Danner, David Snowdon and Wallace Friesen (2001) document a study of the handwritten autobiographies of 180 Catholic nuns, composed when the nuns were in their early twenties. These were scored for emotional content, then the scores were related to survival during the ages of 75 to 95. The researchers discovered a strong inverse association between positive emotional content in these writings and risk of mortality in late life. That is, positive emotional content as evidenced in early-life autobiographies, was strongly associated with longevity six decades later. This study, known at the Nun Study, was part of a longitudinal study of ageing and Alzheimer's disease (Snowdon, 1997). As the authors remark:

> Our investigations raised questions about why the positive emotional content of early-life writings might have such a powerful relationship to longevity. Unfortunately, we had no independent measures of temperament, personality, or emotional tendencies for participants, and we can only speculate that individual differences in emotional content in the autobiographies reflect life-long patterns of emotional response to life events (p. 804–813).

This study forms part of a growing body of research on the influence of emotions, coping strategies, well-being and longevity (Fredrickson and Levenson, 1998; Gross and Levenson, 1997; Seligman, 2000).

It requires mental agility to be empathically intelligent – not unlike the mental agility needed to tell stories and to engage with them. Logic alone will not explain the most complex phenomena of life or the concept of empathic intelligence. Rationality and emotion have to cooperate in that endeavour. In the next chapter I explore the mental agility and imagination involved in narratives and the function of both personal and literary/artistic narratives in developing empathic intelligence.

THE PARADOXES OF LEADERSHIP

Some leaders are clearly identifiable on the world stage and have achieved a high public profile in their leadership roles. While we might need inspiring leaders to motivate us to certain achievements, the quiet leader can be just as important. The psychoanalyst Sigmund Freud, quoted by Gardner (1997, p. xv), said:

> The voice of the intellect is a soft one, but it does not rest until it has gained a hearing. Ultimately, after endlessly repeated rebuffs, it succeeds. This is

one of the few points in which one may be optimistic about the future of mankind (Freud, 1957, p. 96).

Relevant to the issue of leadership in learning is Gardner's argument for familiarising the population with what is entailed in being a leader, as well as what can go wrong and what can go right. He calls this knowledge 'consciousness about the issues and paradoxes of Leadership' (Gardner, 1987, p. xv).

In a compelling paper on leadership recently published in *Harvard Business Review*, Jim Collins (2001) reports the findings of a five-year research project which sought to understand what catapults a company from being a merely good one to being truly great. He concluded:

> The most powerfully transformative executives possess a paradoxical mixture of personal humility and professional will. They are timid and ferocious. Shy and fearless. They are rare – and unstoppable.

Collins speculates that the qualities of a 'Level 5' leader, found in a person who blends extreme personal humility with intense professional will, are 'counter-intuitive' and 'counter-cultural' (p. 68). Indeed, we do tend to expect our leaders to be larger than life figures whose force of personality and material success (usually very visible through expensive purchases) signals their power and influence. For a certain level of leadership, a strong image and a level of competence in both influencing others and managing resources are sufficient. But Collins was interested in sustained greatness.

For that outcome, his research demonstrates that companies need to be led by a person who is more than competent and effective in implementing a vision. He found that great companies were led by a person who could build enduring greatness through a paradoxical combination of personal humility plus professional will. Notice there is no explicit mention of power here. By implication, the power-hungry leader is probably sitting at Level 3 or 4.

There is much to reflect upon from this research. Personal humility and professional will grow out of years of experience honing professional skills and abilities, and years of reflection in developing an ego which can transcend the allure of fame, wealth, prestige and greed. The Level 5 leader has to exemplify the abilities and skills of levels of leadership lower down the hierarchy. In this model, there is no shortcut or charismatic path to the top level of leadership. The Level 5 leader has to allow others to take the praise for success, while still taking responsibility, even blame, for failures. The Level 5 leader has to demonstrate resilience, even while others have grave doubts about the wisdom of a position or strategy. Level 5 leaders cannot ask more of subordinates than they ask of themselves. Not surprisingly, transformative leaders are in an elite group, even though their personal qualities might preclude them from self-nominating for such a select group.

Author Jim Collins (2001) elaborates the qualities of top-level leaders as *personal humility* and *professional will*.

Personal humility:
- demonstrates a compelling modesty, shunning public adulation; [is] never boastful;
- acts with quiet, calm determination: relies on inspired standards, not inspiring charisma, to motivate;
- channels ambition into the company not the self; sets up successors for even more greatness in the next generation;
- looks in the mirror, not out the window, to apportion responsibility for poor results, never blaming other people, external factors, or bad luck.

Professional will:
- creates superb results;
- a clear catalyst in the transformation from good to great;
- demonstrates an unwavering resolve to do whatever must be done to produce the best long-term results, no matter how difficult;
- sets standard of building enduring great company, will settle for no less;
- looks out the window, not in the mirror, to apportion credit for the success of the company – to other people, external factors and good luck (p. 73).

Clearly not all of these qualities are directly applicable to transformative pedagogy, but the focus on values-driven behaviour, sensitivity to constructive group dynamics and the ability to create them, share similarities with empathic intelligence.

THE TRANSFORMATIVE POWER OF LEADERSHIP

Transformation of organisations and individuals through inspirational leadership and education is an outcome of complex dynamics and focused, informed, enduring effort. Once basic human needs for shelter, survival and love are met, transformation, or the achievement of high level psychic integration, may well be within the reach of all humans, whatever their talents, background and opportunities. In spite of many commonalities, humans have unique and individual talents, personalities, mindsets and motivations that function dynamically according to circumstances.

By analogy, the path to personal transformation has unique characteristics, skills, behaviours and requirements. Its achievements might be globally recognised, as in a Nobel Prize, or privately experienced as when a terminally ill person benefits from the heartfelt devoted care of a loved one, or the beneficence of altruistic staff of a hospice.

To accept these parameters of transformation might require some shift in existing notions of its meaning. Readers might well choose to reflect upon their own ideas and feelings about the term. However we choose to elaborate the concept of transformation, it can inspire hope in the ability of the human mind to regenerate when thwarted, respond to enabling conditions and re-shape its structures in beneficial, or transformative ways.

Hope is probably embodied deep in our psyches from the time we first mastered that milestone of standing up and taking the first steps, or articulated our first meaningful utterance. We seem destined to reach up and out, provided the environment is even moderately enabling. And for some heroic people, the challenge might be to overcome disabling environments to take those first steps. Transformation, I argue here, lives within the struggle as much as within the achievement. If we accept that idea, then we allow both self and others to enjoy the profound feeling of pleasure which can accompany the pursuit and process of excellence, or transformation, every bit as much as its achievements. Poets, composers, artists, dancers and creative people regularly transform experience. The poet Robert Browning wrote 'A man's reach must exceed his grasp or what's a heaven for?' In his poem *Auguries of Innocence*, William Blake, (1757–1827) spoke of the capacity:

> To see a World in a grain of sand
> And a Heaven in a Wild flower,
> Hold Infinity in the palm of your hand,
> And Eternity in an hour.

The function of resilience and coping with disappointment has to be accounted for here too. Support for that more complex notion of excellence has to be both personal and institutionalised. We have to believe it ourselves and that belief has to be supported by others. It helps the cause of developing a more complex and functional concept of excellence to reflect that, at heart, most competent humans like to feel alive, effective and worthwhile – the bedrock of excellence. There is more than an altruistic reason for developing an expanded concept of excellence: societies benefit in tangible ways when their citizens have goals to strive for and ideals to inspire them.

It can be liberating to realise that excellence is not only the hallmark of the Olympic gold medallist. It is liberating to think that, because sometimes publicly acclaimed achievements can seem too far out of reach to be useful as examples. Many people have admired and been inspired by human achievements that are less publicly acclaimed. Many achieve excellence in private, complex and enduring ways. Excellence can be an egalitarian notion in a special sense, if we learn to assess it relative to context, effort and outcome. To do so does not deprive it of shine or appeal. Rather it suggests that excellence is a spiralling, lifelong process in which the reach often exceeds the grasp. Pride, hope, determination, goal-setting, perseverance and the ability to recognise the foundations upon which excellence flourishes, are the hallmarks of an inspirational institution and its leaders. Such excellence creates a culture of faith in the worth of the struggle and the joy of achievement, creating an inclusive legacy for members of its community.

Educators have a professional responsibility to promote excellence in ways that are rather more structured and informed than that of the home, even though both settings might share similar values. Educators can promote excellence through their professional expertise. Across the range from pre-school to post-graduate education, educators are required to understand the nature and stages of emotional, social, psychological, moral and cognitive development which underpin human growth. Additionally, they are required to model respect for the cultural diversity represented in educational environments. They need to know how best to recognise and promote the various and complex stages of human development through the appropriate selection of learning processes, experiences, teaching methods and materials.

Given the diversity and inherent dynamics of the professional challenges facing educators, it is understandable that they become exasperated with adults, politicians and stakeholders who simply cite their own edited or selected memories of school days as a rationale for their arguments with educators. Excellence in education is a sophisticated, complex, demanding and therefore, highly desirable outcome for life in the new millennium. Its challenges far exceed those of even our technological age, because it is only achieved through high-level human endeavour. The human quality of striving for development seems timeless. Enthusiasm, expertise, adaptability, persistence and imagination, to say nothing of hunger, drove our ancestors to great achievements, often, quite literally, groundbreaking ones.

The sound professional knowledge that underpins educative leadership develops through research, reflection, professional theory-building and practice in the chosen areas of curriculum expertise. For example, teachers of poetry who write poetry or teachers of woodwork who build parquet floors have an embodied knowledge of the art that informs their teaching in special ways. Such integration between theory and practice means such teachers have valuable insight into the processes of poetry writing or floor building. If they craft their writing or building they will further model excellence for their students as well as advocate it.

EDUCATIVE LEADERSHIP

When I reflect upon the enthusiasm that many educators express for the concept of empathy in educative leadership, and when I listen to their introspections on its important role in their daily work as professionals, I appreciate something of the complexity of both the function and the practice of empathy. When naturally empathic educators encounter the concept of empathy and work it through by applying it to their own professional, and private lives, the concept actually fulfils the very function is describes. It holds stable for these educators a mass of professional experiences that have been informed by an empathic ability, and coalesces those experiences within this word and concept. In creating that coalescence and synthesising these previously free-roaming, embodied memories, it can both soothe and inspire these educative leaders. They feel in touch with their internalised abilities and confident of their potential to draw on those internal resources while developing further both the resources and those whom they influence.

Another way to think of this synthesising experience is to reflect upon the function of metaphor in language. When metaphors work well in language, previously unconnected images, words, concepts, memories and apperceptions fuse into a palpable whole. In this sense, empathy shares much with poetic experiences. It can function to create meaning out of undifferentiated or disconnected experiences. In creating such meaning, tension is released and there is the potential to move forward. The concept of educative leadership with its emphasis on empathy, can function constructively and supportively for its practitioners and their students. Empathic intelligence in action can make sense of certain effective practices in education, just as it can enhance those practices. An ideal outcome for students of empathically intelligent educators is that they can experience certain subtle, but very significant processes of educative human behaviour that provide templates for life-long learning.

Empathic attunement in educative leadership

Considerable attention has already been given to the concept of attunement between parents and their children, as well as between educators and their students. It is the quality of still attention in which one is quietly poised for action and response, depending upon an informed assessment of the dynamics of the situation. In an attuned state of attention to another, one needs to feel poised and focused, even if the person or phenomenon under attention is emotionally charged and potentially volatile. It is not just that the other totally absorbs our attention. Rather, it is that the other is referred to within an awareness of our own physiological responses, fantasies and conscious observations.

Empathic attunement is a skill that, when supported by the ability to learn from analyses of experiences, reflection and introspection, can develop into empathic intelligence. Attunement characterises a performer such as an actor, singer, dancer or public speaker who, prior to and during the performance, tunes into his/her embodied experiences of previous performance dynamics and the nature of the art form in order to achieve excellence. Attunement to the dynamics of the stage and the audience might also guide the performer, whether the performance is artistic, sporting or educative. Attunement is not just a cognitive process, though analysis and reason might be informing processes. Attunement is a fusion of thought and feeling. A competitor in a sporting event may be aware of spectators cheering for her, or against her, and be skilled in turning either case to her advantage.

In situations of choice, most of us choose to engage in activities that are intrinsically or extrinsically rewarding. If we are bored we seek excitement. Boredom scratches the mind in an irritating way, provoking a wish to irritate others as a distraction. If we are over-stimulated or tired, we seek rest. If curious to know how something works, we seek understanding. If satisfaction of that curiosity requires some research, we engage in that research. If we think we'll feel better shaping some meaning from reflection upon experience, we'll engage in that search for meaning. If telling a story about the frightening or funny thing that happened on the way to work helps us come to terms with that event, we'll tell the story. If irritating the teacher in the classroom gains us the respect of our mates, we'll annoy hell out of the teacher. But if paying attention is ultimately more rewarding, even if the reward is far in the future, we'll pay attention. Better still, attuned educators know how to listen to students and how to attract and hold their attention until such time as they experience or trust the long-term rewards. Such educators also know how to pattern learning so that rewards arrive in time to sustain effort.

If educators can model attunement, enthusiasm, expertise and empathy, students may become autonomous, self-motivated learners without even realising it. In such cases, their tacit abilities to learn are stimulated and elaborated, creating a generalised sense of self as a constructive, functional learner. They feel as if they are achievers because their minds and bodies tell them this is so. Joy in mastery has deeply internalised antecedents resonating with milestones in development like talking and walking. For striving individuals, achievement by luck alone, such as in a lottery win, has a very different emotional quality to the joy of personal achievement.

It is not only in traditionally altruistic professions that intrinsic rewards are valued. Stories abound of famous sports achievers who have foregone triumphs and lucrative prizes that would have been gained at the expense of personal integrity or the welfare of others. One famous example was the runner John Landy's gesture of stopping in the 1500 metres race in the 1956 Olympic trials to check on the welfare of fellow runner Ron Clark, whom Landy had accidentally injured slightly at the start. Landy went on to win the race, with the inspiring outcome of matching personal integrity with performance excellence. This story serves as an example of attunement to self. It is reasonable to assume that Landy felt that a win in circumstances at odds with his sense of self-worth would have been a hollow triumph.

CHALLENGING CONTEXTS

Sally and Margaret are empathic educators working in a female juvenile justice school. Both are sensitive and insightful about the particular needs of their students. These girls are living out gaol sentences for a variety of serious crimes. They can choose to attend a school within the juvenile justice campus and most of them make that choice. As you can imagine, the nature of psychic space within a gaol environment is unusual. Incarcerated individuals face particular challenges in creating a sense of personal space and psychological freedom, when the fundamental purpose of such institutions is to curtail freedom. The challenge can be especially difficult for Indigenous prisoners with particular cultural and spiritual concepts of connectedness with environment and community.

Sally and Margaret and their colleagues have to exercise empathic intelligence of the highest order to meet the emotional and educational needs of their students. The balances between control and freedom, self-responsibility and dependence, initiative and direction, fluctuate constantly. Given the differences in age, educational experience, communicative abilities and length of sentence, no one curriculum suits all students. Many of them regress frequently, and without warning, to an infant level of emotional development. Some of them have personal histories that indicate that they have been deprived of critical experiences of empathic attunement in childhood. Their emotional needs and educational needs are equally pressing.

When the staff and educators apply psychodynamic theory and practice (as empathic pedagogy was called in the early stages of its development) to their literacy and emotional development programs, the outcomes are impressive, ('Ombudsman's Report', 1996). When I suggested to Sally, the Acting Principal, that many might see empathic intelligence as a soft option, her response was passionate, articulate and unequivocal. The flash in her eyes would have illuminated a black hole. She manages staff and student issues by enacting psychodynamic practice to understand and create unique spaces for people with whom she engages. Each special encounter, such as in an interview with a student who is rejected from a gaol classroom for unacceptable behaviour, is treated within its own particular parameters. While seeking to understand why a student might have behaved, for example, in a destructive way, Sally and Margaret seek both to understand the reasons for individuals' acting out, and to provide the essential psychological boundaries which can establish and maintain the girls' inner sense of security.

To manage such encounters constructively and empathically is demanding and risky. It is not a job for amateurs or the gutless. It takes courage and insight to function empathically and effectively in a juvenile justice setting. These young women are likely to be en route to despair, if this enforced stop on the brink fails them. Space and empathic intelligence takes on a particular significance when it functions in one of society's most challenging educational environments. Educational leadership in a school where the students have little respect for traditional authority and scant memory of the benefits of learning, has to function in a space which can encompass the emotional needs of an infant, embodied in a grown young woman of eighteen.

At the same time, that young woman has to be accorded the dignity of her age as well as respect for the imperatives of her circumstances. She has to learn to read and write because her life can depend upon it. She has to learn how to present herself in a positive light, with her criminal record stacked against her. She lacks autonomy, a view for the future, a sense of security outside or supportive mentors beyond the custodial walls. The empathic intelligence of the staff has to displace the embodiment of heroin, not only as a substance but also as a way of life. Sally and Margaret understand the stakes, the challenges, the defeats and the anguish of life on the edge. They choose empathic pedagogy as the informing philosophy and practice of this school precisely because there is no place for soft options in this space.

It is ironic, poignant and inspiring that within the confined space of a gaol, there exists a unique space where the most deprived, neglected but desperately hopeful young people discover the source of an education most likely to give them a chance in life. No wonder it is tempting to re-commit crime so they can continue their education in this special space. What a shame and what a comment on our prosperous country, that such spaces are not readily available outside the prison walls!

The point has relevance to the ongoing matter of how best to judge the quality of educational institutions, given the variety of their purposes and goals. Often outcomes are chosen as criteria for excellence, partly on the grounds that they can be readily quantified. It is easy to enumerate the number of high achieving students who graduate from an educational institution by counting the number of first-class honours graduates. It is more difficult, however, to describe and quantify the kinds of enabling processes and strategies that might effectively prepare such graduates for life well beyond the present.

While many high achieving graduates can exhibit a capacity for lifelong learning, a willingness to cooperate with others, and other desirable career attributes, such qualities cannot just be assumed to occur. They appear in the mission statements of excellent corporations and institutions, but rarely is there strong evidence gathered to demonstrate that institutions consciously promote or evaluate the philosophies, ethical thinking or attitudes of their students.

Although there are enormous difficulties in a diverse society in making such evaluations, we cannot ignore the societal expectation that educational institutions should inculcate in their students certain attitudes. These may include, for example, a love of learning, a willingness to engage in learning processes, a respect for diversity of opinion, tolerance for others, and similar values associated with good citizenship. Anecdotes abound of educators who influenced students' life-choices well beyond the school or university gate. The teacher qualities that students often respond to are enthusiasm, expertise, empathy and the quiet pursuit of excellence. Effective educators often have a strong altruistic streak and their students recognise it. It is a quality that conveys an interest in education and their students that far exceeds self-interest. That quality in itself is a powerful form of mentorship.

To be empathic requires a measure of self-understanding and self-acceptance. The individual tortured by guilt or obsessed with power has little psychic space or energy to engage with others or the processes necessary for reflection. Political leaders who cannot apologise for the mistakes of the past presumably expect that their public will blame them for such past mistakes. The primitive idea of finding a scapegoat does reflect a psychological mechanism of projecting blame upon others to spare ourselves the discomfort of guilt. Empathy provides a buffer between understanding and guilt, working as it does in the spaces between private conscience and public justice. At its most sophisticated, empathy would suggest that even the most damaged individuals merit belief in their capacity for redemption. If for no other reason, this is so, simply because I can never know whether, but for the grace of unconditional love experienced at crucial times in my development, could go I. To believe otherwise is to condemn myself to the anguish of existential despair.

Fate cannot be a stronger force than love and redemption unless Gloucester (in *King Lear*) gets it right in his belief that we are simply 'like flies to wanton boys, they kill us for their sport'. Who would reasonably want to regard such a view as anything other than the outpouring of a damaged, hopeless soul? Not a soul beyond redemption, but a soul bereft of hope in its possibility.

Moral imagination, fired by empathy, creates belief in a non-judgmental, benign, transcendent being in whose image humans were created. No wonder breath and inspiration share a connotation of creating or sustaining physical and spiritual life. I have avoided speaking of empathy in spiritual terms, simply because I cannot presume to speak with authority. Nonetheless, several empathic educators who have worked with me have drawn attention to the understanding and practice of empathy by spiritual writers.

HYPOTHETICALS

- Imagine you are in charge of managing resources at either a domestic or corporate level. Think of the arguments others might make for favourable treatment in the resource distribution. It might help to think of children pleading for resources or privileges. Now consider the principles you would follow for the distribution of such resources.

- Prepare a group role-play. The role-play takes the form of a family or work meeting in which the head of the family or group announces that there will be a very significant reduction in expenditure in the next six months. At a meeting, the head presents a planned budget that shows that everyone will have to adjust their spending but some more so than others. During the meeting, each person is invited to comment on the budget. To intensify the situation, winners can swap sides with losers after the first part of the role- play.

    It is important for all participants to debrief and discuss how they felt through out the role-play and to consider how well thoughts and feelings were managed.

- Imagine you are the Principal/Head of an independent school where benefactors contribute to school prizes. You are approached by a high-profile father of one of the school's students. Recently, he made a promise of a very large donation to the school building fund. Now he is offering to fund a prize in an area in which his own daughter excels. He hints that he expects her to be the inaugural prizewinner. If possible, role-play the scenario with another person in which a conversation between the Head and the parent occurs. If a role-play is not possible, imagine the parent sent you a letter indicating his plans. Write your reply to him.

- Does everyone have to be treated in the same way in a paradigm of intelligent caring? How do you manage your own feelings if you are called unfair in adopting certain principles?
- Does transparency curb power fantasies and increase the morale of a group?
- What kinds of curriculum processes allow students to witness and experience democratic processes in action?
- Can you recall a time when someone favoured you and you were very grateful they did? Is favouritism ever in order?
- Do public displays of students' marks contravene an ethic of care and privacy?
- Have you ever discovered that you are biased against persons of particular appearance or background? Are there particular accents or voices you find unappealing? Can you find a source for your bias or is it a personal preference? How would you manage a situation where you become aware of a bias but expression of it would damage your own interests or the interests of others?
- Brainstorm in a group, sentences, phrases or expressions to do with 'care' (See if I care/ Care to join me?/ I couldn't care less). Consider the examples and try to put them in order with the most appealing ones at the top through to the most dismissive at the bottom. What are some appropriately caring remarks one might make in a work situation?

FURTHER READING
Bell, L (2003) Strategies that close the gap, *Educational Leadership*, 60 (4): 32–34.
Cothran, D, Hodges Kulinna, P, & Garrahy, D (2003) This kind of giving a secret away ... : students' perspectives on effective class management, *Teaching and Teacher Education*, 19 (4): 435-443.
Mendes, E (2003a) What empathy can do: Students respond to us because we care – and because they like us, *Journal of Educational Leadership*, p. 57–59.
—— (2003b) What empathy can do, *Educational Leadership*, 61 (1): 56-59.
Rost, J (1991) *Leadership For the Twenty-First Century*, Praeger Publishers, Westport, Connecticut.

CHAPTER SIX

DEVELOPING EMPATHIC CULTURES OF LEARNING

Empathic education creates a milieu within which the educator's non-judgmental, accepting and validating stance allows affects, emotional states and cognitive understandings to be expressed, explored and modulated. The empathic educator's purpose here is to facilitate powerful learning about the world and the mastery of skills. Empathic learning contexts can promote shifts in affective and cognitive states that enlarge our awareness of life's possibilities. Such contexts subtly encourage participants to be centred in their learning, but not self-centred in the pejorative sense. These contexts recognise the developmental potential of centred learning that is meaningful, personalised, and experienced through relationships with others and the culture we inhabit.

The RIGS (Representations of Interactions that have been Generalised – see Chapter Three), which Stern (1985) postulates from his early infant studies, signal a powerful link between affect and the potential development of reflective thought. If an infant has experienced sufficient empathic responsiveness from a mother and significant others, s/he is likely to see the world as relatively safe, manageable and benign – in the absence of evidence to the contrary – and is therefore more able to tolerate the uncertainties of exploratory learning. It is a tenet of empathic responsiveness that if feeling states are tolerable, validated and articulated, then explanation and understanding can follow. In this sense, empathy provides a form of scaffolding for learning.

In the life-long struggle for maturity, empathy is the fundamentally hopeful quality that inspires imagination. To attempt to understand how another thinks and feels, even to search for self-knowledge, is an act of faith inspired by hope. Reaching out to others, to ideas, to the challenges of extended understanding, occurs in the confidence that either the goal will be achieved or the attempt will be worthwhile in its own right. Robbed of that confidence, challenges become overwhelming. To understand the past in its deepest significance is to seek to explain the intricate behaviours, motivations and hopes of our ancestors. It is a quest to apply empathic attunement to the evidence available in order to elaborate the past, inform the present and shape the future. An impossible quest in the limits of logic, but compelling in the fantasies of empathy and imagination.

In the course of writing this book, I was surprised how often examples relevant to its themes presented themselves even in the popular press. Given the stereotypes attached to most politicians, it was encouraging to read that Bob Carr, the Premier of New South Wales (at the time of writing), intends to go into a classroom in Sydney to try teaching history in a school. He expected the experience to be 'terrifying' but hoped that the topic of his proposed lesson, the American civil rights movement, a particular passion of his, would:

> ... appeal to the students' sense of curiosity: I have no full appreciation about how a teacher achieves that skill of understanding where the students are, being able to hold the attention of everyone in that classroom, students of different capacity, and then lead them on to another level of competence, knowing that what they have touched on has been absorbed and that it's safe to move on to the next level ... Think about that for a moment and you can appreciate the level of skill involved in that. (*Sydney Morning Herald*, 12 February 1999, p. 3.)

Through reflection and observation, a person of influence recognises the necessity for empathic attunement to audience needs in order to influence effectively. Empathic comments from leaders have an affirming effect.

It takes a sensitivity to recognise and remedy disruption in normal development. Educators Susan Nicolson (1997), working in a juvenile justice school, and Margarita Maza (1996), teaching the parents of deaf children, have demonstrated that empathically intelligent approaches to learning can result in positive educational benefits, notwithstanding the early deprivations experienced by students.

Empathy (as it functions within empathic intelligence) involves an attunement to both one's own and others' emotional and cognitive states. Such attunement requires self-awareness, imagination, concentration, reflection and practice. Complex as this sounds, empathic attunement can gradually become a habit – and one which is a manageable and rewarding part of professional and personal expertise. However, we must provide safeguards for empathic educators lest they tire of empathic functioning. Because others quickly recognise the altruism inherent in this form of relating, and the potential benefits it can offer them, the temptation to overstep reasonable boundaries can be irresistible. Burn out can occur. Too much can be expected of its advocates. It is a reciprocal engagement between people and cannot work effectively if any form of exploitation, even unconsciously, enters the dynamic.

It is not contradictory to talk about altruism and exploitation in the same breath. Empathic educators are altruistic to the extent that they forego the gratification of their own needs, including ego trips, in the interests of their students. Students themselves are eminently capable of picking educators able to function in this way. Of course, no sane person is ever completely altruistic, but you get the point. It takes considerable discipline for altruistically inclined educators to establish boundaries around their work. But it is essential that they do so. Think for a moment how impossible it is to respond empathically to another when you are exhausted, hungry, cold and disheartened. Empathy is a fallible, complex and demanding form of relating, which merits respect and an acknowledgement of its boundaries.

THE CONDITIONS FOR DEVELOPING EMPATHY

In educational psychology empathy is commonly associated with social and interpersonal skills. Here, however, I argue that empathy is importantly associated with both affective *and* thinking development. It is possible that those who demonstrate an early manifestation of strong interpersonal skills such as warmth towards others, are actually reflecting a particular kind of parenting experience. It is also likely that those infants demonstrating warmth towards others are responded to warmly in return, thus being prompted to develop that predisposition throughout life, even developing into empathically intelligent adults. Much is likely to depend upon the nature and timing of the reinforcement and mirroring infants experience. As with most talents, personal gifts, and predispositions, environmental influences are significant in their long-term development. Given that empathic intelligence requires both inter-personal and intra-personal abilities, its development relies on more than a particular personality or warm disposition.

Who started the mirroring?

The parental and social factors which promote the development of empathy include secure early attachment, parental affection, the availability of empathic models, parental use of inductive discipline encouraging imaginative empathy, encouragement of self-concept as well as perceived similarity to others and discouragement of excessive interpersonal competition (Barnett, 1987).

Educators David Berliner and Robert Calfee (1996) see empathy playing a role in classroom instruction through the necessary skills of prosocial behaviour, cooperation and turn-taking, and affective bonding with teachers and peers. Children who display these capabilities in primary school tend to be better liked by other children and teachers, which helps create more favourable conditions for academic success during adolescence (Wentzel, 1993a, 1993b). In one study, researcher Kathryn Wentzel (1991) found that adolescents who displayed socially responsible behaviour in school had significantly higher grade point averages than students who did not, when cognitive factors and other behaviours were controlled statistically. Given the clear association between socially responsible behaviour, academic achievement and the positive esteem enjoyed by empathic people, the development of empathy in educational programs merits close attention.

Intervention research on empathy has found positive influences for environmental socialisation factors such as affective qualities in parental relationships and friends (Costin and Jones, 1992; Hoffman, 1994). Berliner and Calfee speculate that given its survival value, empathy may have a biological basis as well. Researchers Nancy Eisenberg and R. Lennon (1983) suggest that there appear to be gender differences in empathy, even in newborns. It is hard to determine how this might be so, given the undifferentiated emotional development of newborns and the profound effects on infants of mothering styles. Empathy in this case could be little more than emotional responsiveness – a fairly low-level definition of empathy.

Since mothers, and others, tacitly mirror to infants their own and the infant's affective states, the infant's process of developing sensitivity to the emotional states of self and others is very much influenced by various significant interpersonal relationships. Through these significant relationships, infants, children, adolescents and adults continue to adapt emotional responsiveness according to the ways that responsiveness is affirmed and modulated. While emotional templates developed early in life provide a pattern likely to guide affective responses to situations, those templates themselves can be modified by experience. In that sense, empathy can be developed, provided there is sufficient motivation and modelling to do so. In an important sense, others give permission, or withhold it, to develop both a sense of an individual and a social self. The struggle to keep in balance the sometimes competing demands of individual and social development can be challenging and significant.

Given the positive personal, social and educational benefits of empathy, it is timely to lift the level of the debate beyond issues of heritability and early gender differences to consider, instead, those enabling circumstances most likely to promote its development. This includes considering how different styles of socialisation might well impact on empathic development. I suggest that it is not very productive to confine ourselves to the immediately known or testable. By its very nature, empathic intelligence demands that we integrate thoughtful, affective impulses or responses in creative ways.

ALTRUISM

In considering the function of selflessness or altruism, an aspect of high-level empathy, it is worth reflecting upon some observations from the behaviour of animals. Professor of Primate Behaviour, Frans B. M. de Waal (1998), cites the experience of observing a zoo in Thailand where two medium-sized dogs shared their cage with three fully grown tigers. 'The dogs were walking snacks for the tigers, but the tigers evidently failed to perceive them as such', de Waal reports (p. 38). Mindful that we have to be careful about extrapolating from animal behaviour to human behaviour, de Waal addresses a number of possible explanations for this behaviour and cites other instances of animals behaving in ways where self-interest is wholly absent. These include gorillas who have rescued children in danger and dolphins who have saved men from shark attacks. He concludes:

> Such examples make a deep impression on us mainly because they benefit members of our species. But, in my work on the evolution of empathy and morality, I have found many instances of animals' caring for one another and responding to one another's distress – evidence so rich that I am convinced survival depends not only on strength in combat but also, at times, on cooperation and kindness (p. 39).

Stories of animals exhibiting seemingly selfless behaviour can have a very humbling effect on humans, particularly when colloquial language deploys 'animal acts' as a pejorative term. de Waal argues that when an impulse becomes divorced from the consequences which shaped its evolution – that is, when pay-offs are highly unlikely – then the impulse can be regarded as genuinely unselfish. He concludes:

Paradoxically, the struggle for existence has produced amazingly cooperative species with character traits such as loyalty, trust, sympathy and generosity. Or, as Charles Darwin – always wiser than his followers – stated: 'I use the term Struggle for Existence in a large and metaphorical sense including dependence of one being on another' (p. 39).

In complete contrast to empathy is the construct known as Machiavellianism – the ability to manipulate other people and situations to one's own interests – as characterised by detachment and low emotionality in relations with others (Wrightsman, 1991). Children high in Machiavellianism are less empathic, less helpful and more likely to choose self-oriented reasons for engaging in helpful behaviour (Barnett and Thompson, 1984). Many readers would recognise this as the 'what's-in-it-for-me?' syndrome.

In the large picture of a well-functioning society, that syndrome, and its companion bullying, are perceived as creating situations where everyone, including the bullies and tyrants, ends by losing. Needless to say, it can take considerable work on the part of parents, educators and leaders to influence egocentric thinkers to perceive that larger picture. It requires an ability to perceive long-term, almost abstract consequences of behaviour. Sometimes lack of cognitive ability is the cause of egocentrism, as in the early stages of childhood when it is developmentally relatively normal. But other times, egocentrism is a choice tied to self-interest. The pseudo-team player who chooses not to share information or the means to win a game is a case in point. In such circumstances, peer disapproval can sometimes shift the balance, as can exclusion from the group until the 'rules' are adhered to.

The ability to decentre in thinking and to see another's point of view is regarded as a higher order level of thinking than egocentrism. But whether a person chooses to act on that ability to decentre, and to accommodate another's point of view, is an important measure of empathy. Clearly a Machiavellian student with high cognitive ability could be a very successful examination candidate, and indeed a somewhat 'successful' leader.

Young children who demonstrate embryonic empathic qualities such as compassion (possibly a trait closer to sympathy than empathy) may need to be encouraged to develop their trait further so that they internalise a sense of the intrinsic worth of that quality. Such encouragement would increase the possibility that they will mobilise other traits necessary to develop empathic intelligence. The small child or older student who exhibits concern for the welfare of others, particularly when it can be at the cost of popularity, deserves to be supported, even if not in a public way, should that put the child at further risk. Given that such children are likely to be sensitive to group dynamics, including the possibility that they might be victimised for their altruism, it helps them to know that their attitude and behaviour is noticed and affirmed by adults. How resilient is the trait of compassion in the face of strong threats and bullying? In any climate of blame and punishment it can be difficult for high-order interpersonal traits to flourish. Hence the need for emotional safety to be a priority in family, social, professional and corporate cultures.

BULLYING

Reports persist in the media of bullying in a variety of contexts – for example in schools, in the workplace, in families and in the defence forces. While we tend to think of bullying as the behaviour of ten-year-old boys shoving smaller children in the playground at lunch time, the reality of bullying behaviour is often more persistent, subtle and widespread than the stereotype suggests. Bullying refers to any behaviour whereby one person uses power, status, threats or coercion to force another to comply to the bully's demands.

Adolescent girls who use scorn, ridicule, malice and gossip to pressure others to conform to group norms, or even to leave a group, are exhibiting bullying behaviour. The barrister in the courtroom who uses a sneering tone of voice to question a witness is acting like a bully. The bus driver who deliberately stops or starts the bus abruptly to frighten passengers is bullying them. The apprentices in a workshop, or recruits in the armed services, who force new recruits to endure degrading induction rituals are bullying. The teacher who humiliates students by persistently demonstrating their failings to the class is bullying. The drama director or music conductor who harangues the cast or members of the orchestra in a mistaken belief that such methods improve performance, is bullying.

The persistent pattern in such behaviour is the abuse of a powerful advantage such as physical size, hierarchical position, wealth, or whatever, to gain further personal advantage. Whether the bullying takes the form of physical violence, scorn, threats, withdrawal of privileges or emotional blackmail, it can work because the victim is in no position to respond in kind. The perpetrator has a distinct advantage from the start. Bullying is distinctly different to 'healthy competition' between parties or groups where the struggle for dominance is conducted by certain rules. Bullies conduct combat by one rule only – that they win at all costs. Hitler was the archetypal bully.

In a 1999 radio interview, the Welsh tenor, Bryn Terfel, spoke with some wryness about his experience of becoming a committed singer in the farming village of his childhood in Wales. It is easy to assume that everyone in Wales so admires singing that a gifted young singer would be adulated in the community – even in school. But apparently not. While the adulation certainly came later, Terfel spoke about the school bullies who were only too ready to make life tough for him, except that he was physically strong and won recognition in soccer and other sports. Thankfully, his all-round excellence protected him in his pursuit of a singing career, but one wonders how other less gifted youngsters realise their dreams in the face of bullying.

Combating bullying

Given the persistence of bullying even in these supposed enlightened times when legislation is in place in many countries to counteract it, it is worth considering how it can be combated – and the word is appropriate – in interpersonal encounters. Here empathic intelligence can go some way to understanding the mind of the bully. I'm prepared to suggest that without exception a persistent bully suffers from some defect in self-esteem. In spite of appearances, the bully with the huge physique or devastating, destructive wit feels small or vulnerable inside. When feelings of vulnerability arise, as they do for everyone from time to time, the bully finds them terrifying and unbearable. Bullies take pre-emptive measures to overcome such feelings of vulnerability by manoeuvring to a position where they can exploit whatever powers they have to keep vulnerability at bay. Lacking the confidence, imagination or intelligence to develop socially acceptable winning ways, bullies use force, flattery, ingratiation, money – whatever it takes – to protect themselves from any situation which might stir up those painful feelings of deep, personal inadequacy.

Mind you, understanding why the bully functions in this way offers but small respite from the attentions of the bully. Just sometimes, such as in schools where there is still some hope that bullies might be reformed, empathic teachers can be successful in finding ways to help bullies develop socially acceptable behaviour patterns through positive reinforcement of whatever skills or abilities they have. That takes time and commitment. The problem is often compounded by the fact that bullies are often plainly unlikable people, compounding their own problems by their alienating behaviour.

Increasingly more attention is being given to the issue of bullying in the workplace, since it is recognised as a significant factor in high absenteeism and lower productivity. In a report headed 'Why bad bosses make you sick', a workplace reporter, Jim O'Rourke, discusses the $7 billion cost to industry in a year for sick leave. He reports: 'Labour experts say the main causes of absenteeism, other than illness, include low staff morale and abuse from bullying bosses' (1999, p. 39). Clearly, managers who provide opportunities for workers to communicate their grievances, even if such grievances are difficult to solve and not the 'fault' of management, are more likely to retain the loyalty of their employees. Unhappy workers dread facing work and the slightest illness becomes a reason to take sick leave. The thought of facing a bully at work is enough to make even slightly ill workers feel deathly. You have to feel robust and well-defended to face even subtle slights to self-esteem, to say nothing of the energy needed to face full-on bullying. On the other hand, committed and enthusiastic workers treat minor illness as a passing inconvenience and they come to work anyway. In an empathic, cooperative, caring workplace, the social life of work and the pleasure of achievement and team work can be an attractive alternative to a day off, surprising as it may seem.

In cases of domestic violence, much is made of the fact that many battered wives choose to stay with their bullying spouses. This willingness to stay is often interpreted as a lack of courage or resources on the part of the victim. These can be significant factors, of course. But another factor can come into play also. Empathic spouses often recognise, even intuitively, why the bully behaves that way, just as they recognise the socially-isolating consequences of such behaviour. Sometimes an empathic response to another can actually work against one's own best interests. The plight of the over-empathic 'battered spouse' is a case in point, leaving aside for the moment the complicating issue that the need to be needed is also self-gratifying. But as with all stages of development, in adult life change can only occur if the individual commits to seeking that change. Empathic others can support the wish to change but the process requires the individual's sustained commitment.

How does empathic intelligence help the problem of bullying? If we think that bullying is a gross form of self-gratification at the expense of others, a far-fetched hope might be that better forms of self-gratification might be offered in substitute. With entrenched forms of bullying, that rarely works. The forms of bullying most open to remediation are those where the perpetrator simply cannot think of an alternative way of operating because communication and negotiating skills are underdeveloped. Education can help in such cases. Some bullies do not fully realise the effects of their behaviour, but when confronted with the extent of the distress they have caused they may experience sufficient remorse to seek reform. In private, bullies are often deflated, depressed and dependent. Again, in private, they can sometimes acknowledge the force of their own insecurities and seek help.

The complexities of dealing with bullying are compounded when we realise that not only are bullies unlikable, but also they often stir up feelings of revenge in their victims. I know how enraged I feel when I see an adult mistreating a child or an animal. I react so fiercely to bullying or tantalising behaviour that I have an overwhelming urge to hurt the adult! I want to stop the behaviour instantly and I want the perpetrator to experience the effects of their behaviour. While I don't respond to that primitive urge, I know the compelling force of a wish for revenge. Even though I know rationally that revenge is ultimately pointless, it offers, momentarily, a promise of restoring a power imbalance.

An old cliché sometimes circulates about perpetrators of corporal punishment saying to their victims: 'This hurts me more than it hurts you'. Ironically and in a macabre, sick way, the cliché might actually be correct. By what defect in empathy, imagination and intelligence does one human being want to relate to another through corporal punishment (fortunately outlawed in most schools and institutions now) or humiliation? I am not talking here about the occasional lapses in equilibrium of parents who, overwrought and powerless to think of a better method, slap a child and regret it immediately. I am thinking of consistent, premeditated practices such as initiation rites, reportedly still common in some institutions such as university colleges, defence force academies and apprentice workshops.

CHANGING CULTURES

There are some thought-provoking incidents in literature about the issue of corporal punishment. James Joyce wrote about it in *Portrait of the Artist as a Young Man* (1979). In *Kes (A Kestrel for a Knave)*, a memorable novel by Barry Hines about school and community life in northern England in the 1970s, there is a heart-wrenching account of the caning of an innocent school boy who is in the wrong place at the wrong time. He is sent to the headmaster's office on an errand when he is seized by a group of boys caught smoking in school. They force him to hide their cigarettes in his pockets, and when the headmaster lines the culprits up for inspection, the messenger boy is rounded up too. He has no idea how to defend himself from the combined forces of injustice and can only submit to his fate. Worse, unlike his fellow victims who have learned from experience how to hold out their hands for caning in a manner which reduces some of the effect of the cane, he takes the full impact. 'The first stroke made him cry. The second stroke made him sick' (p. 58).

I used that incident as a letter-writing prompt for fourteen-year-old girls and boys as part of a 1983 writing research project. The students were asked to listen to a teacher read the extract, then to write a letter to a close friend in which they discussed their responses to it. It was somewhat concerning that a number of students, all male as it happened, actually thought that the messenger boy deserved a caning for being stupid enough to get caught. I have often wondered whether cultural forces actually make it very difficult for some students to develop empathy, or even a capacity for its first cousin, sympathy.

To experience and express the vulnerability underpinning such close engagements with others, either in real life or through art, literature and drama, requires particular psychic strength. Part of that strength comes from knowing you will not become so engulfed by the other's pain as to lose psychic equilibrium. Another part of the strength lies in confidence in recovery. This can be supported by the intelligent recognition of the dynamics of intense emotional experiences. They fluctuate in intensity and can be soothed by the sufferer's experience of another's willingness to accept the reality of suffering. The student writers who have to further scapegoat an innocent boy by blaming him for his plight, probably could not afford to identify too closely with a peer for fear of a kind of psychic contamination. To identify with him and feel sympathy could immerse them irredeemably in his agony. They too might become helpless victims of the system. Best to kick him out of sight as one of life's losers. Is this attitude far removed from the dynamics of some boardrooms? Where are the male and female role models of empathic intelligence in the community? Are they applauded and honoured?

Obviously such practices generate negative responses in their victims, even though they might pretend to conform, or even worse, determine to seek revenge by acting as perpetrators themselves in due course (commonly known as the *Lord of the Flies* syndrome after William Golding's 1954 novel). Even if it were not an assault on human dignity and self-worth to condone humiliating practices, it is plainly damaging to the essential fabric of an institution – which after all is no more stable than the combined commitment of its inhabitants – to conduct business in a climate of fear. People cannot think creatively, work effectively or relate constructively if they are living in dread of humiliation. Their psychic energy has to be channelled into defensive strategies such as unrelenting vigilance and compulsive conformity. With technology now capable of eternal vigilance we can well afford to concentrate on eliminating interpersonal behaviour that is destructive and dehumanising. Drama role-plays that allow participants to experience, in a safe climate, the effects of different kinds of interpersonal behaviour, can provide opportunities for developing constructive behaviour patterns. With increased self-awareness one develops sensitivity to others. In hurting them we diminish ourselves.

In Australia, anti-discrimination and industrial legislation governing interpersonal relationships might be regarded as a triumph for empathic understanding, or an acknowledgment that goodwill alone cannot change a culture. When appeals to better nature fail to achieve comfortable levels of tolerance in workplace and community relationships, legislation can now be evoked to further the cause. This is not to suggest that empathy or legislation alone can solve problems – both can actually create them – but empathy has an insistent quality once its claims and consequences are identified. Power brokers who want to reject someone for a position simply because they don't like the applicant's ethnic background or marital status, might still be able to find an argument to mask their bias. But they will at least have to risk exposing that bias to the scrutiny of others.

The Australian Council for Educational Research (ACER) is working to develop and refine frameworks against which schools and school systems might monitor the social, emotional, moral and ethical development of their students (Forster and Anderson, 2003, p. 12). While pen-and-paper tests of values and attitudes can never guarantee a direct correlation between articulated values and actual behaviour in various circumstances, they can indicate predispositions.

EMPATHIC EDUCATION

Theories of pedagogy exist to provide working hypotheses for implementation in practice. As observation and reflection provide evidence to test the underlying hypotheses, so they are modified, or confirmed or abandoned. It is particularly necessary for a dynamic theory of pedagogy that it develops as it influences practice. All the more so because it attempts to explain quite complex, fluid and permeable aspects of educative interactions. For that reason, it is timely now to consider the starting points for educators choosing to work within this model.

Affirmation and critique

Empathic educators are leaders who commit to engaging students and colleagues in educative processes which respect the inherent abilities of humans to learn and which implicitly and explicitly model such values. At its most basic, this means that educators respect the dignity and worth of the individuals under their influence and care. As leaders, they have sound ideas about the desirable direction of discussion and processes, but they are also alert to necessary changes in direction in the light of good evidence. They have a vision of the benefits and processes likely to emerge through their leadership and they can articulate that vision in plausible, convincing and inclusive ways. They see their role as giving their students access to the most significant knowledge, resources and educative experiences possible in the circumstances. They hope and expect that in due course their students might well exceed the achievements of the educator. And they are mindful that should this be the case, they can exult in whatever part they played in enabling another to excel. That sense of exultation might well provide affirmation for the educator that the chosen philosophy was sound, constructive and mutually beneficial. Infants express an enthusiasm for engagement with others and their environment; experienced individuals articulate that enthusiasm through whatever commitment they make to life-long learning.

Revising life scripts

We can access our own constructs of ourselves as leaders, as educators and as parents by recalling those experiences that we believe have been influential in shaping our sense of self and the roles we fulfil. As we reflect upon those influences by writing about them and discussing them with others, we inevitably access more memories than we expected. Across time and place, memory yields up all kinds of interesting, personally meaningful stories. It is as if we have embodied personal dramas in which players, events, feelings and images seemingly live a life of their own in our minds. The more reflective and insightful we become about our personal dramas, the more we come to direct our own scripts and personal theatre, rather than act or live as one of the chorus. Our individual life is the one stage upon which we are entitled to play the lead role, ever mindful that such a role is, paradoxically, always interdependent.

Sometimes it is hard to start reflecting upon significant influences upon our life. Some direction is helpful at the beginning. Focusing on those influences upon current professional life can be a good start. There is usually a person or event which comes to mind easily. Many of us can remember vividly learning to master some skill such as riding a bike, using a compass, a computer or an automatic teller machine. It is well nigh impossible today to avoid new learning situations. Hence our self-concepts as learners are always exercising their influence. We all have some measure of mastery of some skills, but even the most proficient individual can be challenged by new situations. The importance of understanding the dynamics of our personal self-constructs as leaders and educators becomes apparent when we begin to access the richness of those constructs. They have a life as long as our own, and seemingly function with robust intention, notwithstanding our own conscious directions. Even as we think we understand those constructs, they can change colour and force.

Knowing ourselves is every bit as challenging as knowing other people. Just as we think we understand a person or a problem, something shifts and our confidence is challenged. It helps in coming to know our self-concepts to recognise that such constructs can have a certain constancy at their core, with more fluid constellations surrounding that core. For example, we might feel that we are capable leaders and educators overall, but with particular strengths and limitations in certain areas. We might be excellent historians but not very good at operating in mathematical systems. Or we might be equally able in both, but prefer one system to the other. We might work best in teams or enjoy working solo for long periods of time. We might enjoy tasks with a clearly defined outcome or those that are very open-ended. And at different times and in different places our preferences might change. Variability can be a challenge because it seems to suggest constant fluidity, but that paradox itself becomes tolerable with maturity. Such maturity is not necessarily age-linked – witness the ease with which many young people cope with the rapid changes of technology and the dynamics of their own social and cultural lives.

UNDERSTANDING THE DYNAMICS OF LEARNING

There are infinite ways in which we can learn about the world, organise our understandings and symbolise or articulate them. Our senses, our past experiences, our current hopes and the influences of those around us provide multiple permutations for the development of intelligences. For empathic pedagogy it is important that educators feel comfortable exploring their own self-constructs as learners so that they develop a functionally stable sense of the dynamics of those constructs. Since we are all influenced by our internalised self-constructs, it helps if educators, and also students, recognise preferred learning styles or content, or patterns of mastery. Few of us remember the content of our formal schooling but we can often recall the emotional colour of particular classrooms or subjects. In particular, we recall with fear or gratitude, the ways educators dealt with our particular difficulties. If risk-taking was welcomed in the classroom, even if the risk was not productive in its own right, a pattern can be established which influences our attitudes to learning life-long – or at least until the underlying assumptions guiding our current attitudes or self-constructs are explored.

In an important sense, our self-constructs as educators can provide strong motivation for adopting a particular theory and practice. If we operate within a construct that says our function is to teach students a bundle of material which might ensure their success in an examination, we limit our demonstrated effectiveness to a narrow set of criteria with short-term outcomes. If we expand the criteria to include the development and internalisation of learning processes that will be beneficial beyond the confines of a lecture room or laboratory, we gain the benefit or seeing those processes functioning in front of us. Then we can fine-tune them in the light of experience. I notice that judges of sports events such as diving or skating give participants marks for the degree of difficulty in the attempted feat. Educators might well adopt that relative method for assessing their own achievements!

Consider the apparently simple method of having students discuss an issue in small groups with their peers. The reason for choosing that method might be to allow students to express their ideas in language close to themselves, to learn to listen and value the contributions of others, or to reshape existing patterns in a classroom in order to encourage silent members to contribute. In the course of observing students working in small groups, it may become apparent that some students cannot tolerate the uncertainty of an open-ended discussion, or some might deviate from the task at hand but actually discover an entry point to the topic by using personal experience as a kind of scaffold. Whatever the formal outcome of that discussion, there will be all kinds of informal learning for participants in their feelings about the process they were involved in. They might have discovered that they hate having to wait for others to make a point. They may want to focus on something no one else seems interested in.

The dynamics of the group can be powerfully educative, in ways possibly not anticipated at the start. The degree to which these dynamics might be discussed will depend upon the purpose of the experience, but at the very least participants will have discovered something about their own functioning in this small group. At best they might have discovered that others can have perceptions quite at variance with their own. At worst they might have discovered that group work can be slow and circuitous. Where group work becomes unproductive, a leader's ability to structure a discussion might suddenly seem valuable and necessary. Or it might become apparent that small groups work well with some tasks and poorly with others. The point is to recognise that outcomes can vary according to group dynamics. But however participants interact, there will be outcomes of some kind. The most desirable outcomes will lead participants to higher order thinking such as creative problem solving, hypothesising or speculation. In terms of affective outcomes, there might be a desirable recognition and tolerance of even intense feelings associated with some higher order conceptualising, creativity and problem solving.

SELF-REFLECTION IN PROFESSIONAL DEVELOPMENT

Consistent with the beliefs underpinning this theory of pedagogy, students' internalised experiences of the methods by which they learn about the world are more influential in the long term than their formal learning of content. This belief informs the widespread practice in both tertiary education programs for professionals and vocational education for trades, of requiring students to complete practicums or apprenticeships as part of their professional development. Ideally, theory and practice meet during such practicums to create an embodied, lived experience to inform the students' own best practice. The degree to which students reflect on their experiences and engage in the practicum with enthusiasm, commitment and appropriate expertise informed by theory, will significantly influence their professional practice.

Processes of reflection can involve discussion with peers and mentors, written personal journals, extended reflective writing drawing on critical thinking, and the informal testing of hypotheses through exploratory practices. I happen to believe that reflective writing is a particularly powerful form of professional development. It allows us to 'talk' to ourselves, privately, revealingly and in an exploratory way. We can see what we are thinking emerging on the page. The process of reflective writing actually stimulates thinking. We can sometimes be surprised to discover what we think, or even how hard it is to find the words to express what we mean. But at least by engaging in writing, our thoughts are held stable for reflection and revision. And, as with most skills, practice develops writing ability.

Self-reflective undertakings such as these can provide an important link between existing and desired levels of professional ability. Used in meaningful ways, reflections can both articulate current levels of development and signal further aspirations, symbolising the possibility that the covert or tacit can become overt and dynamic. Not all reflections are equally significant, but if they are recorded in writing, they can be scrutinised and evaluated. We can assign renewed significance to whatever is revealed and choose to re-organise it, re-embody it, or relegate it to the past. Each time we re-tell our personal histories their emotional colour and form shifts like a kaleidoscope. We might shudder to discover the laments of our adolescent diaries hidden in the proverbial bottom drawer, but feel relief at the same time that in adulthood we are less tortured by the vagaries of life and love. Nonetheless, our diary writing served an important function then, as it can do in adult life. In our personal, reflective writing we can act as our own indefatigable audience. In our psyches private and public life are seamlessly interwoven, even though we learn through experience and socialisation to choose what it is wise to conceal and reveal.

THE CHANGING ROLE OF TEACHERS

Since most information necessary for modern life is available through technology, it is worth thinking critically about the changed role of educators in the technological revolution. In an empathic model, educators can constructively engage with students to evaluate the worth of information and the worth of interactive, student-centred learning experiences. Such educators can be freed from the drudgery of a transmission role to the stimulation of a mentor role. Students can engage productively in sustained reflection, synthesis of understandings and the generation of creative outcomes. The challenges of such a shift in perspective are both demanding and rewarding. An optimistic and imaginative view of human progress would regard paradigm shifts as positive and enhancing. In such a shift, psychodynamic/empathic leaders and educators become more rather than less necessary.

In the realm of human behaviour with all its complexities and contexts, it is notoriously difficult to generalise about the meanings we create from experiences. Except to acknowledge that we do embody the personal data from our lived experience in highly subjective and idiosyncratic ways. Hence the desirability of accessing our subjective data, through various symbolic and articulated methods, to scrutinise and evaluate it in the light of current realities, hopes and aspirations. In this endeavour, commonly called the search for meaning in life, poetry, drama, music, dance, visual arts, creative mathematics and scientific discoveries enhance our capacities to enjoy and endure that search. Meta-awareness is nothing more than consciously symbolising (naming, structuring, patterning, re-shaping) those higher order engagements we undertake for personally developmental reasons. Whether we like it or not as educators, parents and leaders, those whom we influence create meanings from their encounters with us and the experiences we engage them in. Sometimes such meanings remain unspoken. At other times they surface for scrutiny. Without exception, they are internalised in some way. If we can value the essentially human and awe-inspiring need to make sense of experience and harness that need in the service of person-centred development, it demonstrably enhances constructive cognitive and affective growth.

COMMUNICATING EMPATHICALLY AND STRATEGICALLY

The fairly recent development of email communications is both exciting and challenging. Electronic communication encourages an informal genre of writing which actually requires as much judgment and audience awareness as other more traditional forms. It is easy to be lulled into a false sense of security with emails. They encourage quick, spontaneous messages and an intimate form of communication, yet they can become legal documents like other kinds of written discourse. They tend to take the emotional colour of the moment, and that can be discomforting when time changes the feelings of that moment. Leaders rarely communicate simply to convey information. That is usually done in other ways. Their purposes can be psychologically complex, such as to lift morale or to deflect attention from problem issues. Furthermore, their audiences often listen to them or read their words for subliminal messages about matters quite at odds with the leaders' overt intentions. Hence the need for leaders to have trustworthy colleagues to provide them with feedback on their communicative effectiveness. The leader who cannot abide hearing negative feedback finishes up with little alternative but to become increasingly autocratic. While the leader might intend to motivate colleagues or subordinates to adopt particular strategies or to give support to proposals, the audience could well be assessing whether they trust/like/believe/ doubt/admire or feel inspired by the leader.

We are all exposed to more propaganda daily than we need, so we have learned to be sceptical of appeals for our allegiance. Every advertiser knows how to play to our emotions, our doubts, fears, hopes and propensity for shame and pride. We cannot afford, either financially or emotionally, to respond to every call for allegiance. We are dutifully and necessarily sceptical in our choices. So what is a leader to do?

Educators have been asking themselves that question for several decades as they compete for attention with the instant gratification of mass media and the targeted aesthetics of popular culture. In the domain of communicative effectiveness, successful educators have much to offer leaders in corporations and bureaucracies. Effective educators, and there are legions of them, have had to listen to their students and acknowledge their needs by incorporating them into their teaching strategies. They have developed effective skills and appropriate attitudes to gain and hold the attention of often quite disenchanted students. Appeals to students' long-term goals are rarely effective with those unable to imagine a future. Sometimes empathic listening establishes a foundation of trust upon which pedagogy can build. Such leadership is quiet and unobtrusive, but conveys implicit respect that can be affirming for those unused to being heard or those unskilled in delivering temperate messages.

Effective leaders, parents, carers and educators are often skilled, non-judgmental, patient listeners, even if they do not have all the time in the world to give. While they may not enjoy the emotional force of some of the stories and complaints they have to hear, they know how to contain or moderate that force. Part of the effectiveness of that empathic listening abides in the ability to discipline your own felt responses. Enraged speakers can be enraging, particularly if they can feel in an instant the inflammatory effects of their performance. Mirroring can escalate a situation as effectively as it can soothe it. The empathic listener is not simply in the game of reinforcing another's emotional state. Sound judgment and rationality are part of empathy and can dictate that a wise strategy can be what I call 'going under the prevailing mood'. If a speaker is enraged, or sullen or histrionic and seeking your support for their mood, you can ignore that level of appeal and resist, either overtly or subtly.

The illustration which comes to mind is playing tennis with an opponent who either hits soft balls when you like fast ones, or whose fast balls are intimidating but erratic. The skilled tennis player (which I am not) knows never to underestimate the opponent and how to play their own game within the context of playing against another. In other words, empathy includes choosing how to respond to another, not simply allowing one's self to be manipulated. In leadership, education, sport and life, it is difficult to balance individual needs with corporate or group ones. Hence the need for periods of time-out to reflect on professional and private priorities. It can happen that a highly skilled professional does not necessarily have the requisite abilities to offer leadership in that profession. Sport offers many examples of outstanding athletes who successfully became corporate sports leaders, and many who did not.

Wisely many corporations, educational institutions and caring agencies recognise the necessity of periods of renewal for highly functioning individuals. Such individuals are not only found in public life. They are often also hidden in domestic life, exhibiting competence in managing multiple roles requiring complex skills. It is well known that highly functioning individuals need supporting teams whose combined skills might well exceed those of the leader. Most successful scientific, corporate and educational developments are the result of exceptional team collaboration.

EXCELLENCE AS AN EGALITARIAN IDEAL

The volatile shifts in the public and private dynamics of human relationships require constant, astute evaluation. To choose to be empathic can be risky and challenging, not the least because it involves opening one's self to the mind and feelings of another. That can be a vulnerable position. The choice needs to be routinely scrutinised in the light of all the gains and losses experience delivers. Like most high-order challenges, it is no easy option for anyone engaged in people-orientated professions. It is an influential personal and professional orientation only in so far as it supports and reflects the basic integrity of its adherents. Another way of saying this is to suggest there is a quality of vocation in its practice. That quality is not unique to empathic practitioners, of course. All kinds of work require skill development, practice, deep commitment, endurance, sacrifice and devotion to duty well beyond its call. Those who commit to work with the quiet passion and belief such qualities require, might well regard their work as a vocation. Both humble and exalted positions can have a vocational quality, depending on individuals' personal orientation to their position and its responsibilities.

I am reminded of Ralph, the proprietor of a now-popular coffee shop and food outlet on the university campus where I work. He and his wife, Rose, suffered financial setbacks some years ago but have determinedly recovered by offering the very best coffee and food on campus. They and their devoted team of workers start very early in the morning, filling catering orders and meeting their responsibilities all day. They engage in cheerful talk with their customers, seem to love their work, serve generous helpings of everything and the queues of hopeful customers grow longer by the week. They have more than recovered from their earlier setback. And what do they now do? They give generously to the university community, as if it were responsible for their excellence and commitment. Ralph left school early as a young boy in Italy but wanted to excel in something he loved. He loves seeing people appreciate his food and coffee. He's proudly wearing a gold coffee bean charm on a chain around his neck, an award from a coffee bean distributor to the best coffee maker in Sydney. Rose and Ralph did not wait for their luck to turn – they made it change. They have a well-articulated work ethic and can tell you why they work as they do, how they train their staff, what they know the public expects in service and value, and how they see themselves relating to the wider university community. In essence, their values, commitment, enthusiasm and expertise are similar to that required for any successful enterprise.

The pleasure I feel in telling this story recalls a similar pleasure I felt forty-odd years ago, when my lawyer father drove us to visit some of his Italian clients developing riverside plots of market produce in harsh inland Australia. His clients were the first wave of post-war migration from Europe and in the space of a decade they managed to pay off their debts, expand their holdings, and bring their extended families to join them. My father was very proud of his clients. They cleared the land, tilled, planted and harvested produce every second of daylight in that hot inland country. They were hopeful and determined.

To an eight-year-old girl learning about the world through the fiction of English writers like Enid Blyton, these dark-skinned, exuberant workers, with their white handkerchiefs knotted in four corners on their heads, were inspirational. Dad rarely pursued the payment of his legal fees, but to square the ledger and preserve honour Guiseppe and Paulo insisted we visit them at home on the farm so they could fill the car with watermelons, rockmelons, capsicums and pickled produce. Everyone loved these excursions. We all laughed and tried to speak Italian, miming admiration for the size of the produce and the startling taste of the pickles. We spoke the Esperanto of enthusiasm, pride and joy in the struggle and the achievement of these remarkable survivors. Little wonder that I now espouse a belief in excellence as an egalitarian ideal. It is ageless, genderless, culture-free and pervasive. Perhaps luck plays a part in offering inspiring glimpses of excellence in the ordinary dramas of everyday life.

THE CHALLENGE OF NEW WAYS OF THINKING

It hurts to change your mind. It can be painful to shift your thinking and feeling to see that whatever was held sacred and inviolable as an ideal or construct might actually be wrong or ill-advised. It hurts to admit you might have expended time and energy on a person, an ideal, a mission or a commitment that ultimately proved less than gratifying. But that's just the values and constructs built upon the seemingly loftiest ideals. The others, the vague and slippery ones – they're actually easy to give up. They admit defeat under pressure.

A cautionary tale

Imagine growing up in a family where parents with the best interests of their children at heart, warn their offspring to avoid green-haired people at all costs. The advice is sustained and seemingly astute. 'Such people are known to be prone to violence and utterly untrustworthy. We are a tolerant family but you can't be too careful. Since there are so many good people in the world, don't waste your time on those who are green-haired, but watch their behaviour, and you'll see what we mean. When you watch them carefully they'll become uneasy and probably offer some sign of their proneness to violence. Avoid them particularly when they are in this mood and don't befriend them. You'll notice that they usually keep to themselves or mix only with other green-haired people. They are biased against non-green-haired people'.

One day when you are about seventeen, you are walking home along a suburban street when a carload of youths pulls up beside you and one monster jumps out of the car, knocks you to the gutter, wrenches your bag from your shoulder leaving you dazed, injured, angry and penniless. You vaguely notice that the youths are *not* green-haired. But the person leaning over you inquiring about your injuries *is* green-haired. He's a trainee ambulance driver who knows how to treat shock. You feel grateful, vulnerable and very relieved, particularly as you saw the car turning back towards you until the offenders noticed your helper. Right now green hair doesn't matter at all. But later in that week as you think over the incident, you begin to wonder whether your parents have been very wrong about green-haired people. The shock of the mugging recedes in significance, to be overtaken by shock of another kind. How do you make sense of your internal conflict?

The wiring in your mind that has so ably allowed you to function in a congruent way, suddenly lets you down. New evidence challenges your equilibrium. You can't avoid the pain of the challenge since your feelings and thoughts are not easily pacified. You talk to friends about their encounters with green-haired people but they're not really interested. They don't have anything to do with them, if it can be helped. You can't talk to your family. They are embarrassed that your rescuer was green-haired but there is always an exception to the rule. Meanwhile you remember the concern, generosity and empathy of your Good Samaritan. Worst of all, you can imagine falling in love with a green-haired person. Imagine how that would go down in the family! 'Look what happened to Uncle Walter who married a green-haired woman 30 years ago. The family never forgave him. Do you want to finish up like that? We're just giving you the benefit of our experience. Don't take risks, you'll live to regret it. Besides, you won't be mugged again'.

Nor will you ever forget the bliss of being cared for in a moment of great need.

It hurts to change your mind, just as it hurts to adhere to incongruent concepts. Our nerve endings don't like to be jangled by erratic impulses. Bodies react painfully to psychic upheaval. We feel grief as we contemplate giving up some dearly held belief. We befriend our beliefs. To lose them can create anxiety and fear. We can agonise over changing our minds because it means changing a significant part of ourselves. And it is hard to do that kind of changing alone. Abseiling over a cliff above a ravine for the first time might match the courage required to change your mind. There is always the danger that those who urge us to change our minds or abseil above ravines, might never have done it themselves. Ideally you need experts in that art of human development as empathic mentors.

IDENTIFYING AND PROMOTING EMPATHY

I am often asked how we recognise an empathically intelligent person. I'll resist the temptation to give an obscure and complex answer and suggest a quick initial guide. I have noticed over the many years that I have been researching this subject, that empathically intelligent people often demonstrate a lively sense of humour. They can read the sub-texts of situations, they perceive incongruities and possibilities quickly and they don't take themselves too seriously. Often they can sense how to use humour to shift the emotional paralysis or gravity of some situations. This is not to suggest that every person with a sense of humour will necessarily be empathically intelligent, compassionate and just! Rather I suggest that when you are seeking a person with the kind of intelligence required for complex interpersonal tasks, one with a sense of humour is worth considering more closely.

Once we have identified empathic intelligence as a special kind of inter-intrapersonal ability, we can begin to promote and research it. The culture that eschews empathic intelligence, paralyses its individuals, or, at worst, annihilates them – as history, past and recent, shows. Devastating wars have been fought because one group of people saw another group of people as so threatening or different to them as to deserve extinction. I am not so idealist as to suggest empathic intelligence will promote world peace. Of course, it alone cannot promise that. But it can make it easier to see shared human feelings as superordinate to cultural or tribal differences.

Shakespeare's plays have survived the centuries and been translated into many languages other that the original English in which they were written, because he dramatised the acting out of universal human emotions and the dilemmas they create. Love, hate, rage, envy, shame, disgust, elation, fear and longing lead us into more difficulties, conflicts and resolutions than any amount of rational thought. Artists, musical composers, sculptors, dancers, dramatists and poets communicate to our aesthetic sensitivities. Some scientists, too, like Richard Dawkins (1998) attempt to understand the interface between rational and metaphoric thought. There seems to be increasing confidence that the different ways we can experience and symbolise the world can share a parity of esteem. Science and poetry can co-exist as complementary ways of knowing and experiencing the world. Such collaborative sharing of the territories of wisdom augurs well for the future.

Genocide is an attempt to kill not only the members of a race, but any memory of their existence. This is encapsulated in the phrase 'wiping them off the face of the earth'. Faces are unique and reflect individuality. They can mirror feelings, intelligences and racial and cultural differences. They can both reveal and conceal. The desire to 'save face' defends individuals from the tortures of shame. Ethical and empathic intelligence can protect individuals and groups from potential abuse of the vulnerability driving the need to save face. It educates its aspirants in the literacy of reading voices, faces, spaces and interpersonal energy fields. In so doing, empathic intelligence can explain and expand the cosmos of psychic space. That metaphoric architecture has an embodied existence with foundations, facades and internal structures. These are developed throughout a lifetime of reflection as experiences are internalised, structured and embodied through the process of making sense of them. Needless to say, not everyone engages in such processes.

Spectators can choose to watch events for the transitory entertainment they offer, or they can choose to participate as engaged spectators seeking to determine something of significance from the experience. The former attitude might record the event in memory; the latter attitude might record the experience in a deeply embodied way incorporating thoughts and feelings. Performers watching others perform, whether in sports or dance or drama, can draw upon their embodied memories of similar experiences in an empathic way. Those uninitiated into that particular performance skill can sometimes access their memories of parallel experiences in a challenging feat of empathic intelligence.

The ability to imaginatively apply parallel experiences to new ones can be developed through skilful mentoring. For example, performers such as Olympic athletes, professional dancers, actors, educators and others who wish to make a transition from one arena of excellence to another need mentors to assist the transition phase. Mentors with empathic intelligence can recognise the particular skills, attitudes and psychological attributes that enhanced the performers' current success and scaffold the transition phase appropriately. Highly-developed individuals in all kinds of human achievements need to sustain a level of performance commensurate with their established self-constructs. It may not be as simple as maintaining a public profile or hearing shouts of approval from fans, as feeling a sense of self-development and sustaining challenge. If human development is conceived as an expanding spiral reaching to infinite space, plateaus en route outlive their function if periods of essential rest turn to periods of enforced inertia. Experiences that thwart potential for psychic development can provoke despair. Highly-performing individuals need protection from this possibility.

For the performer who can no longer engage in a particular sport or skill, the transition might well be imagined as a simple move from one physical space to another, mirrored by a more complex shift in personal construct of self, and the creation of new psychological and emotional spaces. It is anticipated that careers in the future will require adaptability to changing career structures and places of work. The ability to function with empathic intelligence not only opens up career opportunities for those involved in training the trainers and providing counselling on careers re-structuring, it can also give professionals a competitive edge in managing their own careers.

It is an enticing fantasy that within the dynamics of the space described here, excellence is inspired. It could well be that such a fantasy one day proves to be a reality.

HYPOTHETICALS

- You have been called for jury duty for a particularly difficult criminal trial. What human behaviour do you find almost unforgivable? Consider a scenario where you might well want to find a way to forgive that behaviour. If you are having trouble finding such a scenario, imagine that the perpetrator of that behaviour is the most beloved person in your life.

- You are in a position of authority in an organisation and you receive a complaint of bullying by a person whom you like, admire, and consider very fair. Part of dealing with this issue involves your raising the matter with this person. Compose the start of the conversation you will have with them.

- In conversation with you in a school setting, a child reveals that her father has mistreated an animal. The child seems to lack any sense of concern or abhorrence at the reported behaviour. How do you deal with this situation?

- In a leadership position you are trying to create a more intelligently caring organisation. You discover that some key personnel are undermining your efforts, spreading rumours about your own behaviour. While you have no real cause to be concerned about the rumours, the rumours have no basis in fact, but they are creating difficulties in developing an appropriate culture. What do you do?

- Imagine you are the primary carer for an elderly mother. You understand how strongly your mother feels about maintaining autonomy in old age. Recently your mother has begun to lose her memory and is demonstrating behaviour which could put her health and safety at some risk. Other family members suggest to you that it is time for your mother to be placed in a nursing home. They tell you that you need to put your own needs ahead of hers. You feel very strongly that were your mother able to express an opinion, she would say she preferred to stay home as long as possible. What is an intelligently caring response to this dilemma? How do you know that you are not simply identifying with your mother rather than representing your point of view (that is, I wouldn't want to go into a nursing home)?

- Imagine an adolescent daughter wants to attend a sleep-over party at the home of your partner's boss. You suspect that alcohol will be consumed at the sleep-over, but you are assured that the parents will be present in the house. Against your partner's wishes, you ring the parents to check and discover that they are intending to be absent for a couple of hours during the evening. You feel highly anxious about the level of supervision but your daughter and partner are pressuring you to ignore the issue. What is the intelligently caring solution to this dilemma?

FURTHER READING

Arnold, R (2004) *How the Arts Impact Learning: Empathic Intelligence and Brain Based Research*, Paper presented at the 5th International Drama & Theatre in Education (IDEA), Ottawa, Canada, July.

—— (2004) *Empathy – the Museums' Missing Link?* Paper presented at the Museums and Galleries Foundation of NSW in collaboration with the Museum of Sydney and The Biennale of Sydney, June.

Barone, T (2000) *Aesthetics, Politics and Educational Inquiry: Essays and Examples*, Peter Lang Publishing, New York.

Cardman, M (2003) Smaller schools foster 'caring climate', Survey. *Education Daily*, 36 (79): 1–2.

Carreiro King, I (2003) Examining middle school inclusion classrooms through the lens of learner-centered principles, *Theory into Practice*, 42 (2): 151–157.

Wrightsman, L (1991) Interpersonal trust and attitudes towards human nature. In Robinson, JP, Shaver, PR & Wrightsman, LS (eds.) *Measures of Personality and Social Psychological Attitudes*, Academic Press, San Diego, CA, pp. 373–412.

CHAPTER SEVEN

CREATING EMPATHICALLY INTELLIGENT ORGANISATIONS

In a sense, it is easier to change an individual than a group but it is also a reality that most individuals are living, learning and working in groups with others. This chapter considers how empathic cultures are developed and nurtured to enhance the lives of individuals and the functioning of groups. Keeping in mind the concept of mirroring, groups can modulate the behaviour of individuals just as individuals can influence the behaviour of groups. When you consider the complex mix of personal histories, individual expectations, hopes, abilities and needs of any group of individuals, it is powerful individuals who can influence change and behaviour but they need the commitment and support of the group to do so.

NEGOTIATING THE RULES OF PROFESSIONAL BEHAVIOUR

I expect that readers who have come this far in the book have done so because they feel comfortable with the themes explored. You might want to effect some changes in personal or professional relationships, spheres of influence or working environment. You are, most likely, an enthusiastic, empathic, engaging and expert leader in an educational or other setting. I include in such settings those parts of any organisation committed to professional development. You are probably looking to enhance your inspirational abilities and your influence. While it is important that those in influential roles reflect upon their own leadership and self-esteem issues, in private or with trusted confidants, it is also important that appropriate professional boundaries are understood and maintained. An empathic workplace, school, hospital or community has to function primarily for the benefit of those whom it serves. The setting of personal goals and the working out of personal dilemmas must always be secondary.

It will take more than reading to create the conditions for personal and professional development, but reading can be both a soothing and a stimulating experience. Reading soothes when it helps us to resolve issues that have been bothering us. We begin to see a pattern to, or reason for, experiences. It stimulates when it challenges us to test out its insights in our own life. Talking and writing about experience can deepen emotional and cognitive development. Writing has several advantages over talking: we can act as our own indefatigable audience in writing, speculate, try out hypotheses, test-run theories and deepen our understanding in the process. We wear others out with our stories long before we wear out ourselves! It is absolutely healthy and functional to be fascinated with our own existence: it's just boring for others if we can't express our fascinations in artistic, engaging ways. Personal writing, like journal writing, is a gift for those who want to discover the patterns and meanings of life.

Of course, it is essential that those engaged in educating, supporting, serving or mentoring others feel inspired, emotionally safe, intellectually stimulated and professionally prepared. But it is not the responsibility of the workplace to tolerate or support behaviours or attitudes that are, frankly, self-serving or detrimental to the well-being of the group. Sometimes the notion of an empathic community can be misinterpreted to mean everyone's personal needs have to be addressed before work can proceed. That would lead to a dysfunctional community in no time. I have written elsewhere (Arnold 1993) about what happened when a participant in a group misread the purpose of an exercise in role-playing and analysing an empathic situation. I argued there that essentially, the group leader has to recognise and refocus the group should an individual 'hijack the stage' for self-serving purposes.

Fortunately, since the days of playing in childhood most of us have been negotiating the rules of behaviour and relationships in groups. Notions of 'fair play' are well internalised in most constructively functioning groups. The dynamics of family, corporate and community life tend to re-play or challenge, in a most sophisticated way, the power games, negotiations, cooperation and competition, defeats and triumphs, observable in embryonic form in any playground. That is, even in childhood we have probably experienced, albeit in childish form, interpersonal dynamics similar to those we encounter later in life. A major difference between the childhood and adulthood experiences is that in childhood we would have been less reflective and aware of the nature of such dynamics. The emotional impact leaves its traces, nonetheless. With maturity, adults can recognise and understand such dynamics, and make choices about appropriate action.

The thinking/feeling dynamic at work

The compelling thing about human maturity is that the impulses propelling it never quite give up. It is uncomfortable to hear that, even as we approach death, there is the potential for growth. Yet so many wise people claim that such is the case, you have to consider it as a possibility. You'd think your growth processes would leave you alone then – quietly anticipating 'the rest in peace' – but the life force deems otherwise. In the spiral model for development proposed earlier, the extent of potential development is infinite. The embodied individual is central to development. So the better we understand how we embody, compose, express and understand our embodied selves, and how others impact on that process, the greater the impetus we give to our own development. When it is functioning at its best, our rational mind tells us to smooth the dynamics between feelings and thoughts by paying attention to the evidence of their functioning inside us. There is no better laboratory for the experiment of living, notwithstanding the courage it takes to befriend our complex, difficult inner world and self.

Should you doubt the scientific respectability of a theory that espouses the efficacy of a dynamic between thought and feeling, listen to Damasio's (1994) view on theory and science in brain/mind research:

> I have a difficult time seeing scientific results, especially in neurobiology,

194 *Empathic Intelligence*

as anything but provisional approximations, to be enjoyed for a while and discarded as soon as better accounts become available (p. xx).

I wish I could say that we know with certainty how the brain goes about the business of making mind, but I cannot – and, I am afraid, no one can ... I hasten to add that the lack of definitive answers on brain/mind matters is not a cause for despair, and is not to be seen as a sign of failure of the scientific fields now engaged in the effort ... The principal reason for the delay – one might even say the only reason – is the sheer complexity of the problems for which we need answers (p. 258).

Or reflect on cosmologist Stephen Hawking's (1988) concluding paragraph to his best selling book *A Brief History of Time:*

If we do discover a complete theory, it should in time be understandable in broad principle by everyone, not just a few scientists. Then we shall all, philosophers, scientists, and just ordinary people, be able to take part in the discussion of why it is that we and the universe exist. If we find the answer to that, it would be the ultimate triumph of human reason – for then we would truly know the mind of God.

In the meanwhile, imagination, art and science continue to contribute to our understanding of the human condition. Tellingly, Damasio concludes *Descartes' Error* with a reference from Tolstoy's *Anna Karenina* (1873–77), implicitly affirming the function of narratives in understanding life, and the research role of novelists and poets who can generalise from experience to offer us creative insights about life and relationships. While the nature of such endeavours might challenge traditional notions of formal research, the discoveries encapsulated and symbolised in cultural forms and art have the advantage of engaging listeners, viewers and readers in an experience of discovery that eschews debates about continuities between brain and mind. Neurobiology takes us a long way towards understanding how brains work but careful qualitative research colours and frames brain scans in unique ways. The mystery inherent to the imagined space between brain and mind is every bit as tantalising to modern explorers of the mind as the infinite spaces of the outer cosmos.

It is worth repeating here that the purpose of empathic intelligence in action is to improve the emotional and intellectual functioning of groups committed to a common purpose. There is evidence from a long-term study of literacy development with adolescents that such an approach has positive outcomes (Arnold, 1991; Nicolson, 1997). A move to this philosophical policy and practice is not even particularly risky, if there is sufficient goodwill and expertise among those influencing the development.

A HYPOTHETICAL LEADERSHIP SCENARIO

Let's imagine a workplace situation and see how the ideas come into play. Imagine you are heading up a small business such as a corporate events company. Your company wins contracts with law firms, insurance firms, arts organisations, university faculties (wealthy ones!) and a few individuals, to manage all the work surrounding particular 'one-off' events – events like a three-day conference for senior executives whose international partners are coming to town for that occasion. Your company has to look after all arrangements to do with the three days – venue bookings, flowers for the keynote speakers, fluffy toy koalas (for visitors to Australia). (I guess 39-flavour jellybeans for US counterparts and Royal guardsmen magnets for those from the UK would also be needed). You can imagine what's involved.

Your company is profitable, relatively stable and you don't really need to implement change right at this moment, but something about the idea of empathic leadership appeals to you. But why would you want to change anything? You are mindful that you are in a risky business to the extent that there are always personnel changes in your client companies and someone, one day, might just decide to try a rival company. Even if that threat doesn't materialise, this idea of empathic leadership might just add value, somehow, to the company. It is a bit like what you do anyway, and with your son coming into the business when he finishes his degree, it's something he'd be able to develop further. (He's full of talk about new management styles. The 'old man' has a few ideas of his own). Yes, it's worth a try so how do you go about it?

It is worth noting here that I have chosen an example of a leader who is already successful but who is also in a position to explore an approach compatible with his management style anyway. This is important because empathic leadership cannot work in a hostile environment. It cannot be imposed from above. It has to evolve in an organisation through cooperation and collaboration. The leader has to feel there are enough people and processes already in place to support the change. It is also worth noting that at this point the leader is not imagining that the company will see a percentage increase in contracts six months after the change is mooted. The motivation to strengthen the company ready for succession, particularly as a son is the likely successor, is a deeply personal, and important reason for change – notwithstanding the playful rivalry adding colour to the scene.

Leading workplace change

As the leader of this organisation, the motivation for change must come from you, but the processes have to involve every part of the organisation as quickly as possible. Let's start with your strengths as the hypothetical leader of the company described above. What is it about your personality that makes you an effective head of an organisation? Perhaps you are deeply committed to this kind of work because you like being in the heart of the buzz around town. You enjoy positive relationships with leaders in other industries and corporations. You can mobilise people to give time and energy to the company and you like the excitement of 'one-off' events. You believe that you have a rich inner life. You enjoy your work but have learned early on in your career to balance work with outside interests. Although your sponsorship of the ballet company links with your work, your patronage of a couple of young dancers has given you an understanding of the discipline and artistry required for success in that field. You thought you'd be the only businessman to enrol in a continuing education course on *Art in Florence* but found an unlikely colleague had made the same choice. You are glad you don't fit the stereotype of an unimaginative, single-minded businessman – if such a person exists!

The company is in good shape but you'd like to think of expanding into franchises one day and if this idea works, you'd have more to sell to the franchisees. Besides, you work well with your son and he'd come into the company with a brief to implement the changes as your likely successor. He won't want to seem to be just stepping into his father's shoes. He is the first person to win over to the idea. 'He's always talking about how much he enjoys working with people who "can see the other guy's point of view". Though he'd kill me for saying it, he's like his mother … feels things deeply … gets taken in a bit sometimes. I, on the other hand … '

Now the focus has shifted in the scenario from a leader functioning alone, to a leader who knows he has to seek an ally in the cause. In this case it is his son, to begin with, but it could be a close colleague or a group of colleagues. Note that the leader is not afraid to move towards a succession plan for the company. No time frame has to be set for that yet. It could be years away. But the plan is evolving and the leader wants to play a significant role in the change process, not necessarily because he'll be the major beneficiary of such change. At this stage the benefits are not absolutely clear-cut but if the company is effective and exceptionally pleasant to deal with, the dollars will most likely follow. Since this is a 'people business', improved interpersonal relationships within and without the company, sounds like the way to go. The leader sounds like someone who is attracted to improving dynamics within the company because of the synchronicity between the nature of the business and the internal dynamics. The leader may not necessarily think to articulate that connectedness, but the inspirational leader knows from experience that it exists.

Our leader is ready to talk to someone, either his son and/or a couple of his close colleagues. He might consider bringing in a change management team or he might want to talk with his personnel manager or team about possibilities. He decides he'll give the idea three months to take hold in the company. He expects that by the end of three months, everyone in the company will be aware of moves to enhance the company's culture through a process of 'empathic leadership'.

You might imagine that at first there is uncertainty among staff who might characterise the change as 'that feel-good stuff'. In the coffee room you'd expect to hear comments reflecting nervousness like: 'Now we can all expect red roses on the desk in the mornings'. Once word is out that change is afoot, the leader and his team need to communicate openly and frankly with staff. A leader serious about developing empathic leadership as part of a group culture has to speak directly to the staff. He has to be prepared to explain the reasons for his commitment and he has to accept that in so doing he must tolerate the inevitable vulnerability of facing staff himself in order to communicate his belief in this idea. That can be a tough call for a leader whose usual mode of communication is written, infrequent and safe. It doesn't matter if the leader decides to ask an expert in the field to explain some of the theory and its background, but his own commitment to the philosophy supporting the change has to be heard first hand. If a briefing session of staff is called, the leader needs to give his closest colleagues some role in that briefing session. This allows staff to see that there is unanimity at the top.

The leader could introduce the theme of the session with something along these lines:

'As you know I have been involved in the development of this company for the past thirty years. We are all familiar with our acknowledged strength in the field of corporate events management and we enjoy a reputation as one of the leaders in the field. As I said at our Christmas party last year, much of that success comes from the fact that we work well together as a team and we have relatively low staff turnover. Things are going well and there is nothing to suggest that will not continue'.

'I know you have heard that I and the leadership team are considering some proactive developments within the company. I say proactive because there is no immediately compelling reason to consider change, except that with a relatively positive workplace environment and a healthy bottom line, I am prepared to put something back into the company in a rather unusual way. I'd like to focus on the ways we think we are an empathic company, and work on elaborating that concept more fully into our relationships with each other and our clients'.

'Now I can hear you thinking "What's empathic … this is not a hospital … we don't have to nurse each other … can I bring my mother to work tomorrow … or my dog, she hates staying alone at home". I've asked Dr Strong to come along today to give you a brief outline of her notion of empathic intelligence with some case histories of how it has worked in service industry companies similar to ours. I have to admit that before I read a bit about empathic intelligence and heard a couple of experts discuss its benefits and applications, I was a bit sceptical too'.

'I am committing some professional development resources to this idea so you will all have an opportunity to attend a workshop in company time on understanding and developing plans around this issue. Because this is an innovative form of change, we have invited a Business Studies Masters student to use this company as a case study for her thesis. We will also be presenting reports on these developments in various business forums and you will be invited to take part in these if you wish. At best, this company will become known as not only successful, but innovative, forward looking, profitable, stable, strongly ethical and a site of professional development within the industry. Even if the changes we propose are slow and somewhat minimal, the relationships between staff will be enhanced and that has personal benefits in terms of well-being and corporate morale'.

'You know I am somewhat conservative. I don't change quickly or easily myself. But as I understand empathic intelligence, I see it in evidence within the company anyway. Enthusiasm, goodwill, respect for constructive relationships, ethical policies and practices, characterise our workplace. I want you to see the evidence too, and build on what you see and experience. Building on these qualities we can become more conscious of thinking and acting sensitively towards each other and our clients. It won't feel good all the time, but we'll analyse the mistakes, tolerate them, and learn from them. That, essentially, is what you are being asked to do in committing to this evolution. The more I talk about this proposed development, the more enthusiastic I become. I hope you begin to feel the same way when you have a chance to hear about the thinking behind, or philosophy, of empathic intelligence'.

Unpacking the strategies

Of course, hypothetical situations never quite fit any particular real situation, but you can imagine the context I am describing. This script is not meant to be a formula. It is simply composed to convey something of the affective quality and strategies an empathic leader might communicate in seeking to capture the attention and goodwill of colleagues. The company director or leader, above, speaks to colleagues with respect (hard to convey just from reading this script, but present in a speaker's tone of voice, body language, obvious preparedness). Such a leader also speaks with authority. That authority comes in part from the colleagues' long-term impressions of that leader, but also here, from the vision he is seeing for the future, from his implicit recognition that the company is only as good as the combined talents and motivations of its personnel, and from the leader's frankness about the purposes of this proposed development. Such frankness has the benefit of mirroring back to listeners their capacity for sound judgment about the blend of corporate and personal benefits this change might promote. Listeners are rarely bluffed for long with false promises, but they are more likely to respond positively to a leader who understands the culture of the organisation and accepts responsibility for effecting improvements.

There are a couple of quite deliberate strategies built into this introduction. Key words such as, 'enthusiasm, goodwill and constructive relationships' are introduced. Words such as 'empathic intelligence' and 'philosophy' are cued, or introduced in a context that hints at their meaning, without being patronising. High-level words do not have to be avoided in audiences presumed to include a variety of educational levels. Most people are well capable of guessing at new meanings if the context is enabling. In educational settings, this form of 'scaffolding' or providing people with enough clues to get things right, is a common and effective teaching and learning method. It has the particular advantage of offering the learner the 'flush of success'. It also cuts right across any power games a teacher or leader might be tempted to play by controlling knowledge or the processes of learning.

This sensitive leader is mindful that listeners can only take in a limited amount of information in this kind of setting. He also knows he must relate warmly but professionally to staff whose goodwill is essential to his project. This has to be an engaging warm-up to set the tone for what follows. Unless the leader is already accomplished in thinking constructively and engaging others warmly, this would not be the time to start practising communication skills. Further, people in organisations learn as much from the implicit modelling provided by their leaders, as they do from formal courses. It is hard to develop credibility in a person-orientated business if you cannot model best practices in communicating and relating – a form of integrity commonly called 'walking the talk' or 'practising what you preach'.

It is very likely that a leader attracted to adding value to a company by improving the quality of its personnel and client interpersonal relationships, has selected a number of staff over time who would be responsive to this kind of leadership. Obviously, leaders tend to select for their teams, people who will fit well with the prevailing culture, or they bring in new people to attempt to influence that culture in some way. It would not be impossible for a shift to an empathic culture to arise from below within the company rather than from the top, but such a shift would have to be endorsed by the effective policy makers at some point. If those policy makers in the group are threatened by change, then it will be sabotaged. Because of the special nature of empathic leadership, it is vulnerable to sabotage through bullying, scorn, passive resistance and all the other power games threatened people engage in.

> Necessary conditions for implementing an empathically intelligent organisation:
- a critical mass of self-reflective, well-integrated individuals committed to growth/change;
- a supportive community of engaged, life-long learners/experiencers;

- commitment to a collective 'good';
- compelling vision (shared narrative/memory);
- self–other – sustaining strategies (for individuals and the group);
- realistic goals; and
- capacity to disengage/disable toxic influences.

CHANGING WORKPLACE CULTURES

Only when there is a critical mass of constructive counter-influence (this can be a significant number of people or effective and strategically placed people) can an empathic culture develop. What can happen is that those who don't like what they see happening, for whatever reasons, and feel powerless to prevent it, begin to seek ways out. It can be hard for some people to realise that once change begins to influence the culture, whether positively or otherwise, nothing ever goes back to the way it was. It is organically impossible. Interestingly, those most resistant to change are, by definition, most unsettled by the thought of having to find a new position. They passionately want things to remain the same and they paralyse themselves with their anxiety. In spite of their protests about how glad they'd be to leave, and how hopeless everything's becoming, if the company wants to retain that staff member, now would be the time to ask a sophisticated and empathic human resources manager or vocational psychologist to offer collegial support. The purpose of the support can be to assist the person to adapt to change or to leave with dignity and sense of autonomy intact. Either outcome benefits all parties.

If the introduction of plans to develop a company's culture are well enough received by staff, there will be some interest, even excitement (along with resistance, perhaps) among those with enthusiasm. It is important to mobilise those feelings into action. Now the staff can be guided to make plans such as conducting some research into aspects of their own workplace practices that might be assessed and changed. The process of conducting this audit (research might be a less intimidating word) can, of itself, generate positive outcomes if it is conducted in a non-threatening way. It is crucial that staff avoid confronting others about their behaviour, attitudes or practices. Ways have to be found to allow people to recognise what is happening in their groups without apportioning blame. Skilful group leaders are needed to model this approach. Even the nastiest person in the company (how did s/he survive so long?) has a right to protection from humiliation. Our purpose is to work towards a psychologically safe workplace to allow creativity and high order thinking to surface. Let the nasty one work out what s/he has to do to adapt to this change. Someone just has to watch to ensure that he/she is not sabotaging the process. If there is a persistent problem, it needs to be addressed privately and by a person in authority. An empathic workplace does not have to accommodate saboteurs.

COMMUNICATING WELL TO BUILD COMMUNITIES

One of the most powerful influences on workplace culture is the nature of communication, both written and spoken, predominant within it. Think of the times you have phoned someone and guessed immediately how they are feeling from their tone of voice. Or the impression you've gleaned of a company or institution from the voice quality of the person answering the phone. It is amazing how much information is conveyed through tone of voice. Subtle shifts in mood are perceptible, as well as age, gender, ethnicity, socio-economic background, education. So too is anxiety, calmness, energy, disaffection, sincerity or phoneyness! We tend to imagine we sound much the same most of the time. But discuss this with your intimates and they'll let you know how much they can 'read' from the variations in your voice. It is actually quite difficult to disguise emotions when speaking, as very good actors will confirm. At every level in an organisation, tones of voice communicate and influence its interpersonal dynamics.

An important factor to pay attention to in an empathic community is the emotional quality of voices. The personality quality of warmth or coldness is conveyed through voice. Are people encouraging or threatening others through tone of voice? Are those with the most engaging voices working in parts of the organisation where their voices can be an asset? You don't need a degree in linguistics to recognise that fact (though it can help for close analyses of work-place communications). Since we first became aware of our mother's voice we have been developing the skill of picking up information from tones of voice. It is both a survival strategy and a highly functional way of understanding some of the complexities of human dynamics. It is important in families, the workplace, hospitals and elsewhere, that people acknowledge the role of language in establishing effective communication styles (Hughes and Hoogstad, 1993).

It is well known that when people are feeling stressed, emotional, anxious or confused, they have great difficulty hearing information or retaining it if they do hear it. Our mind-set and emotional state significantly influence what we hear and remember. This is particularly important to take into account when, for example, information is given to patients in a medical situation or clients in legal contexts. No matter how hard we try to hear accurately and remember important facts or instructions, emotions can block the capacity for accurate processing and recall. Significantly, we seem to have no trouble recalling how we felt about the person who conveyed the information. Emotional responses to others seem to take precedence on such occasions, highlighting the need for message-givers to establish good rapport and empathy as part of the communication. It is essential too that written material, appropriately worded, be given to reinforce the message. In educational settings that takes the form of written summaries; in business the follow-up letter; or in medical contexts, the instruction sheet. All such written communication needs to be scrutinised for its effectiveness, including not only accuracy of information, but tone, length, appearance and 'user-friendliness'.

It is worth remembering that the imperative form of language, such as 'Do not', 'You must not', 'It is forbidden to ... ' tends to turn readers off. They might stop right there and ignore the message. It is better to think of a way to engage the other's cooperation. This can sometimes be achieved by explaining briefly the consequences of the action in question. My local supermarket advertises that the theft of trolleys increases food prices. They ask you to return the trolleys to the holding bays and ring them if trolleys are found in the street. That makes me feel a bit more inclined to do as they ask because it explains the effects on the community of transgressions. The message may not stop the behaviour completely but it would be more effective than a prohibition or threat.

It is also important for organisations to update the language of their written communications because modes of expression change. The image of an organisation is reflected not only through physical spaces, dress codes, logos and typefaces, but also through the style of language used in written communications both within the organisation and to outsiders.

The subjective, dynamic and interpersonal nature of communication means that the way we listen to others is as important as the way we speak to them. Again, we often think we are listening well, but we might not actually be 'hearing' the sub-text of the message. It is possible to hear the content of a message but to be 'tone-deaf' to the masked, but deeply important personal message living below the information. Sometimes we are not ready to hear those messages. We might be already overloaded with our own pressing concerns. It may not be appropriate to respond to some subliminal messages, or the message might be so well masked as to be ambiguous. Or we might want to hear those messages but lack the confidence to interpret them correctly. This is another complex area of human dynamics and those wishing to improve their capacity for attuned listening can work with those whom they trust on clarifying the nature of such messages through 'play-back' or feedback sessions. English and Drama educators are specialists in developing these capacities.

Even without a full-scale commitment to an analysis of the written and spoken communication within an organisation, by increasing awareness of its importance you begin to start the change process. An easy starting point is the public notices to staff on bulletin boards, tearooms, store cupboards and washrooms. If they remind anyone of authoritarian school days they should be removed.

An empathic environment is built on respect for individuality, positive collegial relationships and appropriate measures of autonomy. This is not achieved by pretending that everything runs smoothly and happily all the time. But the empathic leader knows to tolerate insignificant shortcomings, provided there is a group and individual commitment to excellence, and constructive plans for improvement. Within a group most people know, even if they don't admit it, the quality of personnel morale and the level of productive functioning in the place. They know because people constantly signal to each other, either directly or through codes of behaviour, how they feel about the workplace. In a workplace suffering from problems with bullying, newspaper cuttings about workplace bullying were mysteriously left in photocopying rooms. Unusual patterns of sick leave or absenteeism often signal low morale. Morale cannot be mandated. It is a response to the long-term feelings influencing those in the environment. If there is great secrecy about the functioning of an institution and people are speaking in whispers and behind closed doors, things are bad. Fear and anxiety eventually lead to stagnation.

EMPOWERING COMMUNICATION

Inspirational leaders know how to intervene in a stalemate and negotiate commitment to change. They can tolerate the expressions of anger that might follow initial attempts to hear how staff feel about things. The courage and insight it takes to invite constructive feedback, and to tolerate, within limits, the emotions that might be expressed, actually signal a respect for shared responsibility for improved morale and better workplace practices. It takes courage to hear unpalatable truths and it is frightening to be within range of an angry person. It takes insight to know that by listening to an angry person in a non-judgmental way, some of the anger is articulated and soothed. Notice what happens when angry people come to the end of their rage. They take a deep breath. That in itself is relaxing. It is both a physiological need and an expression of relief. Were you to ask them to repeat the performance, they just couldn't do it again with the same emotional force. Much of the anger is spent.

In less intense situations where people are simply irritated, bored and edgy, there is a similar need for someone to address the reasons for their disaffection. Once people begin to talk about the interpersonal dynamics in a constructive context such as a semi-formal meeting with a unit head or a group meeting called for a specific purpose, they become involved in the process of change. Talking about a situation of which we are part inevitably involves us further in it. We commit without really being aware of it, and we also express the thoughts and feelings that can provide the basis for constructive analysis, understanding and change. Provided a leader recognises the need to protect the self esteem of those who speak up, even in difficult or threatening situations, and can model for the group non-confrontational, blame-free analysis of dynamics and communication, improved group or interpersonal functioning can be expected.

Listening to young women in senior school years discussing the group dynamics of their classrooms and social interactions, I have found that the details they observe about their own, the teachers' and their peers' behaviour and motivations are remarkable. They are unerringly accurate and precise in their judgments, leaving little room for anyone to conceal imperfections or anxieties, including the teachers. As a researcher I have wondered whether the talk functions to exacerbate group tensions or to resolve them. Leaders sometimes wonder whether it is better to ignore problems or to open them up to analysis and discussion. Certainly in past decades there was a prevailing fear that to talk about a taboo behaviour, such as sex, would encourage people to engage more vigorously in that behaviour. The primitive fantasy that secrets, desires and power are interdependent is strong in the memory of my generation.

I am aware that when I listen to today's young women frankly discussing subjects that remained private when I was an adolescent, some residual anxiety about taboos is stirred in me. Yet when I observe how empowered and resolute these young women (and men) become through the process of facing reality, accepting its challenges and searching for personal and interpersonal strengths to manage their lives, I can only feel grateful. I realise that as things continue to evolve in family life, social life and education, humans gradually develop intelligent ways to adapt, and some even become pro-active. The young women I have been observing and listening to, will enter the workforce with experience in understanding and negotiating complex interpersonal dynamics. Some of them will have well developed empathic intelligence. The workplace will have to meet their preparedness. I hope their male peers are equally well prepared for a shift towards high level interpersonal communication, driven by empathic intelligence.

Our ability to communicate with others, to hear what they say, to understand simple and complex, written and visual texts, influences profoundly our sense of self-worth, autonomy, and enjoyment of the world. Those who cannot read, write, listen and speak effectively risk feelings of inadequacy, shame, frustration and even rage. You can't enjoy a feeling of agency and autonomy if you can't communicate well with others or understand the communicative codes around you. Reflect on a time when you felt enraged by some incident (think of the aggressive driver who swerved in front of you on a road, risking an accident and terrifying your passenger-children, or the one who swerved to take the spot you were heading for, forcing you to 'gridlock' the intersection). You are lost for words and would like to shake sense into the offending driver. You might even wish the offending driver would suffer harm to learn a lesson. Your sense of fairness is outraged, and your awareness of the possible consequences of thoughtless driving is acute. Well, that feeling of rage, rare but familiar, is something like the feeling commonly experienced by those who lack functional literacy. Everywhere they turn they are confronted by their inadequacies. To them, it doesn't seem fair that they have been deprived of the opportunity to succeed (even though they might well have had chances in school). For some, the only alternative they see to remedy their low self-esteem is irrational, but self-serving aggression. When words fail, you hit out, act out or demand attention somehow.

While such behaviour is ultimately self-destructive and dysfunctional, unless better forms of communication and expression are learned, the downward spiral to despair is inevitable. Even relentlessly aggressive persons often wish to discover a more functional way of coping with life, as evidenced by the successful programs conducted in prison systems to improve inmates' literacy levels (Nicolson, 1997). Empathically intelligent educators know to respect the pressing emotional needs of poor communicators by using methods which allow them to experience a sense of mastery and effectiveness as quickly as possible. Such educators find some skill, ability or interest that will allow the speaker or writer to demonstrate expertise and enthusiasm. It can be as personal as knowing how to flirt well, or how to fly a kite or as esoteric as how to breed tree frogs. An audience will listen if the speaker has even modest expertise and some enthusiasm. The attention of the audience provides mirroring which endorses the speaker's communicative competence.

At first glance the world of advertising seems to demonstrate empathic intelligence at work. Skilled market analysts understand the emotional needs, attention spans and cognitive abilities of vast public audiences. Of course, one cannot set aside all the philosophical and ethical issues this example raises. And, as I have argued earlier, truly empathic intelligence necessarily entails a degree of altruism and a goal of the common good, or at least mutual benefit. This goal, of course, may well be lacking in many, if not most, advertising campaigns. It is nonetheless worth thinking about the skills inherent in successful advertising. When done well, it effectively integrates written, spoken and aural language, together with visual imagery, for the purpose of influencing behaviour in a particular way, namely encouraging consumers to spend money. When you think how difficult it can be to persuade people to part with money, advertising is surprisingly successful. It has discovered how to eliminate the pain of parting with money by promising a boost to self-esteem through the purchase of particular brands, products or services. A certain drink does not just slake thirst; it signifies exclusive membership of a club of associates who share a desirable lifestyle. The fact that we provide manufacturers with untold millions of dollars of free advertising every time we walk around wearing brand names, escapes our critical scrutiny. We unconsciously collude with the producer to broadcast the word. What can we learn from advertising that is relevant to the concept of empathic intelligence and education?

Fundamentally, advertisers understand our deepest desires. They understand our need to feel loved, esteemed and desired by significant others and our need to feel competent in our roles and our progress in life. If we don't feel healthy, wealthy, wise, witty, youthful and beautiful, help is but a credit card away. Advertisers know how to exploit our fears and offer instant gratification when the emotional patterns of life swing the wrong way. How can education compete with the world of consumerism?

There are some strategies that help. For a start, the anxieties that advertisers play on, realistically can't be assuaged by the purchase of a product. Even gullible adolescents recognise, as they buy today's 'hot' brand, that tomorrow a new one will compete for their dollars. They do know that even while one anxiety – such as group acceptance – can be soothed by the purchase of a desirable product, another anxiety surfaces just as quickly. There is anxiety inherent in supporting the buying habit. In English and humanities classrooms throughout the world, students are learning to address these issues by analysing and reflecting upon the language and images they use and respond to. Empathic educators recognise how different kinds of messages appeal to the thoughts, feelings and value systems of their students. They are trained to construct various learning situations, including peer discussions, to encourage students to develop value systems and communicative patterns that are realistic, constructive, personally developmental and socially responsible.

Family and peer values exert a powerful influence upon communicative and empathic abilities. A school cannot remedy deeply entrenched or dysfunctional patterns of communicating without extensive resources of time and personnel. As part of their brief to develop empathic intelligence, good schools communicate their purposes, rationale and expectations to parents and the community. Such communications go further than simply providing information to the wider community. They can inspire others to support the development of excellence and empathic intelligence and to lend their expertise to the endeavour.

LOOKING AND LISTENING WITH EMPATHIC EXPERTISE

Even though it has a primary purpose of educating its students, a classroom can symbolise a microcosm of a dynamic family or corporate group. It is timely, therefore, to consider now the characteristics of an empathic classroom and its teacher. Consistent with the philosophy of empathic intelligence, such a teacher will be enthusiastic about the profession of education, proficient in particular subject areas of expertise, skilled in knowing the many different ways students learn, familiar with the characteristics of thinking, linguistic, social, emotional and social development, and knowledgeable about individual backgrounds, cultures and stages and rates of development. And just as the leader in the corporate world has to engage his or her followers in changing the culture of the workplace, so too does the empathic educator.

With very young children, educators have to model by example the behaviour and attitudes they expect. They will often draw attention to the cause-effect relationship in interpersonal dynamics through role-plays and games with toys – 'Teddy's feeling sad … he was dropped on the floor'. As students progress through the system, subject knowledge and learning skills tend to dominate the focus of the classroom, as is appropriate to developmental stages. However, if the dynamics of the group are overly competitive, hostile to certain clusters within the group, or disaffected with school, the educator has to establish the emotional well-being of the group before effective pedagogy can occur. It can take skill to do this effectively as a too-open discussion of the emotional dynamics of the group can be counter-productive. It is rather like the 'Gosh, you look dreadful, are you sick?' remark which puts you on the defensive immediately.

Faced with the dilemma of addressing a classroom climate which is antagonistic to learning, educators have to observe and try to understand the power plays and shifts in mood of a class, seeking to find an opportune moment to talk with the students about their feelings towards school, their futures and so on. This can sometimes be started in an English or humanities class by seeking written, private answers to a series of hypothetical questions like: 'Given the chance to construct an ideal school day, what would it consist of?' 'What's the best skill you have ever learned and who helped you learn it?' 'What do you admire or like in teachers?'

A task like this has to be set in a context in which the teacher is seen to be genuinely interested in giving the students an opportunity to reflect on these matters, even though they can keep the details private. The point of the exercise is to acknowledge the importance of their attitudes, past experiences and expectations for the future in the dynamic place of the classroom. If students feel hopeful that a teacher can change a dysfunctional classroom towards something more constructive and enjoyable, they will go along with a task that is consistent with that hope. Sometimes excerpts from literature, history, current affairs, photographs or film clips can be a face-saving way to begin discussions about interpersonal dynamics. Ultimately the focus will shift to the classroom itself, but in the meantime sensitive issues may be explored through the safer medium of the external stimulus. Art, drama, literature, dance and music have helped us through the ages to explore and experience issues, feelings and ideas that may be impossible or difficult to communicate through face-to-face talk.

Empathic teachers can find many different entry points to an exploration of the nature of interpersonal and intrapersonal learning. A source of much disaffection for learning in schools stems from students' feelings that such learning is remote from their interests and needs. Therefore, strategies which centre them in the learning experience, either through personal writing, self-directed projects, art work, structured play (including cooperative and competitive games), metalwork, computer games, drama work, or whatever, can be attractive initially because they offer the student the gratification of feeling engaged, autonomous and optimistic about further benefit. Once there is a pattern of reward established, students will persevere that much longer without immediate gain, in the hope of mastering new skills.

HOPE AND DESPAIR

Learning has to generate hope and it has to be underpinned with hope. Hope seems to trigger the mind's readiness to respond to external stimuli. It inspires us to communicate and to learn. Think how you feel when you meet someone whose company you enjoy. Your face lights up, you reach out to embrace or shake hands, you spontaneously want to talk. The conversation is not planned. It is improvised and energised by the feelings of mutuality and joy. The more heightened feelings of such encounters might be somewhat muted to a simple but pleasurable sense of anticipation, such as you might find in a constructive learning or social situation. Nonetheless, imagination is stimulated and important thinking can occur. Corporations around the globe spend millions of dollars taking staff to resorts to engage in playful, team-building activities to recapture the circumstances of childhood. Creative thinkers know that the role-plays and imaginative play of childhood have a profound effect on children's emotional, social and learning development. Regrettably, in the middle and later years of education, the function of play and imagination is ignored. It may be too late to reactivate it in middle-age because by then scepticism about its worth is firmly entrenched. Hurling oneself down a rapid in a canoe or abseiling down a cliff face is one way to break through the fear of risk-taking, but there are other ways to make such breakthroughs, such as confronting the internal fears about self-worth, acceptance and lovability. The Jesuit poet, Gerard Manley Hopkins who introduced me to the despair of the thwarted or unaffirmed artist, knew about the perils of the mind. In *Carrion Comfort*, he wrote:

> O the mind, mind has mountains; cliffs of fall
> Frightful, sheer, no-man-fathomed.

A depressed infant loses the will to respond to others and to the environment, just as depressed children and adults close off from the world. Eyes lose their lustre and limbs hang from the body. Despair is a hopeless educator. This prevails for the leader as with the educator. It is pointless to instigate empathic pedagogy in an environment antipathetical to its philosophy and purpose. If it is unclear whether the culture is receptive to change, some exploratory conversations can test the climate. There are often some students in a classroom who are happy to chat to the teacher about school issues. If their ideas are sought and respected, they become allies, even covertly, for the cause. An issue that does provoke student interest is that of how teachers might best give constructive and helpful feedback on student work. It is one that interests students across the curriculum and into adult or tertiary learning. It reaches into the home, community and workforce also. It influences self-esteem and concepts of self as a learner. It merits considerable attention in any educative environment that takes seriously its mission to prepare students for life-long learning.

How often are students asked what kinds of feedback really help? What is acted upon? What humiliates? What is encouraging and what is ignored? Can students offer peer responses that are empathic? Can teachers? It is hard to imagine a group of students who could not be enticed into responding to those questions. In my experience, students recognise an educator as truly empathic when he or she seeks student advice on those very issues that are an important part of the dynamics of their relationships with teachers, with each other and with their success as learners. Students know who the good teachers are and they know what good pedagogy feels like. Notwithstanding their tendency (and ours) to seek ready gratification in preference to the outcomes of sustained effort, they are capable of critical judgment, imaginative thinking and empathic intelligence, particularly if it is modelled and valued by significant adults.

TRANSFORMATION AND THE IMPORTANCE OF INTIMACY

Transformation is the word chosen to describe aims, outcomes and achievements of the highest order in quite diverse human endeavours. It generally describes achievements that have not just happened by chance, but as a result of effort, dedication, endurance, thought, reflection, skill, talent and practice. Transformation characterises high-level human achievement but the nature of transformation under discussion here can flourish irrespective of class, background, race or gender. It exists where individuals or groups strive to attain worthwhile goals. The truly excellent individual or team usually eschews elitism and exhibits the humility of greatness. Imbued with the modest recognition that good fortune, opportunity and the support of others play their part in most endeavours, excellence is most inspiring and graceful when it stirs hope in its admirers and emulators. Its generative nature ensures its lasting appeal.

It is unusual to connect transformation and inspiration with intimacy – a concept usually associated with close, personal and private relationships. There is good reason for including intimacy in a book of this nature. Empathic intelligence works through trust, integrity, mutual respect and some risk-taking, the bedrocks of intimacy. It is influential in itself, encouraging those within its ambience to take the risks intrinsic to real learning, while providing face-saving strategies in the event of failure. It can paper the cracks between confidence and fear of failure. It does this because of its human history. Our earliest experiences of intimacy were as infants with a mother. The sense of deep love, bonding, relatedness, warmth and security we experienced then, laid down the basis for the development of all the fundamentally important psychological, emotional, expressive, cognitive and relational aspects of life. Naturally, as we develop through childhood, we experience appropriate patterns of separation from mothers, fathers, and family, seeking relatedness with others, with our culture and with our own meaningful work. Some highly-functioning individuals seek a life imbued with a sense of purpose, integration and meaning. They can experience awe in the contemplation of something beyond the temporal and material. This experience can be like an adult version of the merging, fusion and bliss we imagine a feeding infant feels in close intimacy with its mother's body. For the tiny infant, every physiological, sensory and erotic need is fulfilled, for some precious moments.

Throughout the infancy, childhood and adult life of well functioning people, there are moments filled with awe, and longer periods filled with a sense of purpose, integration and meaning. We hold those moments in our minds and bodies as part of our intrasubjective self. We share our quest for repetition of such experiences through our intimate engagements with others, and through our intimate experiences with the world. We make sense of such experiences through reflection, contemplation, conversation, and inner-voice dialogues with our own subjective selves. For all that such moments are private, and disclosed only to chosen intimates, they also profoundly and inevitably influence our public life, albeit in a tacit way. When unexpected demands interrupt routines or new patterns of response are required, even normal defences or patterns of adaptation can falter. Empathic intelligence can come into play as such times, providing the support and strategies to carry matters forward.

We compose our lives through complex engagements between our inner and outer lives, seeking, ultimately, harmony and transcendence. These are my words. Others will compose their own meanings. Poets, artists, musicians, mathematicians, for example, seek to symbolise their understandings of the physical, emotional and sensory world but they are not unique in their quests. Most highly-functioning individuals seek their own means of understanding, experiencing and composing the engagements between their inner and outer life. It is that quest to seek meaning that requires a familiarity with, and acceptance of our own and others' values, feelings and perceptions. To seek that kind of meaning requires a capacity for intimacy.

I will illustrate my point with a story reported by an empathic friend, Lucy. Some years ago Lucy attended the funeral of the mother of one of her closest friends, Emily. Emily's mother and father had divorced about 25 years previously. Her father had re-married and her mother, Eleanor, had continued to suffer the debilitating mental illness that had blighted her life and their marriage. It so happened that when Emily's father quietly slipped into the funeral parlour on the day of Eleanor's funeral, he sat next to Lucy. Lucy had met him a couple of times at family functions over the years but they barely knew each other. Paul was a very formal, elderly, gentleman who had clearly chosen to pay his respects, with dignity and composure, to Eleanor as the woman he had once married.

Emily's husband, a famous and eloquent speaker who had generously supported and loved Eleanor, delivered a moving account of her sad life of chronic mental illness. Inevitably, in outlining the deceased woman's biography, reference had to be made to the fact that she had once been married to the man now sitting alone, next to Lucy. As Lucy anticipated the moment when the failed marriage would be referred to, she became very aware of her own anxiety, and the stillness of her neighbour, the former husband. The moment was charged with meaning and Lucy was temporarily paralysed with its agonising affect. She felt flooded with the sorrow of life, the poignancy of this particular moment and the solitude of the vulnerable man beside her. She guessed he'd be feeling sad and guilty. Everything was unfolding fast. Lucy felt compelled to console the man in his solitude, yet she knew that she risked intruding upon his privacy. Nobody moved or glanced at him as Paul was named as the former husband, yet it felt as if all eyes were on him. As the person closest to him at that second, Lucy felt she just couldn't let him think he was facing this metaphoric day of judgment alone. Unobtrusively, she searched for his hand and held it tentatively. He was surprised by the gesture but seemingly grateful. He held Lucy's hand affirmingly. Neither he nor Lucy spoke but the connection was mutually affirming.

It is hard to know exactly what gives us the grace to make the right decisions in life's more testing moments, but whatever the source of that grace, it blessed Lucy that day. It gave her the ability to make an informed but risky judgment in the interests of another's welfare. She had to act spontaneously and courageously, relying on little more than informed, intuitive, sensitive guesswork. She could have made a wrong move but she knew herself well enough to think that she could tolerate a mistake, if needs be. Lucy acted with empathic intelligence. The quest to understand that intelligence drives the writing of this book. The more this kind of personal/interpersonal intimacy is talked about and valued as an essential part of human development, the more observable it becomes. Many influential people in leadership positions in education, business, the professions and the arts, along with those influential in interpersonal life, function at this altruistic level. It is an achievable ideal. What sets them apart is their capacity to engage with others in mutually beneficial ways. These ways eschew power for its own sake.

INSPIRATION AND MODELLING

Gerard Manley Hopkins, who wrote towards the end of the nineteenth century, expresses in profoundly moving ways something of the richness and the despair of his particularly intense personal, interpersonal and spiritual life. He is inspiring for his sustained quest to compose his life through poetry writing, even when he was forbidden from publishing it. That deeply spiritual man who found God in nature and in his own creativity, was thwarted in his quest to inspire others with his discoveries. The story of his personal difficulties stands alongside the feelings driving his poetry as sources of inspiration. For most of us, a person, an art work, a book, a building, or some experience has acted as an important inspiration to us at some time. Inspiration empowers us beyond our expectations, as long as hope lives within us. Small children unconsciously imitate their elders, learning in the process that sources of modelling exist within their environs. Their elders find within the culture multiple sources of inspiration and modelling through the processes of analogy and identification. By the kinds of analysis and reflection informed by empathic intelligence, unconscious patterns of modelling can be understood and evaluated.

The leaders, educators and influential readers attracted to this kind of book will most likely be comfortable with the themes elaborated here – that public and professional life should be imbued with the same humanistic values which are helpful in private life. In that sense, the development of a capacity for intimacy is one of the aspirations of a quality education. Students who leave a learning institution with no memory of moments of awe, wonder and excitement about the world of learning and their own capacity to engage with it in pleasurable and meaningful ways, have been short-changed. Ironically, they will not have been short-changed because resources were lacking – it doesn't take material resources to meet the need. They will have been short-changed because no one understood the nature of their learning needs, their tacit abilities, nor how capable they could be in enabling situations. Those with whom they engaged failed to recognise their capacity for awe and their need to be inspired. Those fortunate students who can hold dear the moments that inspired them to learn are equipped to become life-long learners. Even more importantly, they will have embodied learning processes that are likely to influence others.

EXCELLENCE IN THE TWENTY-FIRST CENTURY

In striving for excellence, sometimes transformation is the outcome. Excellence is not an ideal achieved primarily through highly competitive means. It is not an exhaustible commodity, but rather an infinite value that can flourish in cooperative endeavours. For example, in educational settings it is well recognised that educators now need to do much more than impart information to their students. They have to develop and model a wide range of learning methods, including problem-solving and research abilities, cooperative skills, communicative and critical abilities, and technological literacy. Indeed, as information becomes more widely available to a large proportion of the world's population, excellence increasingly means an ability to function effectively in flexible, multi-skilled, high-order ways. Excellence, as it relates to empathic intelligence, is not a matter of knowing more or owning more, but of performing impressively in often complex situations. Excellent performance in education, training and leadership includes knowing how to evaluate constructively the relative merits of competing knowledge, processes and ideals. The route to such excellence is marked by long-term analytic abilities and affective sensibilities.

Judgment, risk-taking, imagination, empathy and the constructive use of power might well characterise the excellent performer in the new millennium. Now that technology is taking care of the transmission of information, there is time, space and the incentive to develop a better understanding of the nature and dynamics of global and personal human relationships. We have the language, the concepts and the insights of previously disparate fields such as biology, physics, medicine, literature, art, philosophy and psychology, to manage human, environmental and material resources more constructively than has ever been achieved in the past. Technology is not capable of being visionary or altruistic, but humans are, and always have been. We are the beneficiaries of past excellence and have a responsibility to ensure we advance that record. Empathic intelligence might well offer a way forward.

While the concept of transformation is all too easily equated with instances of winning in competitive fields, the broader, more generative concept of excellence defined here suggests that excellence might be present even in a time of apparent failure. Stories of people who overcome seemingly insurmountable odds to achieve some personal goal, merit the accolade of excellence and serve to inspire others. Figures of significance in world history, science, art, music and literature can serve as global mentors because they create in us, a sense of hope in the worth of human endeavours. While excellence is more readily recognised in the achievement of exceptional results, it is actually more enduringly present in the process of struggle, endurance, risk-taking and choice-making. Winston Churchill is best remembered as the inspiring Prime Minister of Great Britain during World War II who achieved excellence by exceeding, in exceptional circumstances, the challenges of fate's destiny for him. The post-war electoral defeat of his political party is consistently interpreted as the nation's psychological response to war fatigue and a wish for change, rather than a negation of his personal achievements. I recall as a schoolgirl reading his autobiography *My Early Life: 1974–1904*, and feeling inspired that such an inauspicious student could achieve such heights as a world leader and as the author of a massive history of the English-speaking peoples.

A more modern hero was Christopher Reeve, the American actor famous for his role as Superman, who was paralysed when he suffered shocking spinal injuries in a riding accident in 1995. He was confined to a wheelchair, breathing only with the assistance of a ventilator and dependent upon a team of carers to meet his daily needs until his death in 2004. Against all odds, after his accident he continued to hope for a cure for his condition and acted as a mentor for others facing the despair of paralysis. A recent profile described Reeve's effective lobbying of

Congress and other groups for medical research funds for spinal injuries, through the Reeve Foundation, which had its headquarters in Reeve's home. He was cited in the profile as 'the greatest medical fundraiser on the planet ... he has single-handedly created a campaign to heal the 1.25 million people around the world who are as appallingly injured as he is' (Rhodes, 1999, p. 4). As well as committing himself to this public cause, Reeve undertook an extraordinary fitness regime to improve his bone density and prevent muscle wastage. While his story of courage and concern for others is inspiring enough, his reflections upon success are profoundly moving:

> One thing I have learnt is that success is not about money and power ... Real success is about relationships. There's no point in making $50 million a year if your teenager thinks you're a jerk and you spend no time with your wife (Rhodes, p. 6).

The context of these remarks and their ironic poignancy suggest how personal narratives can speak volumes to empathically attuned audiences seeking meaning from experiences, including tragedy.

TRANSFORMATIVE LEADERSHIP

Transformation is an inspiring word. It makes us catch our breath and it stirs up hope. We sit up and take notice when someone offers us excellence because it evokes much of the quality of human aspiration and growth. Unless you are exhausted with striving for excellence, mediocrity is an unappealing concept. The excellence described in this book will be regarded as achievable through increased hope, self-awareness and the mobilising of tacit abilities accessed through insight, understanding and self-belief. The pursuit of excellence does not have to be exhausting. On the contrary, it might be a challenging and pleasurable experience if our goals are realistic and attainable through practice, determination and the encouragement and modelling of others. Then the pursuit of excellence can be exhilarating.

Transformative leadership is a timely topic because corporations and educational institutions are increasingly required to justify their methods and assert their achievements in empirical and, less usually, qualitative measures which can be readily understood by their constituents and the public. It is essential for those aspiring to intellectual and corporate success to develop constructive and trusting relationships with their colleagues, both within and beyond their communities and corporations. It stands to reason that the one resource in a community that is renewable at minimal cost is the competence and goodwill of its members. It is tantalisingly difficult to put a price on this human capital but clearly it is an invaluable asset.

Academic research is now challenged to incorporate high-level outcomes of relating, educating and transforming. It has to create more imaginative ways to recognise and articulate the complexities of inter/intrasubjectivity. Brain-based research using functional magnetic resonance imaging can show how the brain responds to events, but it cannot yet explain exactly what gives rise to those events. Qualitative research methods, including case studies, narratives and ethnography are providing opportunities for researchers to observe and explain the function of affects, thoughts and interpersonal dynamics in the workplace, social life and personal life. We can now legitimately add the narratives of qualitative research to the statistics of quantitative research. In accepting that the complexities of research into human dynamics are best served by dynamic forms of inquiry and research reporting, we allow research to both reflect and expand our understanding of experience. Such research does not simply report what is, it engages its participants, including its readers, in hypothesis testing and hypothesis generation. The report does not end with a QED (*quod erat demonstrandum* – the truth of the hypothesis can be shown to be reliable and valid). A dynamic research report raises new possibilities and teases us with the complexities it has unearthed. We might be provoked with the thought that reality is infinitely complex but enduringly engaging.

For someone as committed as I am to the development of empathic intelligence as a desirable priority in educational research, it is tempting to point out the contradictory thinking here, whereby a 'soft' option is declared as too hard to test! It is also tempting to reflect that we may be developing a tradition in educational research of simply supporting those educational priorities which are easiest to test, in preference to those which are challenging, and, arguably, better. What must be put to rest immediately is the indefensible notion that anything to do with emotions or morality is easy, soft or ignorable. Empathy and moral reasoning are crucial in the development of just, humane and civilised societies. If it is hard to work out how to test the effectiveness of programs designed to educate citizens for such societies, then it is imperative that we meet that challenge – if only to put to rest resolutely, useless dichotomies about soft and hard options.

As we seek to understand the complex nature of felt and known experiences in the practice of excellence in pedagogy, spaces may open up or close. Within these spaces, we can move towards understanding something that is enlightening – that inquiry which reveals some truth is enhanced if it also reveals some beauty.

PRACTICAL STEPS TOWARDS EMPATHIC INTELLIGENCE

The following practical steps may be a useful checklist you can use to reflect on your ongoing development of empathic intelligence and your capacity for transformative leadership.

- **Develop self-consciousness.** I use the term in a non-pejorative sense to mean self-awareness, self-knowledge and self-acceptance. It doesn't help the empathic approach to life and work to be overly self-critical. It can be difficult sometimes for sensitive, altruistic individuals to determine the weight of contributing influences on a situation; hence the value of supportive, constructive networks.

- **Track your own feelings and thought.** The primary source of empathic intelligence is your own feelings, thoughts, relationships, personal narratives, enthusiasm and 'self'-expertise. The practice of labelling your own feelings and expressing them, even through reflective thought, enhances self-understanding. Ideally, you will know yourself better than anyone else because you are aware of the secrets of your heart and mind. Developing an empathically intelligent approach to living is a commitment to a life-long research project on yourself and on human nature.

- **Build a community**. Even a community of three or more like-minded people is sufficient to enhance practice as an empathic professional. To function effectively in a family, a school or an organisation, there has to be sufficient consensus about shared core values for empathic intelligence to work. A mother who is empathic by nature will find it hard to relate empathically to her infant if she is criticised or undermined for her approach. A teacher who is scorned for being 'too soft' will have difficulties also, as will the medical, legal or other professional pressured to deal only with facts when their empathic insight indicates that attuned listening is best practice.

- **Develop the habit of close observation.** Facial expressions, physical movements, dialogues, the ambience of classrooms, consulting rooms, theatres, public transport and shopping centres all signal and influence the ways humans think, feel and behave. Curiosity about the drama of human life is fundamental to the empathic disposition.

- **Practise the habit of reflective thought.** Those curious about human dynamics are never short of experiences to reflect upon. While it can become habitual over time to reflect upon experience, it is also easier to observe and reflect upon those experiences that confirm our mind-set, rather than those which test its robustness. Hence the need to share experiences with others, including those with different value systems and beliefs.

- **Extend the habit of reflective thought to the habit of imaginative, critical thought.** This can be hard to do because the search for meaning, cause and effect is time-consuming and emotionally demanding. But it is worth testing assumptions and remaining alert to the possibility that existing frames of reference can do with an overhaul because that's the nature of personal growth. Playing out imaginatively in the mind 'What might happen if?' or 'What might *have* happened if?' expands the present to the past and future, stimulating problem-solving capacities. Again, to achieve this, it helps to be part of an empathic community.

- **Look to the arts (literature, music, theatre, cinema, sculpture, painting, ballet) for sources of enriching imaginative, aesthetic, sensory experiences.** The life of the imagination is fundamental to empathic intelligence. In addition, experiences that are pleasurable for their own sake often fuel the necessary enthusiasm for professional life. Sometimes it helps to simply become engrossed in watching, listening, reading, observing – suspending judgment on the experience. Judgment requires analytic thought, and for balance in our lives we need both engrossment and distance.

- **Find your own metaphors, symbols and language** to express and shape your professional (and personal) life. That disposition and practice makes experiences dynamic, rich and meaningful, even when they are potentially daunting. Help others to find their metaphors and meanings because that's what empathic education is most about.

- **Find your own space and furnish it**. Professionals are defined, to an extent, by their scope to act autonomously. Within the mandatory responsibilities of a professional, there is always space for some autonomy and much discernment. Find that space and furnish it with your stories, your reflections, your beliefs and your hopes. Then it will be a comfort zone.

FURTHER READING

Arnold, R (2004) *Empathic Intelligence: Leadership through Intelligent Caring, Enthusiasm, Engagement and Relationships,* Paper presented at the Alliance of Girls' Schools (Australasia) Ltd Annual Conference: Leading Women: Leading Girls, SCEGGS Darlinghurst, Sydney, June.

Campbell, E (2003) *The Ethical Teacher,* Published by Open University Press/McGraw-Hill Ryerson, Berkshire, England.

Crisp, J (2000) (reprinted March 2002) *Keeping in Touch With Someone Who Has Alzheimer's,* Ausmed Publications, Victoria.

Kasari, C, Freeman, Stephanny, FN & Bass, W (2003) Empathy and response to distress in children with Down syndrome, *Journal of Child Psychology and Psychiatry,* 44(3): 424–43.

CONCLUSION

Empathic intelligence works in the poetics of practice; in the spaces and metaphors where relationships live both subliminally and overtly, and learning is a holistic, sensory, embodied experience. This is not to say that empathic intelligence informs an esoteric practice. Rather, it can function in the mother-infant relationship that is the source of earliest learning, just as it can function in relationships between teacher and student, doctor and patient, architect and client, actor and audience. It bridges the gap between scientific and arts-based understandings of the world and has the capacity to expand and contract according to its milieu. It struggles in isolation and thrives in communities. It can create, simultaneously, stronger individuals and stronger participants, thriving as it does on the dynamics of intersubjective and intrasubjective life.

Empathic intelligence is based on values which centre on the worth and potential of individuals, the power of care in developing and sustaining human relationships, the potential for such relationships to nurture, and enhance life and to teach us what matters, the importance of process over product in education and the inevitability of change in human life.

Researchers have discovered that a small region on the right side of the brain lights up when people experience a sudden 'Eureka' moment

(Jung-Beeman et al. 2004) Now that it is known that a particular part of the brain is involved in moments of insight (as distinct from those times when answers come gradually), the next challenge is to understand the nature of enabling conditions for such moments. With the encouraging insights of brain-based research and mind development theory (Siegal, 1999), it is timely to demonstrate confidence in the power of enabling relationships to enhance and transform pedagogy. That which was metaphoric, such as a concept of a dynamic between thought and feeling, might soon be found to be an intuitive insight emanating, with good reason, from discernible brain/mind activity. We might soon be able to both see and feel more consciously what lights up as we engage with and attach to others.

Empathic intelligence is a poetic theory that works between the lines and in the spaces housing the ineffable. It privileges the personal as the foundation for public life and gives parity of esteem to feeling and thought as the foundation of dynamically intelligent life. History might indeed repeat itself with the dawn of a new age of enlightenment. In this new age the discovered worlds will be closer to home than we ever imagined: our own dynamic minds shaped by experience and engagement with others.

As I draw this conversation to a close, I am reminded of some lines of a poem I wrote in autumn, the season of change, (Arnold, 1997).

Sometimes the Wind

I reason that I'll carry
for autumn's chill and winter's freeze
intelligence of past experience
leave games and pain behind
for serious pleasure and solemn wisdom
but other leaves fall
and I am bare to bone
born with a structure older than stone
touched by unconscious worlds stranger than seasons
tuned beyond time and rhymed without reason
poised between choices
charged with the change

In shaping the last words in this book, I am aware of parting company with an invisible reader and handing over the page, and the stage, to a new leading actor. The script and direction are now yours.

BIBLIOGRAPHY

Adolphs, R, Tranel, D & Damasio, A (1994) Impaired recognition of emotion in facial expressions following bilateral damage to the human amygdala, *Nature*, 372: 669–672.

Arnold, R (1987) *A longitudinal study of school children's writing abilities (school) Years 6–9 inclusive*, Unpublished PhD Thesis, University of Sydney.

—— (1989) A telling argument from children's arguments and narratives. In Andrews, R (ed.) *Narrative and Argument*, Open University Press, Milton Keynes.

—— (1991) *Writing Development: Magic in the Brain*, Open University Press, Buckingham.

Arnold, R (1993) The nature and role of empathy in human development and in drama in education. In Michaels, W (ed.) *Drama in Education: The State of the Art II*, Educational Drama Association, Sydney.

—— (1993) Managing Unconscious and Affective Responses in English Classes and in Role-plays, NATE *English in Education*, 27, pp. 32–40.

—— (1994a) Drama, psychodynamics and English education, *English in Australia*, July.

—— (1994b) The theory and principles of psychodynamic pedagogy, *Forum of Education*, 49 (2): 21–33, November.

—— (1994c) Research issues, psychodynamic pedagogy and drama in education, *Journal of National Association for Drama in Education*, 18, July.

—— (1997) Sometimes the Wind. In *Mirror the Wind*, St Clair Press, Sydney.

—— (1998) The role of empathy in teaching and learning, *The Education Network*, 14, December.

Austen, J (1995) *Pride and Prejudice*, Penguin, London.

Austen, J (1990) *Emma*, Macmillan, Basingstoke.

Ayers, WC & Miller, JL (1998) *A Light in Dark Times and the Unfinished Conversation: Maxine Greene*, Teachers College Press, New York.

Bannister, D & Fransella, A (1980) *Inquiring Man: The Psychology of Personal Constructs*, 2nd ed, Penguin, Harmondsworth.

Barnes, A & Thagard, P (1997) Empathy and Analogy, *Dialogue: Canadian Philosophical Review*, XXXVI (4): 705–720.

Barnett, MA (1987) *Empathy and related responses in children*. In Eisenberg, N & Strayer N (eds.) *Empathy and its Development*, Cambridge University Press, Cambridge.

Beattie, M (1997) *Redressing the balance in educational research: the possibilities inherent in narrative inquiry for connecting curriculum development, professional development, and educational reform*, Keynote Address to the Australian Curriculum Studies Association Biennial Conference, University of Sydney, July.

Benes, FM (2002) *Brain Anatomy and Development*, Unpublished Paper presented at Learning and the Brain Conference, Boston.

Berliner, D & Calfee, R (eds.) (1996) *Handbook of Educational Psychology*, Simon & Shuster Macmillan, New York.

Bettleheim, B (1978) *The Uses of Enchantment: The Meaning and Importance of Fairy Tales*, Penguin, Harmondsworth.

Blake, W (1977) *The Portable Blake*, The Viking Press/Penguin Books, New York.

Britton, J, Burgess, T, Martin, N, McLeod, A & Rosen, H (1975) *The Development of Writing Abilities (11–18)*, Macmillan Education, London.

Broderick, D (2003), Mind reading the body, *Weekend Australian* [Books extra], September 27–28, p. 11.

Bruner, JS (1972) *The Relevance of Education*, Penguin, Harmondsworth.

—— (1986) *Actual Minds, Possible Worlds*, Harvard University Press, Cambridge, Mass.

—— (1990) *Acts of Meaning*, Harvard University Press, Cambridge, Mass.

Buber, M (1965) *Between Man and Man*, (transl. RG Smith) Macmillan Publishing, New York.

Carpenter, P (2002) *Evidence of Perception, Cognition and Individual Differences*, Unpublished Paper presented at Learning and the Brain Conference, Boston.

Cartwright, L (1999) *The actor's voice: training through performance*, Paper presented at Postgraduate Research Seminar, National Voice Centre, University of Sydney.

Churchill, WS (1930) *My Early Life*, Odhams Press, London.

Clendinnen, I (1998) *Reading the Holocaust*, Text Publishing, Melbourne.

Collins, J (2001a) Level 5 Leadership: the triumph of humility and fierce resolve, *Harvard Business Review*, January.

—— (2001b) *Good to Great: Why Some Companies Make the Leap and Others Don't*, HarperBusiness, New York.

Damasio, A (1994) *Descartes' Error: Emotion, Reason and the Human Brain*, Grosset/Putnam, New York.

—— (2000) *The Feeling of What Happens: Body, Emotion and the Making of Consciousness*, Vintage, London.

—— (2003) *Looking for Spinoza: Joy, Sorrow and the Feeling Brain*, Harcourt Books, Orlando, Flo.

Danner, DD, Snowdon, DA & Friesen, WV (2001) Positive Emotions in Early Life and Longevity: Findings from the Nun Study, *Journal of Personality and Social Psychology*, 80 (5): 804–813.

Darwin, C (1965) *Expression of Emotions in Man and Animal*, University of Chicago Press, Chicago.

Davia, C (2002) *Implications for Cognition, Creativity, and Learning*, Unpublished paper presented at Learning and the Brain Conference, Boston.

Dawkins, R (1998) *Unweaving the Rainbow*, Penguin, Middlesex.
de Chardin, PT (1955) *The Phenomenon of Man*, Collins, London.
de Waal, F (1998) Survival of the kindest, *The Australian*, December 9, p. 38.
Denzin, N & Lincoln, Y (eds.) (2000) *Handbook of Qualitative Research*, 2nd ed. Sage, Thousand Oaks, CA.
Dewey, J (1916) *Democracy and Education: An introduction to the philosophy of education*, Macmillan, New York.
Dewey, J (1963) *Freedom and Culture*, Capricorn Books, New York.
—— (1964) *John Dewey: Selected Writing*, Archambault, R (ed.) Modern Library, New York.
—— (1971) *The Child and the Curriculum and the School and Society*, University of Chicago Press, Chicago.
Doyle, L, & Doyle, P (2003) Building schools as caring communities: Why, what, and how? *The Clearing House*, 76 (5): 259–261.
Duan, C & Hill, D (1996) The current state of empathy research, *Journal of Counselling Psychology*, 43 (3): 261–274.
Eccleston, R (1999) Out for a dux, *The Australian Magazine*, March 27–28, p. 26.
Ekman, P (2003) *Emotions Revealed: Recognizing Faces and Feelings to Improve Communication and Emotional Life*, Henry Holt and Company, New York.
Eisenberg, N & Lennon, J (1983) Sex differences in empathy and related capacities, *Psychological Bulletin*, 94: 100–131.
Eisenberg, N (ed.) (1989) *Empathy and Related Emotional Responses*, Jossey Bass, San Francisco.
Eisenberg, N & Strayer, J (eds.) (1996) *Empathy and Its Development*, Cambridge University Press, Cambridge.
Ellis, C & Bochner, A (2000) Autoethnography, personal narrative, reflexivity. In *Handbook of Qualitative Research*, Second Edition Sage Publications, California, pp. 733–768.
Ensign, J (2002) Weaving Experiential Education into a Preservice Special Education Course: The Klutz Experience, *Teacher Education and Special Education*, 25 (2): 105–113.
Eyre, D, Coates, D, Fitzpatrick, M, Higgins, C, McClure, L, Wilson, H, & Chamberlin, R (2002) Effective teaching of able pupils in the primary school: The findings of the Oxfordshire effective teachers of able pupils' project, *Gifted Education International*, 16 (2): 158–169.
Feshbach, ND (1984) Empathy, Empathy Training and the Regulation of Aggression in Elementary School Children. In Kaplan, RM, Konecni, VJ and Novaco, R (eds), *Aggression in Children and Youth*, Martinus Nijhoff Publishers, The Hague, Netherlands, pp. 192–208.
Feshbach, ND & Feshbach, S (1987) Affective processes and academic achievement, *Child Development*, 58: 1335–1347.
Fineman, S (ed.) (1993) *Emotion in Organizations*, Sage, London.
Forster, M, Anderson, P (2003) Can compassion be measured? *EQ Australia*, Summer, 4: 12–13.
Foucault, M (2000) *Ethics: Subjectivity and Truth*, Vol 1, Penguin Books, London.
Fox, L, Dunlap, G, Hemmeter, ML, Joseph, GE, & Strain, PS (2003) The teaching pyramid: A model for supporting social competence and preventing challenging behaviour in young children, *Young Children*, 58 (4): 48–52.
Fredrickson, BL & Levenson, RW (1998) Positive emotions speed recovery from the

cardiovascular sequelae of negative emotion, *Cognition and Emotion*, 12: 191–220.
Freud, S (1922) Group psychology and the analysis of the ego. In James Strachey (ed.) *Complete Works of Sigmund Freud*, Vol 18, Hogarth Press, London, pp. 69–144.
—— (1957) *The Future of an Illusion*, Anchor Books, New York.
Gardner, H (1983) *Frames of Mind: The Theory of Multiple Intelligences*, Basic Books, New York.
—— (1985) *Leading Minds: An Anatomy of Leadership*, HarperCollins, London.
—— (1993) *Creating Minds*, Basic Books, New York.
—— (1995) *Leading Minds*, HarperCollins, London.
—— (1997) *Extraordinary Minds*, HarperCollins, London.
Gardner, H & Hatch, T (1989) Multiple intelligences go to school: educational theory of multiple intelligences, *Educational Researcher*, 18 (8): 4–9.
Goldstein, L (1999) The relational zone: the role of caring relationships in the co-construction of mind, *American Educational Research Journal*, Fall, 36 (3): 647–673.
Goleman, D (1995) *Emotional Intelligence: It Can Matter More Than IQ*, Bloomsbury, London.
—— (1998) *Working with Emotional Intelligence*, Bantam, New York.
Greene, M (1995) *Releasing the Imagination: Essays on Education, the Arts and Social Change*, Jossey-Bass Inc, San Francisco.
Gross, JJ & Levenson, RW (1997) Hiding feelings: The acute effects of inhibiting negative and positive emotion, *Journal of Abnormal Psychology*, 106: 95–103.
Halliday, MAK (1975) *Learning How to Mean: Explorations in the Development of Language*, Edward Arnold, London.
Hardy, B (1977) Towards a poetics of fiction: an approach through narrative. In Meek, M et.al, *The Cool Web: The Pattern of Children's Reading*, Bodley Head, London.
Harper, D (1998) An argument for visual sociology. In Prosser, J (ed.) *Image-based research: A sourcebook for qualitative researchers*, Falmer, London, pp. 24–41.
—— (2000) *Reimagining Visual Methods: Galileo to Necromancer*. In Denzin, N & Lincoln Y (eds.) *Handbook of Qualitative Research*, 2nd ed. Sage, Thousand Oaks, CA.
Harris, PL (2000) *The Work of the Imagination: Understanding Children's Worlds*, Blackwell Publications, Oxford.
Hattie, J (2003) Teachers make a difference. What is the research evidence? Australian Council for Educational Research, viewed October 2003, <http://www.acer.edu.au/workshops/documents/Teachers_Make_a_Difference_Hattie.pdf>
Hawking, S (1988) *A Brief History of Time*, Bantam, New York.
Heyward, M (1994) Genius of the spirit: the diary of Donald Friend, *The Weekend Review, The Australian*, March, p. 3.
Hines, B (1979) *Kes—A Kestrel for a Knave*, Penguin, Harmondsworth.
Hoffman, ML (1994) Discipline and internalization, *Developmental Psychology*, 30: 26–28.
—— (2000) *Empathy and Moral Development: Implications for Caring and Justice*, Cambridge University Press, Cambridge.
Hopkins, GM (1953) *Poems*, Penguin, Harmondsworth.
Horowitz, MJ, Malmar, D & Wilner, W (1979) Analysis of patient states and state transitions, *Journal of Nervous and Mental Disease*, 167 (2): 91–99.
Hughes, J (2000) Enactment of the Expert: Drama and reading comprehension, *National Association for Drama in Education Journal* 16 (3).
—— (1996) *Enactment of the expert: psychodynamic pedagogy and the role of drama as a*

learning medium, Paper presented at the Australian Association for Research in Education/Educational Research Association Conference, Singapore.

Hughes, J & Hoogstad, V (ed.) (1993) *Communication for Technical, Scientific and Medical Professionals: Theory and Practice,* Macmillan, Melbourne.

Isen, A (1984) Towards understanding the role of affect in cognition. In Wyer R & Srull T (eds.) *Handbook of Social Cognition,* Erlbaum, Hillsdale NJ, pp. 179–237.

Jung-Beeman, M, Bowden E, Haberman, J, Frymiare, JL, Arambel-Liu, S, Greenblatt, R, Reber, PJ, Kounios, J (2004) Neural activity: When people solve verbal problems with insight, *Plos Biology,* 2 (4): 0500.

Kazin, A (1946) (ed.) *The Portable Blake,* Penguin Books, New York.

Kincheloe, J, Steinberg, S & Villaverde, L (eds.) (1999) *Rethinking Intelligence: Confronting Psychological Assumptions about Teaching and Learning,* Routledge, London.

King, KP, Lawler, PA (2003) *New Perspectives on Designing and Implementing Professional Development of Teachers of Adults,* Jossey–Bass San Francisco

Kitson, J (1996) *Psychodynamic Pedagogy: A Celebration of Literacy,* Paper presented at the Australian Literacy Educators Association, Brisbane.

—— (2001) *The Development of an Empathic Educator: Implementing Psychodynamic Pedagogy Through Drama in Education,* Unpublished MEd (Hons) thesis University of Sydney.

Kitwood, T (1997) *Dementia Revisited,* Open University Press, Buckingham.

Kohut, H (1959) Introspection, empathy and psychoanalysis: An examination of the relationship between mode of observation and theory, *Journal of the American Psychoanalytic Association,* 7: 459–483.

—— (1971) *The Analysis of the Self,* International University Press, Madison.

—— (1979) The two analyses of Mr Z, *The International Journal of Psycho-Analysis,* 60(1).

—— (1982) Introspection, empathy, and the semi-circle of mental health, *International Journal of Psycho-Analysis,* 63(395).

—— (1985) *Self Psychology and the Humanities,* WW Norton, New York.

LeDoux, J (1992) Emotion and the amygdala. In AP Agglington, (ed.), *The Amygdala: Neurobiological Aspects of Emotion, Memory and Emotional Dysfunction,* Wiley-Liss New York, pp. 339–51.

—— (1996) The emotional brain: The mysterious underpinnings of emotional life.

Lemonick, MD & Mankato, AP (2001) The nun study, viewed May 2003, <wwwtime-com>

Lippincott, K (1998) *The Sydney Morning Herald, The Good Weekend Magazine,* 24 Oct, p. 58.

Little, G (1999) *The Public Emotions,* Australian Broadcasting Corporation, Sydney.

Manne, R (1999) The Holocaust as a Fairy Tale, *The Sydney Morning Herald,* 15 Feb, p. 13.

Mayer, J & Salovey, P (1997) What is emotional intelligence? In Salovey, P & Sluyter, D (eds.)

Maza, M (1996) *Psychodynamic Pedagogy and Helping the Parents of Deaf Children,* Unpublished paper presented to MEd seminar at the University of Sydney.

McAllister, G, & Irvine, J (2002) The role of empathy in teaching culturally diverse students: A qualitative study of teachers beliefs, *Journal of Teacher Education,* 53(5): 433–443.

McCarthy, P (1998) Operation Oscar, *Sun-Herald,* 18 Oct.

McDonald, R (1996) Face to face justice, *Sydney Morning Herald, Good Weekend*, 18 May, p. 17–23.
Meek M, Warlow, A & Barton, G (eds.) (1977) *The Cool Web: The Pattern of Children's Reading*, The Bodley Head, London.
Moffett, J (1968) *Teaching the Universe of Discourse*, Houghton Mifflin Company, New York.
Nicolson, S (1997) *Psychodynamic Principles in Interactive Pedagogy*, Unpublished, Master in Education major essay, The University of Sydney.
Nieto, S (2003) What keeps teachers going? *Educational Leadership*, 60(8): 14.
Noddings, N (1984) *Caring: A Feminine Approach to Ethics and Moral Education*, University of California Press, Berkeley.
—— (1988) An ethic of caring and its implications for instructional arrangements, *American Journal of Education*, 96(2): 215–30.
—— (1992) *The Challenge to Care In Schools: An Alternative Approach to Education*, Teachers College Press, New York.
—— (1993) *Educating for Intelligent Belief or Unbelief*, Teachers College Press, New York.
—— (1998) Ethics and the imagination. In *A Light in Dark Times and the Unfinished Conversation: Maxine Greene*, Teachers College Press, New York.
Nussbaum, M (1995) *Poetic Justice; The Literary Imagination and Public Life*, Beacon Press, Boston.
—— (1997) *Cultivating Humanity: A Classical Defence of Reform in Liberal Education*, Harvard University Press, Cambridge.
Ombudsman's Report (1996) Inquiry into Juvenile Justice Detention Centres: A special Report to Parliament under Section 31 of Ombudsman's ACT, New South Wales Ombudsman, December.
O'Rourke, J (1999) Why bad bosses make you sick, *Sun-Herald*, 7 March, p. 39.
Piaget, J (1926) *The Language and Thought of the Child*, Harcourt Brace Jovanovich, New York.
Perlman, E (2003) *Seven Types of Ambiguity*, Picador, USA.
Phillips, H (2004) Empathy may not be uniquely human quality, *Neuron*, New Scientist Print Edition, 42: 335.
Piaget, J (1952) *The Child's Conception of Number*, Humanities Press, London.
—— (1963) *Problems of the Social Psychology of Childhood* Translated by Terrance Brown and Michael Gribetz Manuscript originally published in Gurvitch, G (ed.) *Traite de Sociologie*, Presses Universites de France, Paris, pp. 229–54.
—— (1981) *Intelligence and Affectivity: Their Relationship During Child Development*, Annual Reviews, Palo Alto, CA.
Pinar, W. (Ed.) (1998) *The Passionate Mind of Maxine Greene: 'I am ... not yet'*, Falmer Press, Taylor & Francis Inc. Bristol, Pa.
—— (1998) *A Light in Dark Times: Maxine Greene and the Unfinished Conversation*, Teachers College Press, Columbia University, New York and London.
Polanyi, M (1959) *The Study of Man*, University of Chicago Press, Chicago.
—— (1969) *Knowing and Being – Essays by Michael Polanyi*, Greene, M (ed.) University of Chicago Press, Chicago.
—— (1974) *Personal Knowledge: Towards a Post-Critical Philosophy*, University of Chicago Press, Chicago.
—— (1983) *The Tacit Dimension*, Peter Smith, Gloucester, Mass.
Rhodes, T (1999) Cry of a damaged man, *The Weekend Australian*, 9–10 Jan.

Rose, S (1993) *The Making of Memory*, Bantam Books, Toronto.
—— (1998), (ed.) *From Brains to Consciousness: Essays on the New Science of the Mind*, Princeton University Press, Princeton, NJ.
Sousa, DA (2001) *How The Brain Learns*, Second Edition Corwin Press, California.
Salovey, P & Sluyter, D (eds.) (1997) *Emotional Development and Emotional Intelligence: Educational Implications*, Basic Books, New York.
Saxton, J & Miller, C (eds.) (1998) *The Research of Practice: The Practice of Research*, Victoria, BC. IDEA Publications.
Scarr, S Protecting general intelligence: constructs and consequences for interventions. In Linn, P. L (ed.) *Intelligence: Measurement, Theory, and Public Policy*, University of Illinois Press, Urbana, Ill.
Seligman, MEP (2000) Optimism, pessimism, and mortality, *Mayo Clinic Proceedings*, 75, pp. 133–134
Siegal, DJ (1999) *The Developing Mind: How Relationships and the Brain Interact to Shape Who We Are*, The Guilford Press, New York.
Singer, J (2002) *A Role for Imaginative Play in Preparing Inner City Children for School*, Paper presented at Learning and the Brain Conference, Boston, Unpublished.
Singer, T, Seymour, B, O'Doherty, H, Kaube, R, Dolan, RJ, Frith, CD (2004) Empathy for pain involves the affective but not sensory components of pain, *Science*, 303 (5561): 1157–1162.
Sereny, G (1995) *Albert Speer: His Battle with Truth*, Picador, London.
Slattery, L (1998) Rime and reason, *The Weekend Australian*, 21–22 Nov, p. 10.
Snowdon, DA (1997) Aging and Alzheimers Disease: Lessons from the nun study, *Gerontologist*, 37: 150–156.
Snowdon, DA, Greiner, LH, Kemper, SJ, Nanayakkara, N & Mortimer, JA (1999) Linguistic ability in early life and longevity: Findings from the nun study. In Robine, JM, Forette, B, Francheschi, C & Allard, M (eds.), *The Paradoxes of Longevity*, Springer-Verlag, Berlin, Germany, pp. 103–113.
Steiner, C (1997) *Achieving Emotional Literacy*, Bloomsbury, Great Britain.
Stern, D (1985) *The Interpersonal World of the Infant*, Basic Books, New York.
Strauss, A & Corbin, J (1990) *Basics of Qualitative Research: Grounded Theory Procedures and Technique*, Sage, Newbury Park, CA.
Sullivan, M (1998) Presentation to Showcase of Teaching and Learning, Centre for Teaching and Learning, University of Sydney, and personal communication, 23 October, 2001.
Verducci, S (2000a) *A Conceptual History of Empathy and a Question it Raises for Moral Education*, Educational Theory, 50 (1): 63–79.
Verducci, S (2000b) *A Moral Method? Thoughts on Cultivating Empathy Through Method Acting*, Journal of Moral Education, 29 (1): 87–99.
Vischer, F (1994) *Empathy, Form and Space; Problems in German aesthetics, 1873–1893*, Mallgrave, H.F. & Ikonomou, E (eds.), The Getty Center for the History of Art and the Humanities, Los Angeles.
Vogt, F (2002) A caring teacher: Explorations into primary school teachers professional identity and ethic of care, *Gender and Education*, 14 (3): 251264.
Vygotsky, L (1978) *Mind in Society: The Development of Higher Psychological Processes*, Harvard University Press, MA.
—— (1988) *Thought and Language*, The MIT Press, Cambridge, Mass.
Wadsworth, BJ (1989) *Piaget's Theory of Cognitive and Affective Development*, Longman, New York.

Wertsch, J (1985) *Vygotsky and the Social Formation of the Mind*, Harvard University Press, Cambridge, MA.

Wheatley, J (1999) Before the night in June, *The Sydney Morning Herald, The Good Weekend*, 13 Feb, p. 14–21.

White, B (2003) Caring and the teaching of English, *Research in the Teaching of English*, 37 (3): 295–325.

Wilde, O (1905) *De Profundis*, Methuen & Co, London:

—— (1924) *The Ballad of Reading Gaol*, Methuen, London.

Williams, L (2001) *The Emotional Brain*, Address to Science Forum, University of Sydney, 4th April.

Winnicott, D (1965) *The Maturational Processes and the Facilitating Environment: Studies in the Theory of Emotional Development*, Hogarth Press and the Institute of Psychoanalysis, London.

INDEX

ACER tests 140, 174–75
achievements, *see* excellence; rewards
advertising 181, 207–208
affect, *see* emotion
affirmation 36, 175
agency 41–42, 206
Albert Speer (Sereny) 80–82
altruism 142–43, 156, 164, 167–69
analogical thinking 67, 70–72, 114–15
analytic skills 33
Arnold, Roslyn 224
arts 41, 187
   see also literature
   film 77–80
   insights from 53–54, 71–72, 221
   music 123–24
   symbolic systems 21, 50, 145–46
attention, *see* engagement
attitudes, learnt at school 159
attunement 36, 45–49, 59
   early language development 49–52
   educative leadership 155–56
Austen, Jane 73–74
Australian Council of Educational Research tests 140, 174–75
authenticity 43

Ballad of Reading Gaol (Wilde) 74
Barnes, Allison 114–16
Benigni, Roberto 77–80
Biblical references 38, 40
biographical writing 80–82, 149
bonding 41
brain research 16, 60–61, 93, 193–94, 223–24
Brief History of Time (Hawking) 194
Bruner, Jerome 112
bullying 99, 168–72
burnout 137–38, 164

caring 56–61, 142–43, 146–47
   by animals 167
   reciprocity and 36–37
   teaching and 18–19, 97
Carr, Bob 163
case studies 100–102, 133
change 147, 185–86
   leadership scenario 195–201
Chardin, Teilhard de 84
child-centred education, *see* student-centred education
children, *see* infants
choice, *see* decision making
Churchill, Winston 217

classrooms, *see* schools; teachers
Clendinnen, Inga 75–77
cognitive intelligence 20, 25
   see also emotion and cognition
   cognitive templates 33
   imagination and 69–70
   Piaget on 97–99
Collins, Jim 150–51
communication 181–83, 202–08
   see also engagement
   resilience through 137–40
community building 202–04, 220–21
companies, *see* organisations
compassion 74–76, 95, 168–69
composing 65, 127, 145–46, *see also* writing
confidence 39
connectedness, *see* bonding; engagement
cooperation 144, *see also* reciprocity
core relatedness 45
corporal punishment 172–73
corporate events company scenario 195–201
corporations, *see* organisations
creativity 68–69
crime reconciliation meeting 116–17
culture, *see* arts
cultures of learning 162–90
cultures, organisational, *see* organisations
curiosity 70, 146
curriculum materials 58, 68–69, 148
   Mind Matters resource 44

Damasio, Antonio 99–102, 193–94
Damasio, Hanna 100
Darwin, Charles 94, 168
David (case study) 101
Dawkins, Richard 84, 187
de Chardin, Teilhard 84
decision making 46, 121–22
defeat, *see* failure
democratising intelligence 28–29
depression, learning and 211
De Profundis (Wilde) 74–75
Dewey, John 21–22
diary writing 136, 179–80, 192
differentiation in thought and feeling 24–26, 48
domestic violence 171
drama, *see* narrative; role enactments
dynamism (sense of energy) 20, 34–35, 44, 126–27

education
   see also empathic pedagogy; schools; student-centred education; teachers
   affective learning 44–45
   care in 56–61
   leadership 154–56
   mirroring and 41–45
   'new' intelligences and 27
   support for teachers 48–49, 113, 137–38, 164
Ekman, Paul 94–95
Elliot (case study) 100–102
email communications 181
embodiment, identification and 32–33
Emma (Austen) 73–74
emotional intelligence 20, 25–26
emotional templates (affects) 24, 33, 45–49, 129, 166
   ongoing learning 52–53
emotion and cognition 16, 20, 25–26
   about obstacles 111
   analogical thinking 114–15
   Damasio on 99–101
   differentiation in 24–26, 48
   dynamic between 31–35, 88–89, 193–95
   holistic theory 92–94
   in spiral model of empathic development 105
   tracking 220
emotions (affects)
   advertising and 207–208
   fluctuation 135–36
   longevity and 149
   organisational communication and 202–03
   Piaget on development of 97–99
   research on 60–61, 94–95
empathic intelligence 11–30
   cultures of learning 142–43, 162–90
   definitions 19–22
   four components of 22–24
   leadership and 119–61
   research methods 132–35
   steps towards 200–202, 220–22
empathic literacy 119, 145–47
empathic pedagogy 175–77
   energy demands of 137–38
   teachers 20–21, 175–77
   theoretical antecedents of 92–117

empathy 22–24, 31–62
    a 'soft' or 'hard' option 139–40, 219–20
    brain research into 60–61
    compared to sympathy 86, 88–90
    developing through narrative 63–67
    Ekman's three types of 95
    failure of 114–17
    identifying and promoting 186–89
    infancy and 45–52, 164–67
    in literature and the arts 73–83
    social capacity building 143–44
    spiral model of 104–108, 193
energy, see dynamism (sense of energy)
engagement (attention) 19, 22–24,
        38–44, 156, 181–82
    conditions for 123–27
    intimacy and 213
    organisational communication and 203
    with infants 46–48
English teaching
    analysing advertising 208
    gifted students 84–85
    letter-writing exercise 173–74
    research into 132–34
    spelling and handwriting 108–109
enthusiasm 22–24
ethical intentions 25–26, 116, 142, see
        also moral judgements
ethnographic research methods 132–34
excellence 152–54, 216–18
    see also teachers, quality; transformative learning
    an egalitarian ideal 183–84
    aspiring to 128, 130–31
exercises, see hypotheticals
experiences 22, 34–35, 148
    codifying and synthesising 45–47,
        49–50, 154–55
    narratives as vicarious 70–72
    past and present 46, 53–54, 64–66, 71,
        82–83, 122
    reflection on 176–77, 179–80
expertise 22–24, 143
eye contact 124–25
Eyre, Deborah 60

Facing the Demons (ABC) 116–17
failure 108–11, 128–30
feedback to students 211–12
feeling, see emotion

film 77–80
Fog of War (Morris) 78–79
Foucault, Michel 146
Freud, Sigmund 149–50
Friend, Donald 102–103

Gage, Phineas (case study) 100
Gardner, Howard 27, 64, 103, 142–45, 149–50
Gatti, Elio 40
gifted students 84–85
Greene, Maxine 69
green-haired people fable 185–86
group dynamics 56, 85, 169, 178
    talking about tensions 205–206

Halliday, Michael 49
Hamlet 114–15
Hardy, Barbara 66–67
Hattie, John 95–96
Hawking, Stephen 194
Hines, Barry 173–74
holistic theory 92–94
Holmes, Richard 80
Holocaust, books and films about 75–82
hope 93–94, 152, 210–12
    function of 127–31
    myth of creation and 40
Hopkins, Gerard Manley 211, 215
Hughes, John 42
human resource development 55
humour, in empathic people 187
hypotheticals 29–30, 61–62, 91, 118,
        160–61, 189–90

identification 32–33, see also attunement
imagination 32, 63–70, 221
    hope and 211
    in reflection 136
    mirroring and 40–41
infants 17, 45–49, 162, 164–66, 213
    early language development 49–52
influence 121–23, 135
    advertising and 207–208
information technology 17, 143–44, 180
initiation rites 172
inspiration 140, 215–16
intelligence 15, 20, 25–29, 147, see also
        empathic intelligence
internalisation 33, 53, 90
interpersonal intelligence 28, 145

interpersonal relationships 39–41, 124–27
    see also emotional templates; engagement; infants
    classroom dynamics 209–210
    destructive 174
    empowering communication 205–207
    infancy 45–49
    learning and 17–18, 58–61
    research and 132–35
    resilience through 137–40
inter-subjective relatedness 45
intimacy, in transformation 212–15
intrapersonal intelligence 145
introspection 32–34
intuition 47–48, 92–93

journal writing 136, 179–80, 192
juvenile justice schools 156–58

Kes (A Kestrel for a Knave) (Hines) 173–74
Kincheloe, Joe 28–29
King Lear (Shakespeare) 130, 159
Kohut, Heinz 31–32, 47–48

language development, *see* literacy development
leadership 42, 119–61, 205
    education 154–56
    hypothetical scenario 195–201
    paradoxes of 149–51
    transformative 151–54, 218–20
learning 18–19, 22, 52–54, 67–68, 162–90
    see also teachers; transformative learning
    affective 44–45
    classroom climate and 209
    deep learning 148
    dynamics of 177–78
    early experiences and 48
    hope and 210–12
    inspiration and modelling 215–16
    students' perspectives on 96–97, 106–107
Life is Beautiful (Benigni) 77–80
life-long learning 139, 142–43
listening 89–90, 182, 204
    silent witnessing 38–39
literacy development 108–109
    see also empathic literacy
    attentive others and 38–39
    lack of 206–207
    language in infancy 49–52

scaffolding 112–13
literature 73–77, 80–83
    see also narrative
    corporal punishment in 173–74
Lucy (story) 214–15

McAllister, Gretchen 60
Machiavellianism 168
McNamara, Robert 78–79
Manne, Robert 77–80
mastery 41–42, 156, 207
Mayer, John 26–28
mentors 84, 127–31, 188, 217, *see also* leadership; teachers
metaphor, *see* poetry and metaphor
Mind Matters resource 44
mirroring 39–45, 104–105, 132
    false 130–31
    infants 47, 51–52
modelling 215
modulation 39–41
moral judgements 75–76, 90, 140, 142–43
    see also ethical intentions
    crime reconciliation meeting 117
mother–infant relationships, *see* infants
motivation 127–28, 130
movies 77–80
music 123–24

narrative 63–67, 70–72, 82–83, *see also* literature
Nazi Germany 75–80
Nun Study 149
Nussbaum, Martha 65–66

observation 221, *see also* qualitative research; reflection
Once upon a time... 11, 63–64, 83
optimism, *see* hope
organisations 144, 191–222
    see also leadership
    changing cultures 201–202
    outcomes 25–26

Paglia, Camille 42–43
parent–infant relationships, *see* infants
pedagogy, *see* education; empathic pedagogy; teachers
performers 69, 188
personal development 192

personal histories, *see* experiences
personal humility, in leadership 150–51
Piaget, Jean 48, 97–99
play 211
poetry and metaphor 50, 103–104, 121–22, 147, 154–55, 187–88, 215, 221–22
postmodern thinking 17, 148
potential development, *see* zone of proximal development
professional life 54–56, 119–23
    see also teachers
    negotiating rules of behaviour 191–95
    reflection on 83–86, 93, 179–80
    use of theory in 55–56, 86, 103–104, 106, 135–36
    will, in leadership 150–51
psychic development 24–25
psychic spaces 123–27, 222
psychoanalytic approaches 31–32, 46
psychodynamic pedagogy 13, 157

qualitative research 133–34
quantitative research 132–33

reading 63–65, 145–46
Reading the Holocaust (Clendinnen) 75–77
reason, *see* cognitive intelligence; emotion and cognition
reciprocity 36–37, 43–44
reconciliation of crime perpetrators and victims 116–17
Reeve, Christopher 217–18
reflection 136–40, 220–21
    dynamism and 34
    intrapersonal intelligence 145
    on professional life 83–86, 93, 179–80
    revising life scripts 176–77
reinforcement 41, 51–52
relationships, *see* interpersonal relationships
relevance in education 58
Representations of Interactions that have been Generalised (RIGS) 45–47, 162
resilience 137–40, *see also* hope
resistance to change 201–202
resistant performers 128–29
respect 97
revenge 172, 174
rewards 130, 155–56, 210
RIGS 45–47, 162
risk taking in learning 212

role enactments 42, 64, 72, 174
Rose, Steven 102
rules of behaviour 191–95

Salovey, Peter 26–28
scaffolding 103, 112
    in language development 49, 52
    in professional life 56
Scarr, Sandra 28
scenario, leadership 195–201, *see also* hypotheticals
schools
    classroom dynamics 209–210
    development of empathy in 166
    judging quality of 158–59
    juvenile justice 156–58
    mental well-being in 44
    prizes in 130
self-constructs 176–78, 188–89, *see also* experiences
selflessness, *see* altruism
sense making, *see* theory
sense of self 22, 38–39, 44, 47, 220
sensitivity, *see* compassion; empathy
Sereny, Gitta 80–82
Shakespeare, William 73, 187
    Hamlet 114–15
    King Lear 130, 159
silence 35, 38–39, 130
Singer, Tania 60–61
social capacity 144, *see also* ethical intentions
Sometimes the Wind (Arnold) 224
spaces between us 123–27, 222
spectators 188
speculative thought 70, 82–83
spelling 108–109
spiral model of empathic development 104–108, 193
sports 28, 156
Stern, Daniel 45–46, 162
storytelling 65–67, 71, *see also* narrative
strategic communication 181–83
student-centred education 31–32, 107
    Dewey and 21–22
    intelligent caring 58
students
    culturally diverse 60
    disrupted in normal development 163–64

engagement 24, 41–43
factors in achievement 95–96
feedback to 211–12
gifted 84–85
observation of teachers by 17–18, 41
perspectives of 19, 96–97, 106–107, 209–210
reciprocity in relationships 36–37, 43–44
sense of agency 41–42
student teachers 42, 55, 179
Sullivan, Moira 107
symbolic systems 21, 50, 145–46, 180–81
sympathy 86, 88–90

talents 27–28
teachers
  see also education; learning; professional life; schools
  as researchers 132–33
  changing role of 180–81
  classroom dynamics 209–10
  empathic 20–21, 175–77
  inspiration 84–85
  intelligent caring 56–61
  juvenile justice schools 156–58
  professional development 135
  promoting excellence 153–54
  quality 18–19, 60, 67–68, 95–97, 216
  revising life scripts 176–77
  scaffolding 112–13
  self-constructs 176–78
  student teachers 42, 55, 179
  support for 48–49, 113, 137–38, 164
technology 17, 143–44, 180
templates 33, *see also* emotional templates
Thagard, Paul 114–16
theory 122, 131–35, 139
  antecedents of empathic pedagogy 92–117
  self-constructs and choice of 176–78
  use in professional life 55–56, 86, 103–104, 106, 135–36
thinking, *see* cognitive intelligence; emotion and cognition
'time out' 126
tones of voice 202
traits 27–28
transformative learning 17–18, 24, 216–17
  intimacy and 212–15
  leadership and 151–54, 218–22
  mobilisation of 148–49

understanding, *see* empathy
universities, sense of belonging in 54

values 148
vicarious experience 70–72
vicarious introspection 32–33
violence, in bullying 171–73
visualising empathic development 104–108
vocation 183–84
vulnerability 36–37, 170, 173
Vygotsky, Lev 56, 59, 111–13

Wilde, Oscar 74–75
winning 130, 217
workplaces 54–56, 201–204
  see also leadership; organisations; professional life
  anti-discrimination legislation 174
  bullying and 171
writing
  see also English teaching; literature
  diaries 136, 179–80, 192
  organisational communication 203–204
  stories 65
  writers' block 128–29

zone of proximal development 56, 59, 111–13